# Continuing Professional Development

# Continuing Professional Development

A practical guide for teachers and schools

Second edition

## Anna Craft

(Based on Open University postgraduate module *E634: Evaluating and Planning Professional Development,* 1992–1995, written by Rob Bollington and Anna Craft. The first edition of this book was published by Routledge in 1996)

London and New York
in association with The Open University

First published 2000
by RoutledgeFalmer
11 New Fetter Lane, London EC4P 4EE

Simultaneously published in the USA and Canada by
RoutledgeFalmer, 29 West 35th Street, New York, NY 10001

Reprinted 2002

*RoutledgeFalmer is an imprint of the Taylor & Francis Group*

© 2000 Anna Craft

Typeset in Palatino by Bookcraft Ltd, Stroud, Gloucestershire
Printed and bound in Great Britain by TJ International Ltd, Padstow,
Cornwall

*British Library Cataloguing in Publication Data*
A catalogue record for this book is available from the British Library

*Library of Congress Cataloging in Publication Data*
Craft, Anna.
   Continuing professional development : a practical guide for
teachers and schools / Anna Craft – 2nd ed.
   p.cm.
Includes bibliographical references and index.
ISBN 0–415–23770–X
1. Teachers – In-service training – Great Britain.  2. Teachers – Rating
of – Great Britain.  I. Title.

LB1731.C68 2000
370'.71'55–dc21                                          00-030825

ISBN 0–415–23770–X

# Contents

**PART III**
**Planning future professional development**

# Figures

# Tables

# Preface

## A BOOK BASED ON A COURSE

This book is aimed at supporting you in developing as a professional. Much of the material in it originally formed a module in the Open University's Master's level programme. It has been studied and evaluated over several years by students in regions as geographically far flung as Tayside and Norwich, as culturally diverse as Harrow and Warwickshire – and has been re-worked to include student feedback after each group finished their study. This is the second edition of the book, updated in 2000 to take account of many recent changes in policy and practice in the professional development of teachers.

## WHAT THE BOOK WILL HELP YOU DO

This book will enable you to analyse your own experience of professional development, from the perspective of participant or provider. It offers you tools for evaluating a focused aspect of it from the perspectives of both individual and institutional development, and will help you to:

- explore models of professional development provision
- develop your understandings of the principles of appraisal (or, in Scotland, review)
- develop your understanding of professional and institutional development
- review and describe your own professional development (as participant or provider)
- identify a focused aspect of your own professional development to evaluate
- develop and apply criteria for evaluating from both an institutional and/or a personal perspective the quality and value of professional development work you have undertaken
- identify appropriate future professional development work from a personal and institutional perspective.

## WHO IS THE BOOK FOR?

It is designed to be of particular use to teachers and head teachers taking part in professional development. It will also be of interest to those *managing* professional development at school and to LEA personnel engaged on professional development activities as part of their own professional learning. Whichever of these groups you may be part of, the underlying purpose of the module is to encourage you to reflect upon and analyse the professional development work you have undertaken and to think about and plan for your future professional development.

## WHAT DOES IT ADDRESS?

The book is structured in three parts, which each have a different focus and function. Part I, *Theories of teacher and school development,* comprises Chapters 1 to 5. This part of the book looks at the cultural context of professional development, the variety of in-service work and models of effective provision. The nature and role of appraisal in reconciling individual and institutional development needs, and principles of professional and institutional development, including the perspective of pupils, are all explored in Part I as a foundation for evaluating in-service work.

Part II, *Evaluating professional development,* comprises Chapters 6 to 9. This part of the book adopts a practical style and is intended to be a pragmatic guide for you in undertaking the evaluation of a specific tranche of professional development. Accordingly, it covers the context for increasing emphasis on evaluation of in-service work, debates about the purposes of evaluating, and methodology for collecting, analysing and reporting on data.

Part III, *Planning future professional development,* comprises Chapters 10 to 12. This part of the book is designed to support you in making personal, professional and career development plans, with reference to your own needs and the needs of your institution. The areas addressed include views of professionalism and of professional learning, stakeholders in development, change in education, personal factors in personal growth or development including learning preferences and history, contextual changes in career progression, and a look to the future in professional development.

## USING THE BOOK

Reflecting on your experience or provisions of professional development is not an easy task; the greater your own vested interest in the professional development you want to evaluate, the more difficult it is. The book is structured to include lots of practical and reflective tasks, and also includes examples from our Open University students' work to try and make it all more accessible.

Keeping a notebook for your responses to the tasks (in bold) and reflection points (in italics) can be a useful prompt and support for reflection. A loose-leaf style format such as a ring binder may be the most useful, as you will find yourself building up notes on particular aspects of your learning bit by bit as you work through the book.

## Creating a professional portfolio

Developing a portfolio of evidence of professional development is becoming an increasingly important part of the professional's repertoire in education. Although this book is not designed specifically to help you create a personal portfolio, it will support you in logging professional development experiences and reflections on these as well as any feedback on them. This log should not be confused with your notebook and is an activity which will of course go on beyond the life of this book!

## A FINAL WORD

Although I have undertaken the re-working of the course to become the book, and have undertaken the updating of the book for its second edition, I use 'we' from this point onward and throughout, because much of it also reflects and is based on the views and arguments of Rob Bollington, co-author of the original course. Our views were in turn informed by a large development team, drawn from local education authorities collaborating on teaching the material, and from within the University.

# Acknowledgements

I am very grateful to all of the people who contributed to the Open University material on which the first edition of this book was based. These included:

Ray Bolam, University of Swansea (external assessor)
Rob Bollington, Bedfordshire LEA (author)
Lys Bradley, Warwickshire LEA (tutor and member of development team)
Mary Briggs, The Open University (member of development team)
Fred Browning, Essex LEA (tutor and member of development team)
Anne Carter, Oxfordshire LEA (tutor and member of development team)
Viv Casteel, Strathclyde Education Authority (tutor and member of development team)
Margaret Chilvers, Huntingdon Consortium (tutor and member of development team)
Liz Cox, Huntingdon Consortium (tutor and member of development team)
Liz Dawtrey, The Open University (member of development team)
Deborah Eyre, Oxfordshire LEA (tutor and member of development team)
Ian Fletcher, Warwickshire LEA (tutor and member of development team)
Mike Flude, The Open University (member of development team)
Bob Ganson, Tayside Education Authority (tutor and member of development team)
Arthur Horton, Consultant (external evaluator)
Ly Kane, formerly of Hertfordshire LEA (tutor and member of development team)
Lesley Kydd, The Open University (member of development team)
Tom Lyons, Consultant (tutor and member of development team)
Robert McCormick, The Open University (member of development team)
Stuart MacDonald, Strathclyde Education Authority (tutor and member of development team)
Agnes McMahon, Bristol University (external examiner, third year)
Neil McRae (tutor and member of development team)
Deirdre McVean, Tayside Education Authority (tutor and member of development team)

Jan Minchella, Enfield LEA (tutor and member of development team)
David Oldroyd, Bristol University (external examiner, first two years)
Alan Rhodes, Hertfordshire LEA (tutor and member of development team)

The material was painstakingly word-processed and amended over the three-year piloting period by Jo Rogers and Sue Crook. All the course administration from registration to tutor allocation to assessment and evaluation, was undertaken by Brenda Jarvis and Di Harden, Course Managers at the Open University. I thank all four for their support and hard work. In negotiating the transformation of the original course to a book, and for the arrangements surrounding the production of both first and second editions, I am most grateful to Giles Clark and colleagues in the Open University's Co-Publishing Department and, of course, the team at RoutledgeFalmer.

I am very grateful too to all of our colleagues, in the pilot groups in Enfield, Essex, Harrow, Hertfordshire, Huntingdon, Norfolk, Oxfordshire, Tayside, Strathclyde and Warwickshire, too numerous to mention individually by name, and to all of our colleagues in other institutions, who contributed ideas and material.

The module on which this book is based was initially made available by a grant from Hertfordshire LEA. We are grateful to Dennis Mongon and his colleagues in Hertfordshire LEA who worked closely with us on the first year of piloting.

For both first and second editions I am grateful to Maurice and Alma Craft, who acted as willing sounding boards throughout my drafting, on all sorts of matters. For the second edition I am grateful to Lesley Kydd of the Open University who acted as the Scottish adviser on the text. The revision of the book to form a second edition was done in the final few weeks before my second child was born. It could not have been done without the extra help of Ann-Marie Clifford and Kim Rumsey who helped to look after my eldest son, Hugo, whose patience I am also grateful for. My second child, Ella, was good enough to wait until the book was finished before being born, just a few days after the manuscript was handed over.

Finally, a very personal thank-you to my partner, Simon, for his continual understanding, encouragement, inspiration and support.

Anna Craft
The Open University
March 2000

# Part I

# Theories of teacher and school development

# Introduction

Some of the main themes of Part I are:

- the nature of continuing professional development set in the context of teaching as a profession as well as policy positions from government on it,
- factors contributing to effective classrooms, departments and schools and the engagement between the study of effectiveness and the study of improvement,
- factors making for effective individual and school development, and
- the nature of appraisal (sometimes referred to as review, in Scotland) in relation to professional and institutional development.

These themes will be explored in greater depth in Parts II and III. These later parts will also provide detailed guidance on the methods and approaches outlined in Part I.

This part of the book is intended to help you review and describe your own professional development needs and articulate your expectations of professional development and in-service training. It is organised as follows:

*Chapter 1* This chapter deals with cultural and policy shifts in professional development. It looks at definitions of professional development and in-service training. It notes the variety of purposes of professional development and draws attention to the way these can conflict. For example, attention is drawn to tensions between school and individual needs for in-service training and between pressures for in-service training to meet national priorities and those arising within particular schools and for particular individuals. It explores some of the connections between professional development and pupil attainment. Chapter 1 also looks at models of professional development and INSET provision; we consider professional development in terms of purposes, location, length, methods and levels of impact and develop points made in the Introduction. It is designed to help you locate your own experience and reflect on how this corresponds to the models described.

*Chapter 2*   This chapter looks at principles of appraisal. It outlines the differences between contrasting approaches to appraisal. It then explores the relationship between appraisal and professional development, arguing that appraisal can assist in identifying professional development needs, reconciling school and individual pressures for professional development and evaluating professional development. The aim is to help you relate your own experience of appraisal to your professional development.

Even if your experience of appraisal is very limited we take the view that having a personal position on its potential for professional development is important. You should be able to develop a personal position on the role and potential of appraisal even with little experience so far.

**Note**: Some Education Authorities in Scotland carry out teacher review rather than teacher appraisal. This model, Staff Development and Review, has the approval of the Scottish Executive Education Department (SEED).

*Chapter 3*   This chapter looks at principles of professional and institutional development and reviews a range of factors frequently seen as important in promoting individual and school development. It discusses practitioner reflection and professional knowledge and acknowledges the role of the biographical in the process of clarifying your thinking about your own professional development needs. It discusses principles of effective schools and of school improvement, making connections between the two approaches to institutional development and introducing the level of classroom effectiveness, which will be explored further in Chapter 4. The chapter is aimed to support you in identifying your own professional development needs in the context of the school's development plan. It looks at ways in which appraisal may support professional and institutional development.

*Chapter 4*   This chapter looks at the pupil perspective on teacher and school development in the context of the increasing marketisation of education and of a steady increase in emphasis on lifelong learning. It goes on to explore various findings on effective classrooms, departments and schools. We introduce the notions of the evolutionary school and classroom and of the intelligent school. The chapter examines one of the interventionist strategies for professional development originally developed by the Department of Employment , and now being used by many schools: Investors in People, in the light of research on effective classrooms, departments and schools. It also explores further the links between effectiveness and school improvement, introduced in Chapter 3, highlighting the role of middle managers in school improvement and exploring the place and approaches of methodology for investigating and documenting each.

*Chapter 5*    Here we look at the principles behind evaluating specific CPD, to enable you both to 'frame' and 're-frame' your practice. The discussion includes consideration of stakeholders in the evaluation of CPD and exploration of the evaluation of both processes and outcomes. The chapter aims to help you in selecting some professional development which you wish to evaluate.

## Summary of outcomes

At the end of Part I you should have:

- developed your understanding of the purposes and nature of professional development and in-service training in the wider context of policy on CPD;
- explored a range of models of professional development and related these to yourself;
- gained an awareness of key principles of institutional and individual development;
- explored some of the interconnections between classroom, departmental and school effectiveness and improvement;
- explored the links between appraisal and professional development;
- explored the ways in which pupil and teacher learning intermesh, and the potential for developing your contribution to your school's effectiveness, development and improvement;
- explored the relationship between evaluation and professional development.

# Chapter 1

# Models of professional development and provision

## THE CONTEXT: CULTURAL SHIFTS

Professional development has attracted increasing attention in recent years. Faced with rapid change, demands for high standards and calls for improving quality, teachers have a need, as never before, to update and improve their skills through professional development. Formerly known as in-service education and training, or INSET, a phrase now in much wider currency to describe in-service training, is Continuing Professional Development (CPD). Until the mid-1990s, CPD was often taken up as a matter of voluntary commitment or just as something for those with career ambitions. The present climate in education means that this attitude is no longer appropriate. Greater clarity is now needed on what continuing professional development and in-service training are, and what effect they can reasonably be expected to have as more and more teachers become involved.

There are sources of tension in this situation. On the one hand, there are pressures at national and school levels. These arise from demands for increased quality and the need to implement the National Curriculum in England and Wales and, in Scotland advice from the Scottish Consultative Council on the Curriculum (SCCC which is currently being reformed), as well as the impact of public reporting and inspection in education. In addition, at national level there are demands for certain sectors of the teaching population to undertake specific courses of development, some of which are, or will become, statutory. Examples of these are:

- The introduction by the Teacher Training Agency (TTA) of a plan for the National Professional Qualification for Subject Leaders (NPQSL) and implementation of the National Professional Qualification for Special Educational Needs Co-ordinators (SENCO) as part of the National Standards for Teachers (TTA, 1998); in Scotland, the Scottish Executive Education Department (SEED) is also developing a standards framework around three 'standards' – the Fully Registered Teacher Standard (being revised by the teacher education institutions and the General Teaching

Council for Scotland; the Expert Teacher Standard (in development) and the Standard for Headship in Scotland (which was developed in 1998) – together with a profiling system which will be put in place to enable teachers to organise and chart their progress towards achieving the standards.
- The implementation in 1996 of the National Professional Qualification for Head Teachers (NPQH) – which will become a prerequisite for head teachers in 2002 – and the introduction also of the Headship, Leadership and Management Programme (HEADLAMP) and the Leadership Programme for Serving Head Teachers (LPSH). It seems likely (Blandford, 2000) that the government plans that the National College for School Leadership, due to start operations in September 2000, will become a focus for improving the quality of school leadership. In Scotland, a close equivalent of these programmes has been the introduction in 1998 of the Scottish Qualification for Headship (SQH).

Funding is increasingly funnelled by policy bodies that also control funding, toward certain, identified national priorities for teacher development. These arise out of the establishment by the government in 1994 of the TTA in order to review and develop initial and in-service training of teachers. For example, following a MORI poll of teachers' perceptions of the effectiveness of continuing professional development programmes, the TTA introduced a structure of national standards for teachers in a bid to improve provision and its effects. As Blandford has suggested, this particular national standards framework was created in order to:

- establish clear and explicit expectations of teachers;
- help set targets for professional development and career progression;
- help to focus and improve training and staff development at national, local and school levels;
- ensure that the focus at every point is on improving pupil achievement;
- recognise the expertise required of effective headteachers and teachers in schools.                                        (Blandford, 2000 p.66)

At the time of writing (February 2000), the DfEE is consulting the profession on a range of different aspects of CPD (DfEE, 2000), including the introduction of a range of professional standards. These include the identification at policy level of a national performance threshold that will give successful teachers access to a new, upper pay spine and which would map out potential career progression including management and non-management routes into higher responsibility, status and pay. A range of methods for CPD are included in the proposals including teacher exchanges and business placements, sabbaticals from the classroom, peer networks, professional learning teams, mentoring and school cluster work. A part of this consultation is a set of proposals on what areas might need to be prioritised in the investigation of best practice.

The identification of specific priority areas and the identification of specific practice-related standards in each of these, means that providers of in-service learning are enabled in some areas whilst constrained in others. This in turn narrows what teachers may take up as professional learning opportunities. In addition, responsibility for providing the professional development opportunities has transferred from Local Education Authorities (LEAs) to the Department for Education and Employment (DfEE) and the Teacher Training Agency (TTA). At school level, governors and the management team of the school are responsible for ensuring that staff in the school have access to training and development opportunities which will help develop the individual as well as the team and the school. At national level, inspection of provision is carried out by the Office for Standards in Education (OFSTED).

It is likely that the General Teaching Council (GTC), which at the time of writing is yet to be established, will have a role in fostering professional development, in relation to teaching standards. Part of its role will be to lay down a code of conduct, including professional development, and it will also be expected to advise government on a range of issues including professional development, in terms of individuals, teams, schools, subject disciplines, etc. It is expected to be in operation by late 2000.

In Scotland, the situation is similar. The development of the professional standards has been undertaken by SEED in collaboration with other bodies, as indicated above. CPD supporting the development of these is inspected by the Scottish Inspectorate and SHEFC (Scottish Higher Education Funding Council). However, in Scotland, although the General Teaching Council for Scotland has responsibility for the standards for full entry to the teaching profession, including a two-year period of probation, its role in CPD at the time of writing is not clear.

In contrast to what is laid down in policy requirements, there are the individual needs of teachers, who may see in-service learning in terms of job satisfaction and personal or professional growth. In effect, responding to external calls for greater accountability has to be reconciled with the developmental needs of individual teachers, who may wish to act as far as possible as autonomous professionals. At school level, there are tensions between the needs of the school as a whole as well as teams within it, for in-service learning and the needs of individual teachers.

The tension between individual, team, school and national priorities seems likely to increase in England and Wales (and to a much lesser extent in Scotland), with a far greater government involvement in, and intention to be involved in, the identification of teachers' professional development needs and evaluation of how these are met. These issues are discussed further in this chapter and in Chapter 2, where we examine some aspects of what is coming to be called 'performance management'.

## Definitions: what counts as professional development?

*What comes into your mind when you think of professional development? When you think of 'in-service training', or 'INSET'? What do you think your colleagues mean by these labels?*

Professional development, CPD and INSET are terms which are sometimes used loosely and interchangeably. They tend to be used to cover a broad range of activities designed to contribute to the learning of teachers, who have completed their initial training. Although, sometimes INSET is seen in terms of going on an external course or participating in one laid on in a school, the phrase is also used in a broader sense. Likewise, 'professional development' and CPD are sometimes used in a broad sense and seen as covering all forms of learning undertaken by experienced teachers from courses to private reading to job shadowing, but are also sometimes used in the narrower sense of professional courses. The terms 'professional development' and CPD are also sometimes used to describe moving teachers forward in knowledge or skills. In practice, therefore, it is possible for the distinction between professional development, CPD and INSET to break down.

In this book, the terms professional development, continuing professional development, in-service learning, in-service education and in-service training (or INSET) are used interchangeably, to mean all types of professional learning undertaken by teachers beyond the point of initial training. The term 'INSET course' is only used where a narrow definition of what counts as in-service work is intended.

## Why do it?

*Consider the opportunities you have had for professional development in the past. Reflect on the purposes served by these past experiences. Which were the most important purposes? How have they changed for you?*

There are many reasons for undertaking professional development, such as:

- to improve the job performance skills of the whole staff or groups of staff
- to improve the job performance skills of an individual teacher

- to extend the experience of an individual teacher for career development or promotion purposes
- to develop the professional knowledge and understanding of an individual teacher
- to extend the personal or general education of an individual
- to make staff feel valued
- to promote job satisfaction
- to develop an enhanced view of the job
- to enable teachers to anticipate and prepare for change
- to clarify the whole school or department's policy.

Ultimately, all teacher development will have as one of its aims the improvement of pupil learning. Blandford (2000) in addition emphasises that professional development may enable practitioners to widen their understanding of society, in particular of information and communication technology (ICT).

Usually, the emphasis will be on one purpose, but a number of others might be served incidentally. A key issue, both for those planning and participating in professional development, is the match between methods and purpose.

There is a wide range of methods of professional learning. They include:

- action research
- self-directed study as well as teacher research linked to awards such as the Education Doctorate
- using distance-learning materials
- receiving and/or giving on-the-job coaching, mentoring or tutoring
- school-based and off-site courses of various lengths
- job shadowing and rotation
- peer networks
- membership of a working party or task group (these may include what are sometimes called 'professional learning teams' – DfEE 2000 and also 'learning partnerships' which may involve a range of different participants e.g. schools, LEAs and Higher Education – DfEE 2000)
- school cluster projects involving collaboration, development and sharing of experience/skills
- teacher placement including those in business but also those in other schools
- personal reflection
- experiential 'assignments'
- collaborative learning

- information technology-mediated learning (e.g. through e-mail discussion groups, or self-study using multi-media resources).

*Which of these methods of professional learning have you experienced? Which have you enjoyed? Which did you feel were most effective?*

As you reflect on your own experience of professional development, you may find that the approaches and the activities you have been involved in have changed over time in terms of organisation and methods. Traditionally, professional development was dominated by a course-led model of how teachers learn, in other words by INSET courses, usually in colleges, teachers' centres or professional development centres. To some extent, what it means to be a professional has changed over time, too. Whilst responsibility for decision making about curriculum and assessment has become increasingly centralised (embodying, it could be argued, a government-imposed view of the teacher not as a skilled craftsperson, but as 'technician'), there has been a simultaneous shift of funding and responsibility for professional development of teachers on to schools and on to the individuals within them. Being a professional means taking responsibility for identifying and attempting to meet the professional development needs of oneself and one's institution.

And the ways of meeting these needs have changed in their focus, as well as in terms of organisation and methods. The emphasis on competence-based professional learning and assessment has increased in education as it has in other professions, although there remains an acknowledgement at government level that research and award-bearing courses still have a role to play in teacher development (DfEE 1998). Masters' level and doctorate level study remain popular among teachers, particularly since the introduction of the EdD (Doctor of Education) which is a modular course involving less independent research, now offered by a wide range of universities. The TTA itself, although responsible for competence-based professional qualifications which appear to embrace a technicist view of teachers and teaching, is also, it seems, committed to fostering the use of systematic evidence and effective classroom research undertaken by practitioners (Millett, 1996; Cordlingley, 1999).

However, overall, as we have already acknowledged, the individualistic focus on professional development, through the dominant apprenticeship and course-based models of learning, have decreased in dominance. In parallel, the group focus on professional learning, based in and/or focused on the school and its collective needs, have increased in importance. Indeed, schools are now required by government to have a policy on professional development that offers a range of ways of participating as well as forms of opportunity for staff. With the shift, as Bell (1991) has pointed out, come some assumptions:

- that medium and long-term planning is possible
- that policy, once formulated, can be implemented in classrooms
- that resources will be made available
- that whole-school policies are the most effective way of managing and improving schools.

Research during the 1990s suggests strong links between leadership in the effective management of professional development and school improvement and effectiveness; a trend first identified in the 1970s (Rutter *et al.*, 1979; Mortimore *et al.*, 1988; DES, 1990; Sammons *et al.*, 1995). This we will return to in Chapters 3 and 4.

In addition, the fast growing use of new technologies in schools means that modes of professional learning are opening out in ways we could not have foreseen several years ago.

## Changes in professional development

Over recent years a number of strategies have been developed to increase the impact of courses and to encourage a greater variety of approaches to professional development.

Traditional weaknesses in the course-led model of professional development have included:

- being dominated by off-site courses, geared to individuals rather than to groups of staff;
- not being linked to the needs of departments or schools;
- being undertaken on a voluntary basis and, therefore, not necessarily undertaken by those with the greatest need;
- being random in terms of participation and content in relation to the needs of individual schools;
- having limited impact on practice with little or no dissemination or follow-up;
- that courses are often undertaken during the school day and are, therefore, disruptive on teaching that then has to be covered;
- being open to a possible conflict between practising teachers as participants and theorists as deliverers;
- attempting to cater for people at different starting points and, therefore, not being able to satisfy all participants equally well.

Of course, the other side of the picture is that a course can provide stimulating contact with people from a range of backgrounds. It can allow exchange of ideas between institutions and give rise to new perspectives. In many ways, a definition of a good in-service course might be that it is one where those responsible for organising it have adopted deliberate strategies to counteract the potential problems outlined here.

Such strategies are at the heart of a number of recent developments which have the potential to bring about more effective professional development. Recent developments in professional development include:

- greater emphasis on basing professional development on careful needs analysis linked to evidence of existing practice and thus targeted training (linked, increasingly, to evidence of changes in and achievement following professional development);
- moves towards a broader view of what in-service education and professional development are (some examples of this in England and Wales being the funding provided in 1995 by the Teacher Training Agency for training for newly-qualified head teachers, the introduction by the DfEE of the Standards Fund in 1997 to which schools, LEAs and other agencies were encouraged to bid for funding to run professional development on DfEE priority areas and the introduction by the DfEE of funding for fast-track career routes for teachers in 2000 as well as plans for standards framework offering assessed and moderated career progression routes for teachers. An example of this in Scotland is the introduction and revision of a three-level standards framework, referred to earlier – together with a profiling system to enable teachers to track their progress towards attaining these standards.
- a concern to ensure that school and individual needs are addressed through professional development activities;
- the use of school development planning and professional interviews/appraisal to inform the planning of professional development;
- moves towards building evaluation into professional development and of asking questions, through this, about the effects of professional development on practice;
- an increasing interest in seeing initial teacher training, induction and professional development as a continuum for professional competences and personal professional development portfolios providing a structure for planning development work.

In other words, this has been a trend towards a broader view of what constitutes professional development, and towards a greater emphasis on what happens before an in-service training event (needs identification) and afterwards (evaluation and follow-up).

Underlying a number of the recent developments are concerns with raising standards in education and with addressing national needs. Implicit are possible sources of tension between national, school and individual needs.

## Task 1

Compile a record of recent substantial professional development you have undertaken, whether as a provider or as a participant. You may also find it helpful to refer to an Individual Record of Staff Development if you have maintained one, and if you have been responding to the italicised questions, look back over any notes you have made for them.

After compiling this record, analyse the purpose of this work, and the impact it has had.

- How far has your in-service work been related to institution, service or school needs or your own needs?
- What impact has it had on your work in and outside the classroom and on your school, institution or service?

You may find it helpful to compare your own record with Table 1, based on the experience of a teacher who studied the course on which this book is based. He is deputy head of a large primary school, and is responsible for staff development.

## Individual and school development

The view adopted in this book is that individual and school development are inextricably linked and that you cannot have one without the other. Central to this view is the concept of the developing school or the school as a learning organisation. If schools are about promoting the learning of pupils in a changing world and learning is worthwhile and not a static or bounded process, then the learning of education professionals throughout their careers is essential. This is recognised by researchers, commentators and policy makers (Hopkins, Ainscow and West, 1994; Southworth, 1994; Sammons, Hillman and Mortimore, 1995; Green, 1999). The linking of teachers' development to the raising of pupils' standards of achievement is central to policy in this area. As Blandford (2000) puts it,

> The government requires LEAs and schools to ensure:
> - a proper targeting of development opportunities through needs assessment and appraisal;

*Table 1* A record of professional development/INSET

| Professional development activity | Time involved | Needs level | Impact level |
|---|---|---|---|
| Deputy Head's management course (at teachers' centre: lectures, discussions, workshop activity, guided reading) | 13 hours | My own<br><br>The school | Personal professional development<br><br>School level |
| Appraisal of my role as staff development co-ordinator (in school, with head teacher) | 2 hours | My own<br><br>The school | Personal professional development<br><br>School level |
| School development planning (in school with senior management team: meetings, drafting and discussing plans for school development) | 4 hours | The school | The school as a system<br><br>Individual staff members<br><br>Children's learning |
| School development planning (in school, with head teacher and individual members of staff; drafting and discussing plans). | 14 hours | The school<br><br>Individual staff members | The school as a system<br><br>Individual staff members |
| Appraisal in-service work (at teachers' centre: lectures, discussions and role plays) | 5 hours | My own<br><br>My school | Personal professional development<br><br>School level |
| Staff development network meetings (at teachers' centre, with other SDCs: discussions | 6 hours | My own | Personal professional development |

- rigorous quality assurance of provision so that professional development activities address identified needs;
- effective monitoring and evaluation of development activities and the setting of targets for improvement for the maximum impact of professional development on classroom practice;
- that the (annual) five non-contact days are used as part of schools' planned programmes of professional development;
- accountability to school governors for the professional development of staff and its impact.                                    (Blandford, 2000 p.75).

A developmental model of appraisal provides a mechanism for placing professional development or learning on the agenda of all teachers on a regular basis. Appraisal seen in this way can also be a vehicle for balancing individual and organisational needs for professional development. School development plans provide a clearly defined context for decisions on balancing school and individual demands for all forms of in-service education.

Thus, central to the concept of the developing or learning school is the idea that appraisal, school development planning and evaluation of the school's work, including the professional development of its staff, can combine to provide opportunities for teacher and school development. These approaches provide a means for responding to the demands of government and society for education of a high standard and for teachers and schools to be properly accountable. Part of the process of accountability involves the inspection by OFSTED of the extent to which arrangements for induction, appraisal and staff development of staff facilitates their effectiveness.

## NATIONAL PRIORITIES

As the previous discussions have highlighted, it is important to recognise the shift during the late 1990s toward giving national priorities an increasingly powerful role in professional development, alongside both school and individual priorities. The national priorities are currently focused around specific needs such as ICT, literacy, numeracy, special educational needs and headship training – although as indicated above, the DfEE is, as of February 2000, consulting on other possible priority areas (DfEE, 2000).

In selecting professional development opportunities, then, individual teachers balance their own needs against those of both their school and the national framework of priorities and funding for these.

## MODELS OF PROFESSIONAL DEVELOPMENT AND PROVISION

Thinking about professional development from several different perspectives can help you to analyse previous professional development experience, and to clarify future plans. From this point on, we will be introducing a number of models and frameworks developed by specialists in professional development. We intend you to engage with these critically, and to consider how appropriate each is to you, your experience and your context. Feel free to challenge and adapt any or all of them, and to 'own' each for yourself. The models and frameworks should provide you with tools for analysing the professional development you are concerned with – both your own and, if appropriate, the learning of others.

It is possible to look at professional development from a number of different angles:

- purposes
- location
- length
- methods
- levels of impact.

## Purposes

Professor Ray Bolam, a writer in this field, uses the term 'continuing education' (1986) for professional development and sees continuing education serving five main purposes, meeting the needs of individuals as well as requirements of the system they are part of. In this early model, he identifies five purposes of professional development. He places these on a continuum of needs, at one end of which the system's needs are dominant, and at the other end of which the individual's needs are dominant, as follows.

System needs are more dominant at the end of the continuum that caters for what he names 'purpose 1: staff/group performance'. 'Purpose 2', which is 'individual job performance', involves slight dominance of system needs but also individual needs. 'Purpose 3', which is 'career development', he suggests involves a slight dominance of individual over system needs, whereas 'purpose 4' or 'professional knowledge', involves dominance of individual over system needs, and 'purpose 5', or 'personal education', involves strong dominance of individual over system needs.

Bolam's model reminds us that professional development can be more or less geared towards whole school (system) or individual needs. At one end of the continuum, a school might use a closure day to involve all staff in training about a whole school issue. At the other end of the continuum, an individual teacher might engage in personal reading or take up a new interest, which is primarily about their own personal growth. In effect, an individual piece of INSET or a whole programme of professional development can be located on this model. For example, a head teacher may decide that a closure day should be used to address a whole school issue, such as assessment, identified in the school development plan (purpose 1). A head of department (principal teacher in Scotland) or curriculum co-ordinator, newly appointed to his or her post, might be asked to attend a course for new heads of department or co-ordinators to develop their skills (purpose 2). Alternatively, someone might ask to go on a course for prospective deputy heads (purpose 3) or to find out about new developments in a subject (purpose 4). Finally, a tired and jaded English teacher might aim to rekindle their enthusiasm by reading novels or watching plays (purpose 5).

Bolam has more recently (1993) proposed a number of types of professional development activity, which can be seen as a development of the continuum idea described above. He proposes these as: *practitioner development* (which is usually school-based, involving the individual and including such activities as observation, job shadowing, induction and team teaching); *professional education* (which usually involves award-bearing courses offered in higher education institutions, which focus on the interface between theory and practice), *professional training* (which includes such activities as courses, workshops and conferences emphasising practical skills and information – some of which may lead to academic awards or accreditation towards national standards) and *professional support* (which forms part of collegial support in order to fulfil contractual conditions of service and includes such activities as appraisal, promotion, career development, mentoring, team building, equality of opportunity and re-deployment).

The earlier Bolam model in particular focuses upon system vs. individual priorities. In contrast, Howard Bradley (1991) lists the following purposes which focus on specific outcomes:

- to make people feel valued in the job they do
- to enable them to do this job well so that they receive the positive feedback essential for job satisfaction and for motivation
- to help them anticipate and prepare for changes in their work
- to encourage them to derive excitement and satisfaction from their involvement in change
- to make them feel willing and competent to contribute constructively to the development of the school.

As with Bolam's model, there is a recognition that professional development can serve both individual and system needs. This list of purposes can be used to analyse an individual INSET event or a whole programme or series of events. Bradley, however, draws out the additional perspective of how people feel about what they do.

In addition to the contrasts between school and individual needs for the professional development of teachers, is that of needs arising within a team or department. The needs of each relate to the major function of each. So, the needs or priorities of the school or institution as a whole will reflect the role of the school or institution in providing a wide range of learning experiences for a large number of people. The needs of the department will reflect the specialism of the team in providing learning experiences of a particular type for, perhaps, a selected group of people. The needs of the individual professional will reflect not only the professional role they have within the organisation, but also their professional learning, working style, and career aspirations.

Reconciling the different needs of schools, departmental teams and individuals has become an issue, particularly in view of the trend since the late 1980s towards linking national funding for training to specific priority areas. This has meant that on top of the necessarily different and perhaps conflicting perspectives of school/department/individual needs, the way in which priorities are selected is now influenced by a set of national priorities external to the school and, perhaps, remote from its immediate concerns.

We have, therefore, moved from a situation, where it could be argued that professional development was driven to too great an extent by individual needs, to one where individual needs can potentially get squeezed out by school or wider system needs. Indeed, whereas many of the issues or topics for professional development were determined by individual teachers, as discussed earlier in this chapter, these priorities are now determined at other levels, beyond the individual. This might include the reduction of opportunities for a subject specialist to do some work on his or her own subject or alternatively might relate to other ways of developing personal interests. Time for such personal education is a good way for someone to recharge their batteries and it can be argued that a teacher who is excited and motivated by the experience of their own learning is likely to be in a strong position to communicate the excitement of learning to pupils.

## Location

The different ways of organising professional development are often described in a number of categories relating to their location: school-based professional development, school-focused or school-centred professional development and off-site INSET/professional development. As well as relating to location, the distinctions also relate to purposes and orientation.

### Off-site professional development

The dominant model traditionally for professional development has been the off-site professional development course. Here teachers from a number of schools typically come together for varying lengths of time for a training course. Such courses have ranged from short courses of one day or less to longer, award-bearing courses. As indicated in the earlier discussions, since the late 1980s, there has been an increasing interest in the

accreditation of professional development courses, by both higher education institutions and also policy bodies such as the TTA.

We touched earlier on some of the weaknesses of the off-site approach
to professional learning. These include perceived or actual gaps between
theory and practice, and lack of supporting culture in valuing individuals'
off-site experiences for the team or school as a whole. Nevertheless, it is
fair to say that teachers have often found such courses stimulating both in
terms of acquiring new ideas, and also in exchanging experience with
those from other schools.

Other forms of off-site professional development, which became fairly
widespread during the mid- to late 1980s, included teacher placements in
local workplaces. These often involve job shadowing, working on a small
scale project for the company or host organisation, collecting materials
and ideas for curriculum and management in the school and so on.
Teacher placements offer opportunities for teachers to negotiate the terms
and focus of the placement to meet their own and their school's needs.
Other off-site professional development includes cluster or cross-school
development work, working groups and workshops and training courses
on specific issues such as assessment, areas of the curriculum or management. This cluster or cross-school professional development is distinct
from off-site courses, in so far as the needs are collectively identified and
addressed by the schools involved.

### School-based professional development

Moves towards school-based professional development arose out of concerns with the limitations of the course-led model of delivery. One form of
school-based professional development is the in-service course, provided
within the school and targeted at a group of staff. Two sets of aims underpin this approach. One set of aims is about achieving a better match of a
professional development course to the needs and culture of a particular
group of professionals. The second set of aims is about having some direct
impact on practice.

The drawback in the school-based approach to professional development can be that it becomes rather insular, whether it is facilitated by
someone within the school or from outside (e.g. Local Education Authority, higher education, curriculum project, etc.) although by bringing in an
outsider insularity, at least initially, is reduced. On the other hand, when
school-based work is seen as comprising a wide range of professional
development opportunities and not solely in terms of courses, then the
perspective changes. Such thinking has led to the development of a range
of learning opportunities in schools, for example the use of mentoring and
job shadowing, recently documented by Kerry and Mayes (1995).

Of course, the notion of on-the-job learning by teachers has a long history, especially when it comes to reflection on classroom practice. There is a long tradition of teachers undertaking action research and acting as reflective practitioners, and this is a theme returned to below. The School Management Task Force (Styan *et al.*, 1990) drew attention to a wide range of on-the-job opportunities for management development. The approach advocated included much greater use of distance learning materials and other similar information packs, also working on workplace-focused projects or on personal management skills with other members of the management team, rather than depending on residential sessions involving heavy dependence on external speakers.

### School-focused professional development

We take the view that many forms of *school-focused* work are valuable. School-centred or school-focused professional development is similar to school-based professional development, in so far as the target group is some or all the staff of the particular school and the programme of study is related to the needs of the particular group or school. The location is, however, outside the school itself. The distractions of receiving training in school are, therefore, avoided. On the other hand, there is the same danger of insularity as in the school-based approach.

Of course, one of the influences on choice of site and purpose for professional development is the source and extent of funding. The question of whether supply cover will be needed, and of whether government decreed grants or funds are available will of course influence a school's choices. And the source of and reasons for funding will carry different agendas, or intentions, which may need some consideration.

By linking the different *purposes*, outlined in the previous section, to the question of the *location* of professional development, it is possible to develop an analytical matrix such as the one on the next page, completed by a teacher who followed the Open University course on which this book is based.

This matrix was completed by a part-time middle school teacher, responsible for Personal and Social Education (PSE). She undertook two LEA-provided courses at the Teachers' Centre and much development work in school, to help clarify and develop a sex education policy and develop teaching.

In considering the pros and cons of your own professional development experience you may have become more aware of ways that location and purpose of professional development interweave. You may have highlighted how other professional development was less well chosen in

| Purpose | Location | | |
| --- | --- | --- | --- |
| | *Off-site* | *School-based* | *School-focused* |
| Staff/group performance | | School working party: we drafted a process for establishing what we currently do, and targets for development | |
| Individual job performance | 2 LEA PHSE co-ordinator courses: looked at the co-ordinator's role | School working party: I think the experience gave me a chance to become a better co-ordinator | 2 LEA PHSE co-ordinator courses: looked at how to develop PHSE in a whole institution; I action planned for it. |
| Career development | 2 LEA courses: helped me plan my next steps! | School working party: gave me experience in leading a group – I would like to do some more! | |
| Professional knowledge | 2 LEA courses: lots of PHSE info | | 2 LEA courses: info on my obligations as PSE co-ordinator |
| *Personal education* | | | |
| To make staff feel valued | 2 LEA courses: made me feel valued as a P/T member of staff | Working party: I really wanted to collaborate with my colleagues | |
| *Promoting job satisfaction* | | | |
| Developing an enhanced view of the job | 2 LEA courses: widened my perspective | School working party: widened my perspective of what my job involves | |
| Anticipating and planning for change | 2 LEA courses: about developing and implementing policy | School working party: our focus was developing a policy and our practice | 2 LEA courses: looked at how to plan for change at school level |
| Clarifying school or departmental policy | 2 LEA courses: gave info on what could be included in a policy document | School working party: our purpose was to clarify school policy | 2 LEA courses: gave ideas/strategies for developing a whole school policy |

*Figure 1* Analytical matrix of professional development

## Task 2

Use a matrix like the one in Figure 1 to categorise the experiences you compiled in Task 1 into this model of off-site, school-based and school-focused professional development. From these experiences, what are the pros and cons of each approach? If you are school-based how does the way your school uses its 'closure days' fit into this model? Jot down your thoughts in a notebook.

linking the location to its purpose appropriately. As you work through this course, you should become more aware of appropriate ways of linking professional development locations to meet purpose.

## Linking locations for professional development: the cascade

One frequent strategy for linking off-site and school-based training is the 'cascade' approach. Here one or two key people from a school are trained at off-site courses and charged with replicating the training for colleagues back in school, in ways which are appropriate there. In other words, dissemination is built into the initial learning process. Cascade training tends to involve the dissemination of a central 'message' or 'approach'. Two classic examples of this approach are the way it was used for GCSE training and later for SAT training in 1991, both in England and Wales. An example from Scotland would be the Standard Grade Development Programme. HMI (1988) offered a critique of the GCSE training and their comments point to some of the factors that need to be addressed if the cascade approach is to be used successfully:

> The cascade model envisages a series of consecutive training processes, each occurring as a result of the previous one, and designed to impart an agreed and consistent body of knowledge, skills and attitudes. Flexibility in training methods is an integral part of the model. In theory and in practice the successful implementation of the model requires that:
> - The audiences are well defined and their particular needs carefully targeted;
> - Clear training objectives are set and the training materials are of high quality, well structured, logical, credible and consistent. Detailed and comprehensive training notes, common to all involved, are used;
> - The trainers are carefully selected for their support of the aims of the programme, the match between their experience and expertise and particular stages of the training programme; their competence as

trainers and their understanding of the knowledge and skills to be imparted; each stage of the programme provides time to prepare thoroughly and for trainees to absorb and reflect on the training;

- The risk of idiosyncratic personal interpretations of the training objectives is minimised by setting each stage of the whole process within a firm structure and removing any ambiguity in the objectives and the training materials. (HMI, 1988)

These factors could, of course, be applied to any professional development and not just the cascade model. But perhaps the most fundamental requirement for the cascade model, made under point 3 in the HMI extract, is to show participants how to run sessions and other dissemination activities with their colleagues, and to give them ideas, materials, formats and activities for this purpose. The complexity of the task of dissemination also relates to whether the training is primarily concerned with imparting knowledge, changing attitudes, or developing skills, with dissemination of knowledge being the most straightforward. Where changes in skill and attitude are involved, then support and training over time are likely to be needed and the interactions between external or school trainers and the trainees are likely to be more complex. The need for schools to support the implementation of cascade training is also identified by the government in its recent Green Paper (1998).

The cascade approach is not the only, or always the most appropriate, way of linking locations for professional development. Where there is a central message to convey it can be useful. However, the model would be less appropriate for a more developmental focus for professional learning.

## Summary

So far we have considered the purposes and location of professional development, and to what extent these are linked.

The argument we have developed so far is that each location for professional development has its strengths and weaknesses; for example, the cross-fertilisation of ideas and the opportunities for detailed study over time of the off-site approach are strengths. The point to remember, however, is to adopt a strategy which ensures that the off-site work is linked to what happens in school. On the other hand, opportunities to ensure relevance to needs and practice of the school-based and school-focused professional development need to be combined with strategies to avoid insularity or pooling collective ignorance.

These strategies will include involving individuals who work in a wider context than simply your own school or institution.

## Length

*Reflect on the professional development work you identified in Task 1. Of what duration was each opportunity you undertook or created? Consider the sequence in which they took place. What kinds of continuity were there between the different experiences?*

It is also possible to consider professional development in terms of its duration, or length, and also in terms of the related issues of sequence and continuity. Fullan (1982) coined the phrase that 'change is a process, not an event', portraying change as a complex process, that takes place over time and involves the interaction of an array of factors and individuals. He argued that, 'if we are interested in a theory of "changing" – in identifying those factors most possible to alter and most instrumental in bringing about change at the level of practice – professional development would be at the very top of the list.' Given that change takes place over time, those involved in change are also likely to need support and training over time. In other words, there is a need to think in terms of continuity and sequence in professional development.

The range of professional development opportunities available to teachers does not necessarily fit this ideal. Table 2 provides a summary of typical opportunities and groups them in terms of length; most will be 'part-time' rather than full-time; and some will be face to face, others 'distance' learning.

In practice the 'process' that Fullan refers to happens through the meshing together of professional development experience over time, and the development of some continuity. In other words, the topics of professional development may be the same; or the experiences may involve the same group of people; or be concerned with the same purpose; or involve the same method or location, etc. The continuities are sometimes not obvious until after the event.

You may find it helpful to compare your own experience with this example drawn from a reception teacher in an infant school who studied the Open University course which formed the basis for this book. She was reflecting on the continuity in some of her professional development experience, and drew the diagram shown in Table 3 in her notebook.

The reception teacher's analysis of the diagram read as follows:

> I realise now that the continuities were to do with purpose – i.e. all three professional development experiences contributed to:
> - my career development
> - promoting my job satisfaction
> - giving me confidence to contribute to school policy on reading, and work with adults other than teachers

*Table 2* A range of professional development opportunities

| Long opportunities | 1–3 years |
| --- | --- |
| Following through school development plan; MA, MBA, MEd, Advanced Diploma, etc.; job rotation; school-based, local or national curriculum development. A range of practice-focused self-development activities facilitated by a provider, in order to meet National Standards. | |

| Short opportunities | 2–20 days |
| --- | --- |
| Working groups; 20 day courses, award-bearing courses delivered at a number of sessions spread over time; short university courses such as certificate modules; summer residentials; teacher placements. | |

| Incidental opportunities | 1 day or less |
| --- | --- |
| Study days; one day courses; twilight briefing sessions; moderation sessions; job shadowing; attending association conferences. | |

Although I started the book review group first, then organised the parents' evening, and then had Polly as a student, by the time Polly came I now realise I was much more able to share my expertise on school reading policy and wider books available for this age group. I was also much more confident about supporting her as an adult other than a teacher. The interface between professional and quasi-professional really interests me.

## Methods

*Consider one substantial element of your own professional development (you may find it useful to refer to Tasks 1 and 2). What different kinds of activities did it involve? Which kinds of activity did you most enjoy? Which did you learn most from? What contrasting professional development activities have you experienced through other aspects of your professional learning?*

You will of course be aware of the varied methods, or the processes involved in different forms of professional development. You are probably fairly aware of the ones you find accessible and useful, too.

Now consider this model developed by two American experts in professional development, Joyce and Showers (1988), where they relate kinds of activity during professional development, to the impact they each have. They identify the following components of professional development:

*Table 3* Example of a reception teacher's professional development experience

| Short opportunities | Having a student teacher in my class | January–March 10 weeks (4 days a week) |
|---|---|---|
| Incidental opportunities | Joining the LEA's infant book review group | September–July (9 twilight INSETS at the teachers' centre over the year) |
| | Organising a parents' evening on reading with infants | October (1 evening; 2 twilights preparing) |

- presentation/theory
- demonstration
- practice in simulated settings
- feedback on performance
- coaching/assistance in the classroom.

They then suggest that each of these components of professional development has impact on different levels, which they name as:

- awareness
- knowledge
- skills
- application.

Their model goes as follows:

| *Presentation/theory* | impacts on awareness. |
|---|---|
| *Demonstration* | impacts on awareness and knowledge. |
| *Practice in simulated settings* | impacts on awareness and knowledge. |
| *Feedback on performance* | impacts on awareness, knowledge, skills and application. |
| *Assistance in the classroom* | impacts on awareness, knowledge, skills and application. |

The Joyce and Showers model is not necessarily complete, or even a 'truth', as we will explore in Chapter 11 and the Appendix, although it is a useful reference point on which to reflect. For example, you might wonder whether presentation/theory components of professional development do not have the capacity to increase knowledge as well as awareness, and similarly whether practice in simulated settings does not have the capacity to develop skills. We could, also, add to the 'components' which Joyce and Showers identify, for example we might add brainstorming, pooling, guided reading, and so on – although these could perhaps be subsumed under Joyce and Showers' categories.

Their contention is that the most effective training activities should combine theory, modelling, practice, feedback and coaching for application.

*Consider again a substantial element of your professional development experience. Which methods named by Joyce and Showers did it involve? What is your perception of the levels of impact of the methods you experienced or created? From your own experience, consider whether or not you would agree with Joyce and Showers that the most effective professional development activities should combine theory, modelling, practice, feedback and coaching for application.*

Other methods, not named in the Joyce and Showers model, include action research, working group discussions, planning activities, visits to other schools, visits to museums/galleries, teacher placements, the creative use of ICT, mentoring, peer networks, and job shadowing, rotation or exchange. We explore action research in some detail, and then touch on working with others, visits/placements, the creative use of ICT and job definition/comparison.

### Action research

For many teachers, a particularly rewarding form of professional development that is directly linked with practice has been action research. Here the teacher aims to identify an aspect of his or her work for investigation in order to develop, implement and evaluate a new approach as shown in Figure 2.

In action research, a teacher would start by collecting data and analysing his/her classroom practice and aim if possible to compare his/her perceptions with those of pupils or an observer. The aim is to use the analysis to identify issues for possible development. Once the analysis has taken place, then a problem or issue would be selected and a strategy identified for improving practice in this area. This action hypothesis would then be introduced by the teacher into his/her teaching, the data collected and analysed again. This could result in the strategy being modified, retained or rejected. The next cycle of activity could, therefore, centre on a new issue or the development of a refined strategy. The interesting point about action research is that it links together professional development and evaluation. Professional development through action research is grounded in a careful analysis of the situation in which a teacher operates and the various interactions involved.

Action research has tended to involve a wide range of approaches for gathering data about a teacher's work. It is a systematic attempt to ensure that personal reflection is carried out in valid way. The focus is very much on the concerns and issues of the individual teacher, but the possibility is

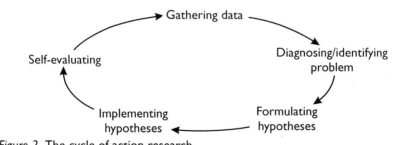

*Figure 2* The cycle of action research

open for peer support and collaborative learning. Such ongoing personal reflection and even less formal equivalents are important strands of teacher learning. There is no reason why such approaches cannot complement professional development arising from whole school needs as it is possible to set up action research projects to investigate whole school issues in individual classrooms.

For example, one secondary teacher who followed the Open University version of this book, co-ordinated the development and implementation of a cross-curricular health education module in her school. She collected data from some classes and some colleagues in order to evaluate it.

### Working with colleagues

Many teachers undergo professional development through working with colleagues on a defined task or set of problems such as during working-group discussions or planning activities. This kind of professional development is often underestimated; and yet learning from successes and failures of strategies and working relationships can lead to professional growth and learning for individuals, groups and schools as organisations.

Hargreaves (1994a and b) has described the way in which the culture of individualism is powerfully built into the ways in which many schools operate (where teaching itself is a 'private' activity, reflected in the very layout of the building). He argues that one of the roots of the desire for individualism in teacher culture comes not from self-assurance, but rather from a hesitancy and lack of confidence in their own development as teachers. Other writers such as Ruiz and Parez (1997) suggest that the need for teachers to work together is increasingly powerful, and indeed, that much professional development relies on a collaborative model, where problems faced by schools are tackled by the collective synergy of communal effort.

Some aspects of the teacher's role automatically involve working with others and can be sources of professional development even if this is not the stated aim of them. For example, a teacher acting as a mentor to a colleague both offers professional development and also experiences it at a different level, and from different perspectives, for themselves.

### Visits and placements

Visits provide another form of in-service and professional development; whether visits to other schools, to resource centres such as museums or galleries, or to other kinds of workplace such as can be organised through a teacher placement. The key feature of any visit, however, if it is to provide professional development, is being clear about why you are undertaking it, and precisely what you hope to learn, gain, achieve or find out. A visit to another school might, for instance, be in order to find out about the way a specific part of the curriculum is planned, taught, learned, assessed or resourced. It might focus on the staffing structures in the school. It might focus on the way the budget is allocated and managed. It might focus on the relationship between governors, parents and the staff or children, and so on. Such visits might range from short to long, and could include exchanges of staff for specific purposes; indeed the DfEE hopes to begin funding international study visits (DfEE, 2000). Closer to home, a visit to a resource centre might focus on the potential of the centre to enrich teaching generally in the department or school in a particular curriculum area, or might be much more narrowly focused on a particular event, activity, class or part of that subject. Equally it might focus on your capacity to advise and develop the facilities offered by the resource centre. A teacher placement might, similarly, have a curriculum focus, a management/people related focus, or a financial one – and again could involve both learning from the workplace and contributing to it, for either school-related or for personal development.

### The creative use of ICT

Information and communication technology offers an increasing range of ways of linking with professional development opportunities, including simple data/resource collection, supported open learning programmes which have interactive elements built in via electronic conferencing and e-mail support with a tutor and fellow students, as well as personally initiated dialogues with colleagues about practice. Russell & Bullock (1999) for example cite a project in which a university teacher and one of his teacher training students set up an e-mail dialogue in which, over a bounded period of time, they shared electronically their reflections on their own practice, the one as a novice and the other as an expert, and gave one another feedback on these. Other projects, such as the Open University's Learning Schools Programme, offer facilities whereby teachers can join electronic conferences themed around particular issues, and both share and develop practice in this way, either as part of an award-bearing course or separate from it.

The potential for all kinds of 'virtual' support centres ranging from those offering 'teaching tips' to those fostering the deeper examination of practice and its effectiveness, through a virtual environment, is being explored at a number of levels. Some funding is being set aside to support teachers in accessing such initiatives (DfEE, 2000).

### Job definition/comparison

Some professional development opportunities involve defining one's own work role and that of others. Job shadowing and job rotation are two ways of achieving this. 'Shadowing' somebody else at work in your own school or outside it helps to build up a picture of the role and the way a particular individual carries it out; the reasons for doing this might range from preparing yourself to take on that role (for instance, in moving from deputy head to head; from class teacher to class teacher and co-ordinator for an aspect of school life such as assessment), to exploring ways in which you and the person you are shadowing can work more closely/effectively (for instance, in the case of a 'parallel' teaching class, in a secondary school; or a teacher of the year above or below you in a primary school). Equally, job shadowing could form part of the needs-identification stage for in-service work and professional development for a whole team or indeed a whole school.

Job rotation, often employed in small schools such as in the primary sector, is a way of extending professional experience, and of developing new areas of professional strength and expertise as well as using existing ones. Comparing jobs may also take place as a consequence of visits to other schools, as well as exchanges of staff.

*Which methods of professional development have you experienced – as producer or as participant? Which do you prefer? What are the strengths and weaknesses of each, in your opinion? Which methods (if any) you do not choose or have access to but would consider in the future?*

## Levels of impact

*Choose a part of your own professional development. What levels of impact do you consider were intended, and actually resulted, from this professional development?*

Professional development is designed to help people change. As noted above when we considered Joyce and Showers, change can be thought of in terms of change in awareness, knowledge, attitudes and skills. Earlier in this chapter we considered the purposes, and levels of intended impact of in-service work, which included:

- whole staff, team, department or faculty performance
- an individual teacher's practice
- an individual teacher's role or career
- an individual teacher's professional knowledge
- an individual teacher's personal education or growth.

It is also possible to look at professional development in terms of its direct and indirect impact on:

- children's learning and achievement in the classroom
- school or team management and organisation.

Both of these latter two are currently emphasised by policy bodies and the holders of funding, as discussed earlier in the chapter. Clearly the intended impact may be direct or indirect. Significant impact is likely to depend on matching professional development methods to purposes by considering intended levels of impact, and thinking in terms of professional development as a continuous process sequenced over time, rather than as a one-off event. In other words, in selecting professional development, you should be as aware as possible of what the impact is, i.e. whether you are seeking impact in changing awareness, knowledge, attitudes or skills, who this involves, (i.e. individuals/group, teachers or other adults or children) and in what ways (i.e. career/role/practice/personal growth).

## Task 3

**Look back at the records and notes you compiled for Task 1 where you considered the purposes and impact of the professional development you have brought to this course, reviewing your thoughts. Consider how appropriate your own professional development was, in terms of purposes, location, length, methods and levels of impact.**

**Summary of Chapter 1**

- We have explored the wider cultural and policy context for continuing professional development and in-service training, and created a working definition of professional learning which incorporates a very broad range of activities designed to support the learning of teachers who have completed their initial training.
- We have explored some ways in which teacher professional development is related to pupil attainment.
- We have looked at a number of dimensions to consider in professional development relating to its:
  - purposes
  - location
  - length
  - methods, and
  - levels of impact.
- We have outlined the range of purposes for professional development and the tension between system and individual needs, including increasing accountability to government in this set of relationships.
- We have presented you with a critique of school-based, off-site and school-centred professional development.
- We have raised the issues of length and continuity in professional development.
- We have discussed the variety of methods that can be used for professional development; in particular we have drawn attention to the Joyce and Showers components of effective training, but we have also raised the issue of the extent to which professional development may be an individualistic activity or a collective one, and the ways in which new technologies are bringing about new possibilities for professional development.

We have raised the issue of different levels of impact of professional development in terms of *what* the impact is (knowledge, attitude, awareness, skills) and *who* is affected (teachers, schools, children and stakeholders such as government/policy makers) and *how* (i.e. career/personal).

# Chapter 2

# Principles of appraisal

In this chapter, we consider the process of appraisal (or staff development and review, as it is sometimes known in Scotland). We take the stance that it offers, potentially, both a way of identifying professional development needs and also of reconciling tensions between individual and school priorities. The process of appraisal provides a way of moving from identifying needs to setting up a series of actions which aim to do something about fulfilling them.

## THE NATURE OF APPRAISAL

The introduction of teacher and head teacher appraisal in England and Wales has been a long and tortuous process. The 1980s witnessed a steady growth of school-based appraisal schemes and increasing interest in moving towards a national framework. The national School Teacher Appraisal Pilot Study of 1987–89 was set up following lengthy consultation between government and teacher unions from 1982–86. The pilot study was designed to inform the design of national appraisal guidelines and played a major role in developing the model that was eventually introduced by the government in the 1991 appraisal regulations and circular (Secretary of State for Education and Science, 1991a and b). It remains a contentious and debated area, since the publication of the Green Paper in 1998 (DfEE, 1998).

The path has been similar in Scotland. In 1984, the National Committee for the In-service Training of Teachers (NCITT) published a report entitled 'Arrangements for the Staff Development of Teachers'. As part of its concern for the quality of pupils' education this report made two important statements. It defined staff development as the full range of planned activities and experiences which contribute to maintaining and developing professional expertise. The report also stated that there was a need to establish better management arrangements for planning and co-ordinating the wide range of training and development activities.

In the period following publication, there was a growing awareness of the implications of the new, wider definition. There was also an increased emphasis, in all parts of the country at both authority and institutional levels, on finding better ways to manage staff development. In some authorities there were initiatives specifically designed to achieve these objectives. In session 1988–89 pilot studies were run on staff development and appraisal in various parts of the country. All local authorities now have schemes in place and a considerable number of teaching staff have been appraised.

Evidence from current practice confirmed that staff development was seen to be vital for ensuring the quality of learning and teaching in schools; it provided a means of continuing the development of teachers as members of a profession operating in a changing educational world. Successful models for managing staff development have been implemented.

Staff development and review is seen by many in Scotland as a positive process, intended to raise the quality of education by providing teachers with better job satisfaction, more appropriate staff development and better planned career development based upon more informed decisions.

## Appraisal for accountability, or for development?

Throughout these developments in bringing in appraisal schemes, there has been considerable debate on the appropriate nature of an appraisal scheme for teachers. Different views on the purposes and nature of appraisal have been put forward. These have tended to fall along a continuum, with the view of appraisal as being about accountability at one end and the view of appraisal as being about development at the other, as illustrated in Figure 3. These differences of opinion about appraisal are not just restricted to education.

| *Accountability Model* | *Development Model* |
|---|---|
| Appraisal is seen as: | Appraisal is seen as: |
| • informing decisions on duties, pay, promotion and tenure | • a process of review and development about improvement; performance enhancement through performance management |
| • backward looking/general one-way | |
| • involving judgement by a superior | • forward looking/focused and selective |
| • linked to rating or grading | • two-way, involving shared evaluation |
| • based on standardised criteria | • centred on agreeing targets |
| • being validated by a written record | • individualised, with criteria being open to negotiation and contextualisation |
| | • being validated by effective outcomes |

*Figure 3* The two ends of the appraisal spectrum

Indeed, the extent to which appraisal is a requirement influences opinion on what it can or should be used for. For example, where support services in England and Wales have not been obliged to introduce appraisal, it may perhaps be perceived under the developmental model more readily.

It has been argued (Bennett, Lister and McManus, 1992), that the two elements of appraisal have completely different philosophical roots from one another, these reaching back into the 1970s. Bennett *et al.* suggest that the accountability route is traceable to James Callaghan's Ruskin College speech in 1976, where he exhorted teachers to ensure that what they were doing with children in schools met the needs and requirements of both parents and the economy. They suggest that this lay the philosophical groundwork for a view of teaching as the efficient deployment of resource for society's good, where teachers and schools were accountable to wider society. The developmental approach to appraisal on the other hand can be traced back to the James Report (James, 1972) which explored the nature of and need for teacher development. The increasingly systematic identification of teachers' INSET needs and the allocation of specific resources address these needs. Early national funding formulae such as TRIST, GRIST, LEATGs and GEST (being, Bennett *et al.* suggest, the precursors of appraisal in the sense of funding professional development systematically) can be seen as flowing from that original starting point in the James Report. The commitment to appraising performance and the need to inform and plan future professional development is key.

The process of appraising can, in our view, be interpreted as having both a formative and a summative function. Appraising in order to improve practice and performance then, might be seen as formative. It also leans more toward appraisal for developmental purposes. On the other hand, judging performance at a particular point in time without reference to improvement is a summative act – and leans more toward appraisal for accountability purposes. In practice, appraisal in your own context may be a mixture of the two. As the climate has gradually shifted during the 1990s toward accountability in the context of nationally-defined standards and criteria for performance, it has been suggested that, to survive, the developmental model must be continuously scrutinised and evaluated by schools, their governing bodies, LEAs, OFSTED, trainers and evaluators (Blandford, 2000).

## TRANSLATING POLICY INTO PRACTICE

Under the appraisal regulations, LEAs in the case of maintained schools and governing bodies in the case of grant-maintained schools are seen as the 'appraising body' responsible for ensuring that appraisal is introduced and operated properly and effectively. In effect, schools are operating appraisal in the light of both national and local guidance.

Bollington, Hopkins and West (1990), reviewing a range of pilot and pre-pilot studies in appraisal, suggested the following key principles in implementing appraisal:

1   the need for commitment to the process and credibility in those presenting and introducing the scheme;
2   the need to consult with and involve all interested parties in planning for appraisal;
3   the need for the scheme to be developmental, constructive and positive;
4   the need to provide adequate training for those involved in appraisal;
5   the need to actively involve teachers not only in the design of the process but also in discussing criteria used and the areas chosen for appraisal;
6   the need for the process to be two-way and related to the individual school context and the appraisee's own stage of development.
                        (Bollington, Hopkins and West, 1990, p. 9–10)

In their comments Bollington *et al.* focus on the level of the school as an institution, although they are not explicit about all of the staff who need to be involved – including governors. More recently, Blandford (2000) has added to these suggested guidelines by proposing that the appraisal scheme also needs to be acceptable to LEA personnel. Blandford also suggests that appraisal schemes should be integral to the school's own development strategy, should avoid over-bureaucratisation and should draw on a range of data sources. The NUT's advice on appraisal (1993) identifies the ways in which appraisees and appraisers can be protected from abuse of the system. It also emphasises the importance of follow-up action and review which takes into account the targets set for the individual in their own right as well as within the overall school system.

The national School Teacher Appraisal Pilot Study showed that a developmental model of appraisal can work effectively and overcome some of the traditional shortcomings of appraisal schemes. It recommended a biennial cycle of appraisal with the following components:

*Year 1*   Initial meeting between appraiser(s) and appraisee.
- Collection of evidence:
  - appraisee self-appraisal
  - classroom/task observation(s)
  - collection of other appropriate data.
- Appraisal interview, to include target setting and leading to the production of an appraisal statement.
- Follow-up discussions/meetings between appraiser(s) and appraisee, and follow up action such as professional development activities.

*Year 2*   Formal review meeting to include:
- Additions to appraisal statement
- Recommendations for follow-up support and professional development.

The review element in the cycle is significant as this contributes to the potential for the cycle's compatibility with a developmental approach. Those involved in the pilot study of school teacher appraisal frequently reported a range of positive outcomes of appraisal.

*Consider the biennial model described above. How far is this model followed in your own experience of appraisal? Take each component part of the cycle you have been through, and reflect on the value, and use, of each.*

The National Steering Group responsible for oversight of the pilot study in England and Wales summarised the benefits of appraisal in the pilot study as follows (NSG, 1989):

- greater confidence and improved morale for individual teachers
- better professional relations and communication within schools
- better planning and delivery of the curriculum
- wider participation in and better targeting of in-service training
- better career planning, and
- better informed references.

During the 1990s the emphasis has increasingly focused on the need for outcomes to inform the institution's effectiveness and, ultimately, the raising of pupil standards of achievement, meaning that inevitably the tensions between developmental and accountability models of appraisal have been maintained and potentially increased. For managers responsible for carrying out appraisal, there has been an increased recognition of *their* need for appropriate training and support.

## Task 4

Read:

(i)   the appraisal regulations

(ii)  your school's appraisal policy

Focus particularly on what is said in each document about:

- Purposes, including links with pay
- Documentation
- Evidence
- The respective roles of appraiser and appraisee
- Outcomes: for the individual and for the institution

Which model/s does your own school adopt in the documentation? How is the process of appraisal implemented in practice? To what extent does your own experience of appraisal reflect the principles outlined by Bollington *et al.? To what extent does it reflect the additional suggestions made by Blandford?*
Spend a few minutes writing down your own position on appraisal. How do you think it should be implemented, and what should it be used for?

Evaluation of staff development and review in Scotland has indicated that a development model can be effective and overcome some of the traditional shortcomings of the accountability model. Teachers who have been appraised/reviewed comment on the positive nature of the process.

These included benefits for the individual such as the way appraisal encouraged reflection and helped to clarify thinking on a range of issues, from the way to do the job to more general career and professional issues. In addition, appraisal was often welcomed as an opportunity for recognising and valuing the work of individuals. Appraisal was also seen as a mechanism for improving communication within a school and for enabling senior staff to receive feedback on how the management of the school affected a teacher's work. Often people spoke of appraisal leading to a clearer and shared understanding of key aims and greater clarity on roles and responsibilities. They also often felt that appraisal led to a more precise identification of INSET needs. Those involved were able to point to improvements in classroom practice, arising from working on areas identified and discussed in the appraisal process. Targets agreed in the appraisal process tended to centre on changes in classroom practice, changes in role and range of professional development activities.

Given the developmental interpretation of appraisal it is possible to identify four dimensions in this relationship. These are:

1   *Motivation and communication*: appraisal systems enable staff to discuss with their line managers the aims and objectives of current school policies and practices. Such discussions should be beneficial to staff motivation as they should aid the understanding of existing policies and provide an opportunity for staff to comment on their implementation, and to influence future developments.

2   *Review, evaluation and development of professional performance*: appraisal procedures can provide a formal occasion when staff can review and evaluate all aspects of their contributions to the team. During such reviews, managers should give formal recognition to achievements and encourage any further necessary support and, where appropriate, explore with staff how performance in some aspects of their work could be enhanced and what steps might be taken to bring this about. The possible introduction of performance management by the government, however, may change this picture to a much more accountability-based one, as discussed later in this chapter.

3   *Identification of personal staff development needs*: appraisal interviews can provide a formal opportunity for staff, in conjunction with management, to identify their personal development needs and to discuss how these needs may be met.

4   *Career review*: for all teachers, appraisal can provide a regular and systematic procedure for reviewing their career development and for providing appropriate advice and support. For some staff, appraisal procedures provide a first indication of their suitability for future promotion and of the need to prepare for such an eventuality.

As acknowledged in Chapter 1, appraisal can also be a means of reconciling whole school needs and individual staff development needs. In any needs analysis there will always be the tension between whole school and individual needs for development. Set within the context of the school development plan it is easier for an institution to decide on its priorities both for itself and for the individuals within it. The introduction of the School Development Planning process has helped to place Staff Development and Appraisal in a whole school context.

The basic purpose of the developmental model of appraisal is to encourage teachers to identify targets and to identify staff development activities in order to achieve these targets. The government has emphasised the need for professional learning in the fulfilment of the targets and vision of the whole school (DfEE, 1998).

## APPRAISAL AND PROFESSIONAL DEVELOPMENT

Whether we adopt the developmental or accountability interpretation of appraisal, it is not surprising that there are links between appraisal and professional development. It is possible to identify at least five dimensions in this relationship, as follows:

- Appraisal provides *opportunities* for professional development (reflection, paired observation and feedback, collaboration involving the exchange of ideas and mutual support);
- Appraisal can be a precise way of *identifying* professional development needs;
- Appraisal can be a means of *reconciling* school and individual professional development needs (within financial constraints) by logging and making explicit differences and the reasons for them;
- Appraisal can be used to *evaluate* the effectiveness of professional development, particularly at the review meeting in year 2 of the process;
- Appraisal puts professional development on the *agenda* of all teachers on a regular basis.

Appraisal is not simply about identifying professional development needs. The basic purpose of the review and development model of appraisal, which most current LEA schemes embody, is to help teachers identify priorities or targets for future action. A necessary follow-on then is how to give teachers the support they need in order to achieve their targets. Such support may or may not include professional development. Whether or not the targets of an individual teacher include professional development support, the process of appraisal can be a valuable development opportunity in its own right.

Experience of working on appraisal both in the pilot study and since, summarised by Bollington *et al.* (1990), demonstrates that appraisal should not become an end in itself. Rather it is a means to an end in that it provides an opportunity for detailed discussion and reflection on individual and school priorities. There is not much point in becoming good at appraisal for its own sake; the key is to use appraisal to provide support for development in the areas of curriculum, management, teaching and learning. Using the process to look at a manageable number of priority areas is likely to be more satisfactory than using it to carry out a general yet superficial review of all aspects of someone's work. Clearly the presence of a well-constructed school development plan can facilitate the role of appraisal in harmonising individual and school priorities.

A model for doing this has been documented by Jones (1993); on the one hand, appraisal has the potential for helping individuals' effectiveness, skills and motivation. On the other, it has the potential for enabling a school to make better use of people, to develop and grow, and to ensure that individuals perceive their jobs and roles in the context of the needs of the whole.

The introduction by the government of the proposal for individual learning accounts for teachers to pursue their professional development (DfEE, 1998) recognises this. On the other hand, the government is also planning to introduce professional development contracts in order to ensure that objectives for performance improvement set at appraisal, are followed through. One force behind the professional development contracts is the government's wish to respond to criticism by OFSTED that appraisal systems lack rigour (OFSTED, 1999).

An additional area that has been identified in recent years as needing attention in the context of appraisal and professional development, is middle management in schools. In part, the existence of staff who operate in middle management has emerged from the less hierarchical organisational structures which many schools have adopted since the late 1980s. As Blandford (1997) has identified, being a middle manager in a school means being able to identify at appropriate times with potentially conflicting perspectives on school life: teacher, leader and team member. The government has recognised the contribution of curriculum leaders and heads of departments and has advised that schools recognise their need for training when allocating professional development budgets (DfEE, 1999a).

## PERFORMANCE MANAGEMENT AND APPRAISAL

The government appears (DfEE, 1999b) to be moving in the direction of tying appraisal far more centrally into the process of teacher and head teacher career progress and to their pay, relating these far more directly than before to their performance. The plans for the appraisal of head teachers, for which the governors are responsible, also include a recommendation that high quality external advice should be sought, and that the outcomes of head teacher appraisal are directly linked to head teachers' pay.

The government has made it clear (DfEE, 1998) that the role and process of teacher and head teacher appraisal in England and Wales is being reviewed, in the context of the TTA's national professional standards which were discussed in Chapter 1. A number of developments seem likely to come out of the review process, on which a new framework will be published when the process is complete. These include:

- the introduction of appraisal as an annual process, linked closely to the school's development plan targets
- the use of clear, measurable objectives
- the direct relationship between some targets and pupils' progress and performance
- the identification of specific targets attached to stages in a teacher's career
- the explicit relating of teachers' performance to their own individual strengths and weaknesses in the context of national professional standards
- the linking of performance outcomes to both decisions about professional development and about pay
- further training and support for those responsible for appraisal to ensure fairness and justice in the process.

The review and planning process, which at the time of writing is not yet complete, seems likely then to herald a far more accountability driven model of appraisal than is currently in place in England and Wales.

*Think of three aspects of your work that it would be important to focus on in your appraisal or review. You might like to select one area which is a school priority, one which is a team issue and one which is an individual matter of interest. Do you feel that using appraisal to focus selectively on a small number of priority areas will help encourage a development approach to appraisal/ review? What else do you feel is necessary from your own experience and in the light of the points made in this text? How would your views on the above questions change if there was a stronger accountability model of appraisal/review, particularly if your performance was pay related? Jot down your thoughts.*

## APPRAISAL AND PUPILS

*How much do the pupils you teach know about your professional learning and development? How relevant is it for them to know about their teachers' development?*

A school is a learning community, where the adults as well as the pupils, are learning new knowledge, improving skills, being evaluated by themselves and others (children are assessed; teachers appraised). Evidence from the primary sector (National Primary Centre, 1990; Alexander, 1984) suggests that central to effective *pupil* learning is the relationship between pupil and teacher. The effective schools literature (all phases), which we will explore further in Chapter 3, suggests that part of being an effective school is maximum communication between teachers and pupils (Stoll, 1992) and genuinely caring about the individuals in the school (Fullan, 1985). The school improvement literature, which we will also look at in Chapters 3 and 4, suggests that a powerful feature of an improving school is the focus on pupils' involvement and achievement (MacGilchrist, *et al.,* 1995; MacGilchrist, *et al.,* 1997).

Even if you do not overtly share your professional development with pupils, they may well have expectations of it. Knowing what pupils do expect may help inform choices you make about undertaking professional development or implementing ideas from it. Certainly since pupils are the main reasons for schools existing, teachers are in some ways 'accountable' to pupils they teach for their professional development. Yet, for most teachers, their own professional development does not enter into what they share with pupils. We would argue that it is time to reconceptualise the teacher/pupil relationship, acknowledging both as learners, whilst acknowledging their different roles. Accepting and making explicit to pupils that teachers are also learners does not mean altering the teacher's role from being the teacher; on the other hand, you may learn a lot about your own performance if you choose to seek your pupils' views on it and the professional development you undertake.

We would argue that the process and system of appraisal for teachers is parallel to the record of achievement which pupils in many schools now have. Usually compiled by the pupil in partnership with teachers, and documenting achievements over a set period of time (usually the length of time over which they attend a particular school or phase of schooling), there is a parallel between it and the record of professional development which many teachers are beginning to keep, partly as one source of evidence for appraisal.

One of the most powerful ideas behind teachers and pupils keeping records of their own learning, is taking greater personal charge of their own next steps. For teachers, the written record (especially if it is carefully compiled, with input, verification, advice and agreement where appropriate from key people involved in their learning), offers a detailed support for continuous professional development, because it is constantly being added to. It helps teachers to reflect on particular experiences, identify their own professional development needs and the needs of their school, and to find ways of meeting them.

Professional portfolios may contain evidence from pupils. The idea of involving pupils in your professional development is to give you feedback on the impact of your learning on pupils, and to give you an additional perspective to consider when planning professional development, either for yourself or for your school. It also reinforces the idea of school as a learning community where adults as well as children are learning continuously.

Recent research with pupils aged between six and fifteen, in a variety of locations across the UK, (Craft, 1995) suggests pupils have a clear understanding, even at the age of six, that teachers are also learners, that their attainments and some of their learning needs are identified through the process of appraisal. In the schools where the pupil's perspective on their teacher's work was valued, the children were aware of this.

We would argue that involving pupils in the appraisal process can contribute powerfully to the model of appraisal which your school leans toward. Evidence from pupils can be used within a school which has an ethos of clear and acknowledging communication between all members of it, as a tool for the developmental process of appraisal. By contrast, in a school where a part of the ethos includes an attitude of greater separation between the perspectives of pupil and teacher, the evidence from pupils could contribute to a more acountability-based model of appraisal. And, as we noted during our discussion of the accountability and developmental models of appraisal, pupil evidence may contribute to both models within the same school, as in practice your school may adopt a mixture of the two purposes for appraisal.

**Summary of Chapter 2**

- This chapter has been concerned with appraisal/review.
- We have outlined the recent policy context to appraisal/review in England, Wales and Scotland, noting that an accountability model, based on a technicist view of pedagogy, is increasingly dominant.
- We have made a key distinction between appraisal/review schemes which emphasise accountability and those which emphasise development.
- We have identified a number of ways in which a developmental model of appraisal/review can be used to encourage, promote and evaluate professional development, whilst meeting government-imposed demands for accountability.
- We have advocated a consultative and collaborative approach to developing appraisal/review schemes.
- We have explored briefly some issues for senior managers in schools of policy moves toward tying their performance to pay, through the appraisal system.
- Drawing on the overlapping but distinct school effectiveness and school improvement literatures, we have argued that the pupils' perspectives on appraisal inform purposes.

# Chapter 3

# Principles of professional and institutional development

In this chapter we explore some general principles for effective teacher and school development. It is written in the belief that:

- individuals find it hard to develop in static schools
- schools are unable to develop without teachers changing what they do
- if teachers do develop professionally, but individually, they may not be able to change their schools
- sometimes when schools change, teachers do not change with them. (Bradley, 1991)
- learning organisations are filled with individuals who, alongside the performance of their main duties, also have opportunities to learn (Blandford, 2000)
- teacher education or teacher development is a career-long continuum from the earliest through to the latest stages of being a teacher (Watson and Fullan, 1992) and that this is an application of lifelong learning
- the absorption of new information and successful encounters with new situations is central to lifelong learning (Fryer, 1998)
- change is a process, not an event (Fullan, 1982)
- every person is a change agent (Fullan, 1993); and that
- theories of change and theories of education need each other (Fullan, 1999).

## CHARACTERISTICS OF EFFECTIVE INDIVIDUAL DEVELOPMENT

Loucks-Horsley *et al.* (1987) identified ten characteristics of successful teacher development which involve a mixture of individual and institutional development:

- collegiality and collaboration
- experimentation and risk-taking
- incorporation of available knowledge bases

- appropriate participant involvement in goal-setting, implementation, evaluation, and decision-making
- time to work on staff development and assimilate new learnings
- leadership and sustained administrative support
- appropriate incentives and rewards
- designs built on principles of adult learning and the change process
- integration of individual goals with school and district goals, and
- formal placement of the programme within the philosophy and organisational structure of the school and district.

This list assumes that professional development should be based on a view of how teachers learn both as individuals and as members of a whole school or team and recognises that such learning involves changes, during which teachers need a mixture of support, success, pressure and involvement. Change which occurs during or following professional development may involve the curriculum, the school as an organisation, and individuals within it.

*Think about a positive and a negative professional development experience that you have had, either from the perspective of provider, or from the perspective of participant. What made the positive experience positive, and the negative one unsatisfactory? To what extent were the characteristics of Loucks-Horsey et al. for successful teacher development to be found in your positive experience? How far were they missing or ignored in your negative experience? You may find it useful to write down your thoughts.*

Assumptions which appear to underlie both individual and school-based professional development involve a commitment by individuals toward one another's professional development *and* toward the development of the school. Les Bell (1991), whose comments on the shift from individual to collective emphasis in in-service we touched on in Chapter 1, argues that this is not in fact the reality. For although this dual commitment is in fact part of the conditions of service of teachers (in England and Wales) he cites evidence to suggest that, at least in the late 1980s, some forms of professional development did not appear to embody this commitment in practice. For example, school-based professional development may, in reality, under-emphasise the commitment to the individual's professional development needs, in comparison with the school's.

A key requirement of professional development is to ensure that there is a link between the professional development programme and the teacher's practice. Indeed, the MORI poll (1995) undertaken for the TTA in 1995, found that although 89 per cent of respondents believed that professional development was useful, only 26 per cent thought it had much impact on classroom practice. To achieve the development of practice as well as the personal professional development of the individual teacher, involves basing professional development on a careful and precise analysis of a teacher's previous learning and his or her professional development needs, just as you would for pupils. As change takes place over time and as new issues arise as people implement new approaches, effective professional development needs to be seen as ongoing and continuous. There is a need to avoid a split between training and doing the job. For example, a course of professional study needs to combine practice and reflection on it. Learning on the job, for example through mentoring, needs to be done with reflection. In addition, it is often useful to reflect on practice within a theoretical framework. This enables you to intellectually engage with the assumptions and values behind new or changing practice.

Reference has already been made in Chapter 1 to the Joyce and Showers (1988) model of five components of effective INSET and the need when developing skills to combine different strategies such as lectures, practical activities and coaching.

Not only does the use of a combination of methods lead to better mastery of new skills but it also recognises, as we noted following Loucks-Horsley et al.'s list, the fact that different people have different preferred ways of learning. Broadly speaking, the following ways of learning need to be considered, when planning a programme:

- learning from concrete experience, e.g. from doing things in the classroom; or from doing things during the professional development itself, such as being placed in the same role as the child learner
- learning through reflection in action (i.e. reflecting as you do a job) or through reflection on action (i.e. reflecting on what you have done, perhaps with the help of feedback from a colleague)
- learning through experimentation, i.e. assimilating a new idea, trying it out and making it part of your practice
- learning through conceptualising, i.e. exploring ideas, relating them to a theoretical framework.

The point is that different approaches to learning and therefore teaching will need to be included during a professional development programme in order to make people with different preferences of learning style feel comfortable. This will be the case whatever form the professional development takes. In their work on pupils, Gipps and Murphy (1994) note that learners need to be able to develop ownership and relevance in their learning. Our contention here is that the same is true for adult learners. In addition, the emotional element to learning, for both adults and children, should not be ignored, as Goleman (1996) argues. In other words, the need to feel emotionally secure applies as much to learning as it does to any other environment an individual may participate in.

In relating your own experience of professional development to the principles for effective individual development outlined above you may find the following comment of Rudduck (1981) helpful. She uses the concept of the 'logic of learning' to tie together the various principles for effective development that need to be considered when planning an INSET event; although she is talking about courses, we take the view that her points apply to any form of professional development.

> It seems that course leaders and course members need to understand the logic of learning that each course as a unique in-service event offers those who are present. The logic of learning is arrived at by a careful balancing of the relationships between the following elements; the aims of the course; the interests and the experience of the course members; the structure of the content; the working style of the course; the setting of the course, including the shape and size of rooms; the resources needed, including handouts and audio-visual equipment; the total working time available at the course and the disposition of that time; the time of year and the time of day at which the course is run; the continuity and the coherence of the course as a total event; the relationship between the course and the classroom or between the course and the school.
>
> It is important that the short course is perceived as one episode in a process in which preparation and implementation constitute other equally important episodes.

To conclude this discussion of factors involved in effective individual professional development as central to educational change, we turn to Rudduck again:

> All promoters of professional development should pay attention to and worry about two fundamental requirements: (1) incorporating the attributes of successful professional development (à la Loucks-Horsley) in as many activities as possible, and (2) ensuring that the ultimate purpose of professional development is less to implement a specific innovation or policy and more to create individual and organisational habits and structures that make continuous learning a valued and endemic part of the culture of schools and teaching.

Throughout this book, we explore the different elements of personal and school development. Day (1991) usefully summarised the factors

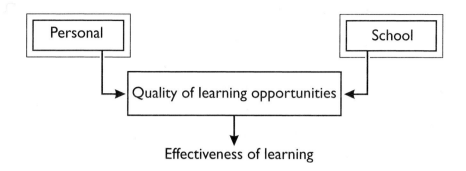

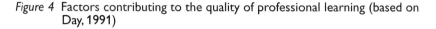

*Figure 4* Factors contributing to the quality of professional learning (based on Day, 1991)

contributing to the quality of professional learning as divided into those two areas. The personal factors include life-cycle stage and career-cycle stage, which influence the biography of the individual teacher's professional learning. Together, he suggested, these influence the individual's learning attitudes and value preferences. From the system side, the school culture influences the provision of professional learning opportunities. Together, then, the personal and school factors contribute to the quality of professional learning opportunities, and to the effectiveness of the learning. We can summarise the two sets of influences thus:

Figure 4 suggests the need to match what is provided by way of professional development to a participant's experience and attitudes, and indicates that what is provided is just a fraction of the school's approach to professional development. When all the factors are in harmony, effective professional learning is likely to take place.

## PRACTITIONER REFLECTION, PERSONAL BIOGRAPHY AND PROFESSIONAL KNOWLEDGE

Whatever an individual teacher's preferred combination of learning styles, reflection on practice inevitably forms a part of their development. Reflection may be a collaborative activity and not necessarily purely individualistic. The notion of the reflective practitioner can be sourced back to Schon's work (1983). He highlighted the distinction between technical rationality (abstract knowledge learned from sources external to the self) and experiential knowledge (knowledge developed through professional experience), suggesting that the latter is a vital part of learning as a professional. Drawing on the work of Dewey, Schon suggested that in order to learn from experiential knowledge, reflection was essential. He distinguished between reflection on action (similar to Dewey's concept of reflection – that is, thinking about one's own professional conduct and decision making) and reflection in action ('thinking on your feet'). Schön's concept of the reflective practitioner influenced teachers across the world, notably in the USA, UK, Australia and New Zealand. Teacher development traditions which have drawn on Schön's ideas include those which utilise life history, narrative and personal biography to investigate changes in one's own views and practice with respect to pedagogy. These approaches tend to focus on the individual and self-knowledge rather than emphasising the possibilities for collaborative reflection, although there are plenty of ways in which reflection may be done collaboratively.

Reflection, whether done individually or collaboratively, is not of course done in a vacuum; it involves the use of evidence. The debate on what constitutes evidence, and how it can be interpreted, has developed over the last few years in education as well as in other professions. Within education, the question of what constitutes evidence was raised by Hargeaves (1996) when he suggested that education might have something to learn from medicine. This has stimulated a debate about appropriate forms of evidence, which is still ongoing (Davies, 1999). In this book we take the view that professional knowledge is sourced through a range of evidence sources which include personal experience of teaching and learning as well as large-scale systematic enquiry which attempts to control specific variables. Other evidence sources include journals, online discussions with colleagues and others, books, world wide web and other databases. What is significant is the relationship between the data source and the questions you are posing. We return to the posing of questions in Part II of the book.

As discussed in Chapter 1, professional knowledge is increasingly defined externally by policy bodies which define knowledge as including professional competence. This is in addition to the ways in which local education authorities (LEAs), trainers and higher education institutions have traditionally created professional knowledge external to the teacher too. However, these modes of knowledge creation often assume an easy relationship with application to practice which does not take account of the ways in which teachers actually use knowledge (Eraut, 1994). For although teachers may need to make reference to external definitions of knowledge for a variety of reasons (some of which are to do with the statutory nature of that knowledge), their own meaning making is equally significant in terms of how the knowledge affects their practice. This is so for both individual teachers and also within the culture of departments and schools. The holding of individual meaning by individuals is one of the barriers, suggests Eraut, to institutional change in schools for, he argues, the introduction of new knowledge with the potential to change institutional norms and routines will usually be greeted by inertia and attempts to minimise change. In this way, the introduction and use by individuals of new knowledge can be very difficult.

We take the view, however, that professional development and planning for it, needs to take account of a person's own biography and their own personal response to professional knowledge creation and its use. For it is only by making space for the individual within the system of the school, LEA and wider education service, that new knowledge is actually applied in practice by the individual practitioner. And it is through the application of professional knowledge that classrooms and schools develop.

## PRINCIPLES OF EFFECTIVE SCHOOL DEVELOPMENT

Professional development relates to both the experience, attitudes and capabilities of an individual on the one hand and to the culture of a school or other organisation on the other. A school in which teachers individually and collectively are seeking to develop and extend their expertise, is one that is likely to value professional growth. It is, therefore, possible to think of creating a climate within a school conducive to both individual and school development. Over recent years, it has become fashionable to describe a school with such a climate as a learning organisation (and to link learning organisations with school improvement). Holly and Southworth (1989) summarise the characteristics of the learning school in the following way. They say it aims to be like learning itself:

- interactive and negotiative
- creative and problem solving
- proactive and responsive
- participative and collaborative
- flexible and challenging
- risk-taking and enterprising
- evaluative and reflective
- supportive and developmental.

In Scotland, the concept of the learning organisation has been taken up in recent years by a number of education authorities, particularly the smaller ones, which are moving toward the creation of such communities of learners.

If we relate Holly and Southworth's views back to Loucks-Horsley's characteristics of effective professional development, we begin to see a picture of the learning school as one which both fosters and is a product of professional development. Embedded in much writing about institutional development is the assumption that learning schools are effective schools, implying then that effective schools require and produce a commitment to professional development. Fullan (1985) identifies four process factors to be found in effective schools, which extend this picture:

- a feel for the process of leadership
- a guiding value system
- intense interaction and communication
- collaborative planning and implementation.

Others support the importance to school and teacher development of developing a shared mission or framework of values to guide the work of the school. For example, the LEAP 4 materials on Quality in Schools (1992) identify the following aspects of effective management:

- shared values and mission
- consultation
- participation and teamwork
- accountability, and
- a concern for quality.

Such processes create a foundation for individual development and help the school to improve as an organisation. Between them they create a culture or climate in which opportunities for professional development occur and are encouraged.

Teachers 'working together to improve practice' also needs to be distinguished from teachers 'being nice to each other'. Barth (1990) refers to this as a distinction between collegiality and congeniality. MacGilchrist *et al.* (1997) refer to the notion of 'corporate intelligence' as involving a range of different and inter-related intelligences, which they name as:

| | |
|---|---|
| *Contextual intelligence* | the ability of a school to view itself in relation to the world of which it is a part |
| *Strategic intelligence* | the capacity to engender clarity about and a shared responsibility toward goals |
| *Academic intelligence* | placing high value on achievement and scholarship, in both children and teachers |
| *Reflective intelligence* | monitoring and evaluating the school's overall effectiveness |
| *Pedagogical intelligence* | continuous learning by staff about pedagogy |

| *Collegial intelligence* | staff working together to improve classroom practice |
| *Emotional intelligence* | a school's ability to enable the feelings of pupils and staff to be acknowledged |
| *Spiritual intelligence* | valuing all within a school community in the context of a wider, mysterious universe |
| *Ethical intelligence* | recognition of each pupil's rights and the valuing of justice and equality |

*Reflect on your own school or institution. Using the factors identified by Holly and Southworth, Fullan, LEAP and MacGilchrist et al., how far would you say it is a learning institution? In Scotland, a useful resource for this might be the SOED ethos indicators folders and accompanying video. What are the barriers, if any?*

## SCHOOL IMPROVEMENT

During the 1990s the focus has increasingly turned from the foundations of school development planning, to school improvement, connecting this with school effectiveness. Although clearly linked, the sources of knowledge and data for each process are significantly different, as Bollen (1996) has pointed out. For the research on school effectiveness, with its ultimate goal being to gather knowledge about what makes schools operate successfully, has tended to seek characteristics which are of a measurable and generalisable nature, generally from large-scale quantitative studies. Although programmes for school improvement are often based on such lists of factors produced externally to the institution, the translation of effective school characteristics can be problematic. One aspect of the challenge is in reaching mutual understanding of the meaning of terms and what they involve in practice. There are also ongoing debates about the reliability of the methodologies used in school effectiveness research which are well summarised by Sammons (1999). These issues will be explored further in Chapter 4.

School improvement on the other hand tends to be concerned with the processes and internal knowledge base of a particular institution, where individual cases of departments and schools are used to develop practical knowledge which has traditionally not necessarily been tied to any strong methodological approach or standards. School improvement is focused on developing practical strategies to change practice. Hopkins (1996) and Hopkins and Lagerweij (1996) suggest a number of propositions on which to base school improvement strategies:

- The internal conditions of the school must provide a powerful focus for improvement strategies (these include placing the achievement of pupils at the heart of the project, as well as making a commitment to staff development, the involvement of staff, pupils and wider community in school decisions and policies, the use of lateral and transformational management strategies, effective strategies for co-ordination, attention to the benefits of enquiry and reflection and a commitment to collaborative planning activity – Hopkins *et al.*, 1994).
- Decisions must be made about the development of specific changes and the maintenance of existing aspects of a school's functioning – a distinction made by Hargreaves and Hopkins (1991) (this means resources being allocated to dedicated areas for development, whilst acknowledging that the majority of a school's resources will continue to be spent on the maintenance of existing activities; for developmental activities which cut across established meeting patterns, hierarchies, timetables and curriculum areas often fail).
- External change needs to be adapted for internal purposes (Hopkins and Lagerweij suggest that schools which see externally generated change as offering opportunities which can be harnessed to improve pupil learning are the most successful in managing school improvement).
- Change must be based on the school unit but recognise the teacher as the pivot in change (Hopkins and Lagerweij suggest that school improvement strategies need to be aimed at the level of the whole school, the individual teacher and also at the level of working groups).
- Energy for developing the school's performance needs to be based on data (Ainscow *et al.*, 1994 argue that systematic collection, interpretation and use of school-generated data accompanied by underpinning ground rules, are essential in decision making about school improvement together with review strategies and the involvement of all staff in the processes).
- A language about teaching and change will be developed in successful school improvement efforts (the existence of a vocabulary which draws on pedagogy and improvements in classroom practice helps to initiate and empower change: Hopkins and Lagerweij suggest this includes the discussion of teaching strategies, the establishment of guidelines for these, mutual agreement between staff on standards used to assess pupils' progress and mutual observation and partnership teaching).

Over the late 1990s, the two fields of school effectiveness and school improvement have been brought closer together despite their very different origins and traditions (see for example, Hopkins *et al.*, 1994; Stoll and Fink, 1996). Some of the most significant work exploring how quantitative and qualitative approaches to evidence gathering can inform both school effectiveness and school improvement has come out of the Improving School Effectiveness Project funded by the then Scottish Office Education & Industry Department (SOEID). This project examined three major themes: teaching and learning, ethos and school development (Robertson and Sammons, 1997a, b) and brought together a value-added school effectiveness framework with use of case study.

The inter-relationships of school improvement, school effectiveness and classroom effectiveness, will be further explored in Chapter 4.

## IDENTIFYING NEEDS: SCHOOL DEVELOPMENT PLANNING

One of the difficulties facing any organisation is how to handle the process of change and development when there are multiple internal and external pressures or requirements to do so. The introduction at the start of the 1990s of school development planning is an interesting example of an approach that is designed to help schools handle multiple change (it also provided the foundation for what some have called the school improvement era (Gray *et al.*, 1999). In effect it is an innovation with implications for the way a school is managed and for the culture or climate of the school. It is an approach that can both be used to provide professional development opportunities as staff collaborate on the plan and to identify future professional development needs – in both the short and, in theory, the longer term.

Essentially there are four broad phases in the school development planning cycle:

1   Audit: a school reviews its strengths and weaknesses
2   Construction: priorities for development are selected and then turned into specific action plans, targets and tasks, each with clearly identified success criteria
3   Implementation: the planned priorities and targets are implemented
4   Evaluation: the successes of implementation are checked. (Hargreaves and Hopkins, 1991).

Development planning has been presented as a way of handling change in a co-ordinated and manageable way. It has been seen as a vehicle by which schools can develop themselves as organisations by refining their sense of vision and purpose and turning these into action. As Hargreaves and Hopkins (1991) argue: development planning is not just about implementing innovation and change, but about changing the culture of a school – or in more concrete terms the management arrangements of a school – to improve the school's capacity to manage other changes.

Blandford (1997) has described a slightly wider view of the planning process. Hers acknowledges the starting point of a school's development planning as the definition of its policy and aims, and which also acknowledges the need for identifying criteria by which to evaluate the success of specific actions delineated in the plan. The role of criteria is explored in this book in Chapter 8.

The capacity of school development planning for enabling schools to handle change and for planning for and promoting professional development depends, as Blandford (1997) has highlighted, on the plan being rooted in a vision of where the school is heading, and supported by a developmental approach to appraisal. Schools with effective planning and appraisal systems and a coherent policy for professional development are likely to be learning schools in that they are likely to be developing both as institutions and in terms of the individuals within them. Appraisal and development planning have the capacity not only for helping individuals and schools develop but also for moving the culture of schools towards the ideal of the learning organisation. In doing so they provide a means of both assessing and responding to external pressures for improved standards and accountability and of identifying internal individual and whole school needs.

It is imperative that the needs identified help to implement a school's development plan and develop individuals in that institution in a planned and progressive way. McMahon (1999) has noted the increasing awareness of senior managers of the tensions which exist between whole-school

---

## Task 5

Refer to a copy of your school or institution's most recent development plan.

- How far does the plan address issues to do with the organisation and management of the school?
- How far is it based on the school's aims or vision?
- Consider who was involved in the construction of it and how individuals will be involved in implementing it.
- If you can, carry out an investigation to find out what colleagues feel are the main benefits/drawbacks of school development planning in either your own or another school or institution.
- How far has it been constrained by outside factors, e.g. curriculum changes, or changes in funding arrangements?

and individual development needs. Blandford (2000) suggests that when in balance, the two will feed one another.

### Identifying school and individual development needs

At the heart of effective development planning, and therefore of development itself, is the audit, or analysis of *what development is needed* and the starting points for development.

A development need can be thought of in five ways:

1    the area for development (e.g. a topic, subject, issue)
2    the kind of development (e.g. awareness raising, importing knowledge, changing attitudes, developing skills)
3    the starting point for development (what learning has already taken place)
4    the audience for development (an individual, department, team or whole staff)
5    the pressure for development (individual, department, team, school, LEA/EA or national priority).

The following list includes approaches that can each be used to identify development needs and can be set up to take account of the five dimensions above. We have classified them in terms of those used primarily to identify whole school needs and those where the emphasis tends to be on identifying individual needs. Once needs for professional development arising from an individual, group, school or external priority have been identified, they in turn will need to be analysed and decisions on setting priorities and targets for action made.

#### Identifying needs at school level

* School review or audit, (sometimes time consuming and not very helpful in moving from identifying problems towards ensuring appropriate action is taken; can be used for accountability and for developmental purposes; can be used in an evaluative and developmental way that ensures action follows review or audit e.g. as GRIDS aims to; can encourage collaboration). Note: In Scotland, a useful resource for review/audit is the *School Development Planning Support Materials* (HM Inspectors of Schools, 1992): *Using Performance Indicators in Secondary School Self-evaluation, Using Performance Indicators in Primary School Self-Evaluation, Using Ethos Indicators in Secondary School Self-evaluation* (taking account of the views of pupils, parents and teachers), *Using Ethos Indicators in Primary School Self-evaluation* (taking account of the views of pupils, parents and teachers).

- School development planning (aims to keep the review or audit stage quick; can encourage collaboration and the development of a shared sense of vision and purpose, but can backfire if carried out by senior staff without consultation or dissemination).

### Identifying individual needs

Approaches that can be used to identify individual development needs include:

- audit (as part of school review/development planning)
- professional development inventories. (This can be helpful in structuring thinking and encouraging people to take a broad view of their professional development; it can lead to individual needs being seen as more important than school needs; it can depend for their success on how well the form fits the school and the individual teacher; and it is not always filled in fully if teachers are concerned about issues of confidentiality or do not have a good rapport with the person processing the form). Figure 5 is an example of a professional development inventory; it could well form the basis of, or be included in, a professional portfolio.
- professional development discussions or interviews. (These depend on the relationship between those involved, on adequate use of time, preparation and effective use of communication skills, and are subject to the same issues as professional development inventories);
- appraisal/review. (This is subject to same issues as professional development interview; dependent for its effectiveness on clarity on the purposes of the model used and using the process to balance individual and school needs).
- using a list of competence statements of what an effective teacher or manager should do as a basis of assessing present performance and identifying future professional development needs including, where appropriate, the development of management competences. Competences associated with a variety of qualifications can provide a helpful vehicle for analysing areas for professional development but care may sometimes be needed to ensure that they fit a particular context.

*Which of these approaches to identifying development needs have you experienced – from the perspective of either manager of, provider or participant in professional development? How far does your experience tally with what is described here?*

## Task 6

This task involves identifying your own professional development needs. You will need to develop working notes. Using Figure 5 (page 62) as a template, complete your own professional development inventory, as a means of identifying your own development needs.

Once you have carried out an identification of your professional development needs, consider the following:

- How did the approach you used for this task compare, for example, with your previous experience of needs identification (for example, through institutional audit using a professional discussion or interview, appraisal or competences?)
- Did it reveal anything you were not conscious of?
- How do your own needs/concerns relate to team and school priorities?

Your notes should include an explanation and analysis of your current professional development needs. You may also like to make a copy of your notes to put in your professional portfolio to use beyond your study of this book.

---

You may find the following comments helpful once you have completed the task involving Figure 5 (on page 62).

- Any pro forma designed for a range of situations may not fit a particular situation exactly. You may have felt you needed to modify the pro forma or list of competences to fit your own situation;
- Using a pro forma for identifying professional development needs is often useful in helping an individual to focus and reflect. It is, however, a solitary approach. Would you have found it helpful to work through the form or the lists with a colleague or your line manager?

The essential point about any approach to identifying professional development needs is that it allows you to reflect on your needs in an organised and comprehensive way and to relate your needs to your own concerns and to team and school priorities.

**PROFESSIONAL DEVELOPMENT INVENTORY**

**NAME:**                              **DATE:**

1   What are the main tasks for which you are responsible?

2   What are your main priorities for the coming year:

   (a) as a classroom teacher?

   (b) as a manager? (e.g. curriculum co-ordinator, head of year, assistant head teacher, head of department, principal teacher, etc.)

3   Please indicate below where you feel you would benefit from additional professional development. (You may find the attached list helpful as a prompt.)

   (a) Classroom practice:

   (b) Curriculum area:

   (c) Pastoral care/Personal Social and Health Education (Social Education/Personal Social Development in Scotland):

   (d) Cross-curricular themes:

   (e) Management issues:

   (f) Career development:

   (g) Other areas:

*continued* ...

*Figure 5* Professional development inventory

# POSSIBLE AREAS FOR PROFESSIONAL DEVELOPMENT

The following list suggests some areas you might find it useful to reflect on when considering your professional development needs. It is meant as a source of ideas and is not seen as a prescriptive or exhaustive list.

(a) *Classroom practice*
Assessment
Classroom control and discipline
Flexible learning
Learning environment
Lesson organisation
Planning and preparation
Relationships with pupils
Supporting pupils with special needs
Teaching and learning styles
Use of resources

(b) *Curriculum areas:*
Early years education
Foreign and community languages
GCSE/'A' level (Standard Grade/
    Higher Grade in Scotland)
National curriculum – subjects,
    processes, assessment (5–14
    Development Programme in
    Scotland)
Other subject area
    Post-16 education (Post-
    compulsory education in
    Scotland)

(c) *Pastoral care/PSHE (SE/PSD in
    Scotland)*
Anti-bullying
Child abuse
Counselling skills
First aid/Health and Safety
Guidance/careers work
Leading pastoral teams
Pastoral programme
Profiling

Role of head of year/tutor
    (role of AHT/guidance teacher in
    Scotland)

(d) *Cross-curricular themes*
Economic and industrial
    understanding/Education Industry
    links in Scotland
Information and communication
    technology
Literacy
Citizenship
Numeracy
European developments

(e) *Management issues*
Appraisal/review and staff
    development
Communication
Development planning
Equal opportunities
Financial management
Handling stress
Leadership
Managing change
Managing teams
Marketing
Monitoring and evaluation
Personal and inter-personal skills
Time management
Timetabling

(f) *Career development*
Job applications
Job interviews
Preparing for your next post

## APPRAISAL AND PROFESSIONAL AND INSTITUTIONAL DEVELOPMENT

*In your own institution, what do you consider to be the driving force behind appraisal – the identification of individual needs, or those of the school, or a combination of both? Do you think your colleagues would have the same response as you to this question?*

As discussed in Chapter 2, appraisal provides one tool for identifying and attempting to reconcile both individual and institutional development needs. As Scott (1985) has argued in discussing the political locus of change, in a democratic and free society, this process of reconciliation can only come about meaningfully and fruitfully when the individuals concerned are truly part of setting objectives for the larger whole as well as for themselves.

This is viewed by some as a challenge within today's financial and values environment. Jennings (1995) argues, from long experience of curriculum development himself, that the combination of a series of factors means that individuals' professional development needs compete unequally with the school's needs. The factors he cites are:

- the devolvement of the majority of funds for in-service work to schools
- the restrictions on the use of this funding, so that in effect expenditure is set within centrally defined national priorities
- the market approach to providing school education, so that schools are competing for pupils
- the regular inspection of schools, the outcomes of which in practice contribute to the popularity of the school within this marketplace
- the impact of inspection outcomes on expenditure.

Clearly, the outcomes of this model of resourcing may be that individual teachers are in a less valued position for personal professional development than the school as a collective. Since Jennings published his analysis in 1995, the position in England and Wales has shifted to make this potential for under-valuing the individual arguably even greater, given the direct influence of policy makers in defining professional development activities, as discussed in Chapter 1.

Nevertheless, we take the view in this book that a reconciliation of needs is both essential and possible. And as the world in which education exists demands increasingly that the individual takes responsibility for developing a multi-skilled flexibility, it is perhaps more important than ever before that individuals within organisations see to it that their needs are met. Fullan calls this process of reconciling the individual with the institution: 'institutional renewal' (1992), and as he puts it:

> Successful individuals will be highly involved with their environments, inflencing and being influenced in this continuous exchange ... Paradoxically the way ahead is through melding individual and institutional renewal. One cannot wait for the other. Both must be pursued simultaneously and aggressively ... institutions will have to provide both pressure on and support for individuals.

Whichever model of appraisal you adopt, the developmental approach or the accountability one, that process is, in our view, the locus of that 'melding'.

---

### Summary of Chapter 3

- In this chapter we have considered principles of individual and institutional development, and their relationship to approaches to classroom and school effectiveness and improvement.
- We have put forward the view that effective development for individuals depends on a range of factors including effective needs identification, relating development to practice and sensitivity to individual learning styles and experience.
- We have explored briefly the role of practitioner reflection and personal biography in the development of professional knowledge.
- We have proposed that individual and school development can be linked and for satisfactory development of both, should be.
- We have used the concept of the 'learning school' to help tie together a range of factors important both to individual and school development, exploring the notion of 'corporate intelligence' proposed by MacGilchrist *et al.*
- We have explored aspects of the school improvement movement, drawing links between school improvement, school effectiveness and individual development.
- We have argued that individual and institutional development must proceed hand in hand despite pressures which militate against the individual, and appraisal provides a focus for the negotiation of different sets of needs.

# Chapter 4

# Teachers, pupils, effectiveness and improvement

This chapter looks at the pupil perspective on teacher and school development, and then explores various findings on effective classrooms and effective schools. It examines one of the interventionist strategies for professional development originally developed by the Employment Department, and now being used by many schools: *Investors in People*, in the light of research on effective classrooms and schools. It also explores further the links between school effectiveness and school improvement, introduced in Chapter 3.

## THE PUPIL PERSPECTIVE ON PROFESSIONAL LEARNING AND INSTITUTIONAL DEVELOPMENT

There are some parallels between the learning of pupils and teachers in schools, and the ways their achievements or performance are documented, as discussed in Chapter 2, which considered appraisal. Consider now the ways in which pupils are affected by and aware of their teachers' professional learning, and the development of their institution.

### Teachers' learning

*What forms of professional development have you been involved in over the recent past? Which of these did you inform pupils about, and why? How do you think your pupils perceive your professional development? How might their perceptions help your learning – and theirs?*

Pupils experience teachers learning in many different ways; for example, from student teachers and NQTs (newly qualified teachers) working alongside and with the support of teachers or mentors in the school; teachers' meetings and working groups held on site during school hours; staff coaching one another in the classroom; school closure days; teachers being released from the classroom to go and work elsewhere in the school, or to leave the school site. Those of the experiences which have a direct link with classroom practice may lend themselves more automatically to being shared with pupils (particularly those which generate materials or experimental ways of working). But how often *are* your plans for and experiences of professional development shared with pupils?

Some people who have monitored INSET (for example, Harland, 1990; Harland and Kinder, 1991) suggest that the model of teachers undertaking professional development on a different site during school hours has been, and continues to be a popular one. This often means providing either internal cover, or a supply teacher, for the teacher who has been released. How often do pupils know why this is? At other times, for example, when an inexperienced or student teacher is learning from the experience of teaching and/or being coached in the classroom, it is possibly more obvious to pupils that this adult is learning. Making this learning explicit may foster positive relationships, and thus contribute to school effectiveness, in terms of individuals understanding one another, but also from the point of view of mirroring to pupils what the environment beyond school demands of them.

As the opportunities offered to pupils in schools shift, they represent wider societal changes in what kinds of knowledge are valued. Competence is gaining in currency, and importance, for pupils and teachers. As the economy and society require more multi-skilled individuals, so learning, re-learning, up-skilling and re-skilling are becoming a part of adult life. For pupils, school is just the beginning of formalised ways of learning; there will be many opportunities for and requirements on them to be continuous lifelong learners beyond school, particularly if they are able to enter employment.

As teachers, we need to encourage children to acknowledge that personal development is continuous throughout life, and that they have some responsibility for and choice over it. During the 1990s the inexorable move toward the 'marketisation' of education, where pupils are now seen as clients of provision, has meant a need for an increasing emphasis on acknowledging to them the CPD their teachers are undertaking whilst encouraging the development of a positive attitude toward their own lifelong learning.

## School development

Consider how the pupil's perspective is taken account of during the process of school development planning, and as the institution itself evolves. How appropriately can pupils' views be heard? Clearly, the pupil's learning is at the centre of development planning and in theory at the heart of what drives the development (and improvement) of the school. This was described in a model developed by Hertfordshire County Council

Education Services (1995), as a series of overlapping circles around a central circle representing the pupils. The circles around the edge represented the parents, the community, the LEA or Funding Agency for Schools, the governors and the senior management team.

Questions which schools must therefore ask include how evidence from pupil learning informs the way the school development plan is constructed. Pupil evidence may include:

- discussion, analysis and feedback from daily routine
- pupils' records of achievement and action plans
- outcomes of teacher assessments and Key Stage tests
- recommendations of pupils' school council (or other democratic forum)
- (with older pupils) the use of questionnaires, followed by sampling interviews

In seeking the perspective of pupils on teacher professional development, there is an increasing body of literature on gender and communication which as a profession we need to take note of (Craft, 1994; Gilligan, 1982, 1986, 1988; Tannen, 1995). The literature suggests that there are marked gender differences in the way girls and boys tend to relate – girls demonstrating a greater self- and other- protection in the way they relate, showing in their interactions greater empathy and sensitivity to expectations and interpersonal dynamics than boys. Boys on the other hand tend to adopt a more independent approach, to prefer to try and work out problems for themselves, to take a direct approach (including making statements rather than asking questions), to see interactions in terms of winning and losing, and to use humour more in their interactions.

## INVESTORS IN PEOPLE AND APPROACHES TO EFFECTIVE CLASSROOMS AND SCHOOLS

*What do you predict would be the answers to the following three questions if asked of staff in your own institution:*

- *Does everyone working for the school understand what we are trying to achieve?*
- *Does everyone working for the school understand how their own role contributes to the school's success?*
- *Is everyone working for the school competent to fulfil their role effectively?*

Some schools are starting to work toward the Investors in People standard (IIP). Developed on the basis of a very wide survey and analysis of 'best practice' in management, IIP recognises organisations whose policies and practices demonstrate a tangible commitment to staff training and development for all who work in them. According to the CBI Education Foundation which has produced materials (Chambers *et al.*, 1995) to support schools who are undertaking IIP, it is intended as both a way of linking planning, implementation and evaluation within an organisation, and also a step toward becoming a learning organisation: a view which has been actively adopted by Training and Enterprise Councils (TECs) in collaboration with LEAs, such as the partnership between Avon LEA and Westec, which by summer 1995 was working on IIP with 70 per cent of Avon's secondary schools, 45 per cent of Avon's special schools and 8 per cent of Avon's primary schools (some 86 schools in total).

With support from all three major political parties in the UK, the TUC and the CBI, adopting the IIP framework enables a school to ask questions such as the three at the beginning of this section.

The process of implementing IIP involves the negotiation of understanding, assessment of competence and identification of individual needs throughout all aspects of the school's activity. It can also be seen as helping individuals within schools to address some of the key elements of the 1994 OFSTED inspection framework in England and Wales, particularly those concerning the efficiency of the school, quality of teaching, management and administration, and resources and their management.

Involving pupils is important, in our view, even though IIP is about looking at the professional development needs of the staff in schools. We take this view because one of the qualities identified both sides of the Atlantic over the past twenty years of research into school effectiveness is the depth and reality of relationships between all the people in the school, pupils included.

## Effective classrooms

What makes a classroom (and a teacher) effective is a question which has exercised researchers for many years. For the purposes of this book, by an effective classroom we mean an environment where pupils achieve highly, are motivated and happy and where change and improvement is seen as 'evolutionary', a term used by Joyce *et al.* (1999) to refer to improving schools. It is important to note that definitions of effective classrooms and schools do vary as highlighted by Sammons, Hillman and Mortimore (1995), being dependent on a variety of factors summarised by Sammons (1994), including the sample of schools examined, the choice of outcome measures, adequate control for differences between schools in intakes to ensure comparison of 'like with like', methodology and timescale. We return to school effectiveness later in the chapter.

Many studies of effective classrooms in the second half of the century focused on separate elements of classroom teaching, and resulted in recommendations to teachers which did not take account of other aspects of the pedagogical setting. In 1994, Creemers suggested a model which attempted to integrate several components within pedagogy in an attempt to create a framework for effective classroom teaching. These were:

- curriculum
- grouping procedures
- teacher behaviour.

Drawing on previous studies, Creemers identifies a range of factors most of which have strong or moderate empirical evidence to suggest they are important in effective classrooms. A few factors had no empirical evidence to back them up but seemed plausible. These were: offering corrective instruction to pupils, co-operative learning arrangements, using differentiated material for pupils, and emphasising cognitive learning and transfer of skills and knowledge across domains of learning.

The other factors for which there is either strong or moderate empirical evidence, he summarised as follows:

### Curriculum

- explicit and ordered learning goals
- structure and clarity in content
- carefully ordered explanation of concepts, relating to the structure of what is being taught as well as to pupils' prior knowledge – what Asubel (1968) called 'advance organisers'
- evaluation (assessment) of learning
- feedback from teacher to pupil
- corrective instruction

### Grouping procedures

- placing high value on helping children to master concepts specified at a high level, before moving on ('mastery' learning – Bloom, 1976)
- grouping by ability
- fostering co-operative learning (this is highly dependent on using differentiated materials, assessing pupils' learning, giving feedback and also giving corrective instruction)

*Teacher behaviour*

- maintaining an orderly and quiet atmosphere in the classroom
- setting homework
- having high expectations of pupils
- setting clear goals (with a restricted number of objectives, emphasis on basic skills, emphasis on cognitive learning and transfer)
- structuring content (ordering goals and content, using advance organisers, building on pupils' prior knowledge)
- offering clear presentation
- using questioning with pupils
- setting immediate exercises following introduction of specific concepts
- assessing/evaluating pupil learning
- giving feedback
- offering corrective instruction.

Creemers' list is drawn from a range of research studies done over a period of twenty or more years from the 1970s onward and from a range of national contexts. MacGilchrist *et al.* (1997) offer another three dimensions to teachers' skills in understanding how classrooms may be most effective. They are implicit in what Creemers lists. They are:

- *The role of subject knowledge:* teachers' own subject knowledge in terms of content, progression and continuity as well as links with other subjects – must be adequate to enable them to support pupils' learning. This is what enables teachers to build on pupils' prior knowledge. Curriculum planning should be informed by an understanding of both the curriculum and individual children's grasp of aspects of individual subjects. This includes teachers understanding how to help their pupils establish and develop learning skills including how to explore the subject matter under focus – in other words research and analysis skills as well as skills of writing information, structuring arguments, etc.).
- *Knowledge and understanding about how pupils learn:* what is to be learned, together with observation of ways in which specific pupils learn best, should underpin pedagogy, rather than individual teachers' personal preferences. Thus pedagogy needs to be chosen to reflect the purpose in hand. Consequently they suggest learning experiences should be designed so that all teaching has clear intentions, is well structured, is well organised and is well matched to pupils' previous learning and is appropriate to their stage of development.
- *The role of managing the process of teaching and learning:* this includes a pedagogical style which emphasises instruction as well as reflection, and which encompasses respect for the learners and their learning process.

*How far would you agree with the factors identified by Creemers and by MacGilchrist et al., for an effective classroom? Jot down the areas in which you feel that your own practice is strong, and those in which you need to develop further. How could you foster further development and how might colleagues assist you in that process?*

## Principles of an effective school

Studies of school effectiveness have become increasingly fashionable in the UK since the start of the 1980s, although as Reynolds (1992) and Creemers (1996) point out, elsewhere, such as the United States and the Netherlands, both school improvement and school effectiveness have been areas of study since the 1970s. In addition to the findings of Her Majesty's Inspectorate of Schools (HMI), the three major studies carried out in the UK have focused on a wide range of indicators for school effectiveness in secondary schools (Rutter *et al.*, 1979), Reynolds (1976, 1982) and primary schools (Mortimore *et al.*, 1988). We quote some of the key findings from each to demonstrate how together they underline the importance of valuing each of the individuals within the school, staff and pupils included.

The Rutter study found eight within-school factors to be important:

1   The way intellectually able and less able children were grouped and the match of tasks to capability (setting standards at a level which a majority of pupils were not likely to attain producing anti-authority or anti-academic peer group cultures)
2   The way in which achievement was rewarded; ample encouragement, praise and appreciation being important
3   The amount of care given to the upkeep of the physical surroundings
4   Plenty of opportunities for children to take responsibility for leadership and participation in the running of their school lives
5   Good use of homework, clear academic goals and demonstration of confidence in pupils' capacities
6   Teachers modelled 'good behaviour' such as good timekeeping and willingness to deal with pupil problems
7   Teachers prepared lessons in advance, kept the attention of the whole class, kept discipline unobtrusively and focused on rewarding good behaviour, but took swift action to deal with disruption
8   A combination of firm leadership with a decision-making process, where all teachers felt their views were represented

The Reynolds work with eight secondary modern schools in South Wales produced parallel results to Rutter, including the following factors being associated with school effectiveness:

1   High level of pupil involvement in the running of the school
2   Low levels of institutional control including more relaxed attitudes to enforcing school rules, especially to do with dress, manners and morality
3   Positive academic expectations
4   Small overall school size
5   An attitude toward the pupils of involvement rather than coercion
6   At the heart of the school's norms a respect for the development of interpersonal rather than impersonal relationships
7   A therapeutic rather than coercive response to pupil 'deviance'
8   Positive teacher perceptions and expectations.

Mortimore *et al.* identified a number of primary schools which were effective in both academic and social areas, and which demonstrated the following qualities:

1    Purposeful leadership by the head teacher
2    Involvement of the deputy head
3    Involvement of teachers
4    Consistency among teachers
5    A structured day
6    Intellectually challenging teaching
7    A work-centred environment
8    A limited focus during sessions
9    Maximum communication between teachers and pupils
10   Thorough record-keeping
11   Parental involvement
12   A positive climate.

The debate on effective schools continues, as policy-making bodies such as SCAA, OFSTED and the DFE attempt to define indicators of effectiveness, which include pupil achievement. Studies of 'classroom effectiveness' have been introduced into the frame for defining effective schools. Attempts have been made to examine the extent to which school effectiveness can be seen as a culturally transferable concept – this latter notion we would dispute.

For as well as there being inconsistencies within the studies cited above, there were also inconsistencies between these studies and some of those carried out in other countries. For example, Rutter *et al.* (1979) found that high levels of staff turnover in secondary schools was associated with secondary school effectiveness, the opposite of which was found in the Reynolds study. Another finding which is replicated over and over again within the American literature, namely assertive leadership by the school head which is associated with positive pupil achievement, is not replicated in similar research in the Netherlands (Creemers, 1992, 1997).

Looking however at the three studies cited above, what is noticeable are the areas of commonality, which really turn on effective communication and confident relationships (a point which has drawn criticism from some, such as Scott, 1997, as curriculum factors appear to be neglected).

## Task 7

**Create a written map of the different relationships within your school. How would you describe the way people relate to each other?**

**For each type of relationship, consider which of the variables from the studies by Rutter *et al.*, Reynolds and Mortimore *et al.*, are present. If you can, ask a colleague to do the same exercise and compare your views.**

- **How could you seek the views of other adults and also of pupils?**
- **Which relationships could be improved?**

Since the publication of the three major studies discussed above, attempts have been made by Scheerens and Creemers (1989) to develop a comprehensive model of educational effectiveness, which takes into account data from a number of different levels: the pupil, the classroom, the school and the wider context. Creemers (1996) describes the following factors as being important for school effectiveness at each level. He draws for this model on his earlier work (1994) described above. The factors which he identifies at each level are as follows:

### Pupils

- *Background, motivation and aptitudes,* all of which affect pupil motivation.
- *Time on task,* affected by motivation and also supply of learning materials, appropriate experiences through which to gain skills and knowledge (that is, the provided curriculum) together with the pupils' use of these (i.e. pupil take-up of the provided curriculum).

### Classroom

As might be expected, the three major areas identified by Creemers overlap:

- *Curriculum,* which needs to include explicit and ordered goals and content, structure and clarity, the use of strategies for organising study, the use of assessment feeding into learning.
- *Grouping procedures* which need to reflect specific learning goals, the most effective forms of grouping being ability grouping, and those devised for mastery learning and co-operative learning.
- *Teacher behaviours,* which need to include the maintenance of a quiet and orderly environment; appropriate use of homework; high expectations; explicit setting of goals which are not too broad; which emphasise basic skills and the transfer of knowledge and skills across domains; a structured curriculum content which builds on pupils' prior knowledge and is ordered in a logical way; clear presentation; frequent questioning; immediate use of exercises in order to apply new content; the use of assessment for formative purposes in learning.

## School

Creemers notes that many of the factors identified by previous studies as indicators of school effectiveness in fact reflect classroom practice. Trying to separate the school factors from the classroom level ones, he proposes that conditions for effectiveness can be grouped as follows:

- *Educational aspects,* which include rules and agreements between staff about all aspects of pedagogy, including use of materials, grouping approaches, teacher behaviour and consistency between staff on all of these.
- *Quality of instruction,* which includes a school level policy on co-ordination and supervision of teachers and senior staff together with explicit strategies for what happens where staff do not live up to the agreed standards, and also a school culture which encourages and supports a quest for effectiveness.
- *Time,* which includes the development of a proper schedule or timetable for all subjects in the curriculum, shared rules about time use, including time on homework, pupil absence and the cancellation of lessons; also the general maintenance in the school of an orderly and quiet atmosphere conducive to study.
- *Opportunities to learn,* which include a school curriculum plan, concensus about the school's mission, rules and agreements about how the curriculum plan is to be followed particularly in the transition from one domain to another or one year to another.

He notes that rules and policies should not be frequently changed, so that constancy , stability and ownership in all, staff and pupils, is maintained.

*Context*

Creemers identifies similar factors at context level to those at school level:

- *Quality,* which includes a national policy focusing on educational effectiveness; the existence of an indicator system or national policy on evaluation; appropriate support and training focused on effectiveness in instruction and effective schools; funding of schools based on pupil learning outcomes.
- *Time,* which includes national guidelines on how schools should allocate time to curriculum areas and the supervision and maintenance of schools' schedules of time allocation.
- *Opportunity,* which includes the development of national guidelines and rules concerning what is to be learned – for example, a national curriculum.

As with school level, Creemers suggests that consistency, constancy and control are important characteristics in helping to enable synchronicity between levels.

One of the problems with the school effectiveness research and literature, as Hargreaves (1994) notes, is that, although we have an increasingly clear picture of what effective schools look like, we are not very clear about how to create and maintain them. Other writers such as Reynolds and Parker (1992), Scott (1997), Fielding (1997), also note a number of increasingly apparent problems in the school effectiveness area. These include the following:

- Checklists do not give a full picture of a school's culture; they lack holism (Reynolds and Parker, 1992).
- Definitions of what makes a school effective have tended to be narrow (academic/basic skills related). The characteristics of what made a school effective in the past may not be appropriate for the rapid change and multi-skilled demands of the post-modern world (Reynolds and Parker, 1992).
- Cultural specificity has characterised definitions of school effectiveness (for example, notions of strong leadership which are considered effective in the US and the UK are at odds with what is considered effective in Holland) (Reynolds and Parker, 1992).
- Some influential lists of factors supposedly involved in school effectiveness badly neglect the curriculum dimension of effective education (Scott, 1997).
- The measurement of pupil performance in the context of school effectiveness studies tends to rely on standardised performance tests, the validity of which may be challenged (Gipps, 1994; Scott, 1997).

- The exploration of school effectiveness relies on a 'behavioural objectives' model of teacher behaviour which has been criticised as neglecting complex learning outcomes by trivialising them, encouraging inflexibility in pedagogy and making the false assumption that if something cannot be measured then it cannot be assessed or, by implication, learned (Scott, 1997).
- School effectiveness studies offer an overly rational approach to understanding teachers' work and do not follow through how such findings are or could be integrated into teachers' pedagogy (Fielding, 1997).

On the question of the cultural relativity of different effectiveness models, Scheerens (1992), a Dutch researcher, has suggested several models of organisational effectiveness, which reflect differing cultural values, as follows:

*Economic rationality*   Under this model, the organisation is thought of as rationalist. The main focus is on output (such as exam results) and the level at which the question of effectiveness is asked is organisational. 'Productivity' is highly valued in this model.

*Organic system theory*   Under this model, the organisation is likened to a complex biological organism which adapts to its environment. Flexibility and adaptability are highly valued; the level at which the question of 'effectiveness' is posed is again organisational, but the main focus is on what is put into the system, in other words its environment or context.

*Human relations approach*   Under this model, the organisation itself focuses inwardly. It emphasises the wellbeing of the individuals, their relationships and motivation, and values human resource development. The focus is on motivation and the level at which the question of 'effectiveness' is asked is individual.

*Bureaucratic theory*   Under this approach the organisation is viewed as the interconnected sum of many parts, or relatively autonomous sub-units. Continuity of departments and of the whole, is valued. The focus of 'effectiveness' is at the level of the organisation and also the individual units within it. The formal structure is valued.

*Political theory*   Under this approach, the organisation is viewed as a political battlefield. The different parts of the organisation compete against one another for external recognition, according to implicit or even hidden agendas. Power and interdependence are valued, as is responsiveness to external stakeholders. The level at which the question of effectiveness is addressed is the sub-group, and individuals.

## Task 8

Using Scheerens' models of school effectiveness, consider which model:

- is used by your school/institution
- you most identify with.

---

Clearly, in considering school effectiveness, we must consider the political, economic and cultural context. This has been stressed by leading writers in the field such as Hopkins, Ainscow and West (1994) , including those involved in major international studies of school effectiveness (for example, Creemers *et al.*, 1991; Reynolds *et al.*, 1994; Teddlie and Reynolds, 1998).

From the International School Effectiveness Research Programme (ISERP), Creemers (1997) reports that there exist the following characteristics of effective schools, which are independent of country, socio-economic, and student ability and gender contexts:

- strong commitment to academic goals
- controlled environment showing cohesion, consistency, constancy and stability
- proactive approach to schooling (exhibiting no elements of reactive activity)
- effective management of time including high time on task, break times and lesson transition times being well organised
- good relationships between teachers and high level of curriculum knowledge
- highly interactive pedagogy in classrooms enabling students to take a high degree of control and autonomy.

We would argue that given the transforming nature of society the world over, which is widely documented (Edwards, 1995), the capacity and willingness to create effective relationships will remain key. Thus, in Scheerens' terms, we would adopt the 'human relations' approach to creating and maintaining effective schools.

## School, classroom and departmental effectiveness and improvement

In Chapter 3 we discussed briefly the fields of school improvement and school effectiveness. We acknowledged the tendency of the two to use different methodologies to draw their conclusions, the former tending to use large-scale, quantitative approaches with the aim of demonstrating reliability across different contexts and the latter tending to draw on cases and case studies which emphasise validity. The methodologies of both are under continuous debate and scrutiny and each has its strengths and weaknesses, and also neither can be said exclusively to have used only one approach (i.e. either quantitative or qualitative); in practice it has really been a 'mixed economy'. The two approaches are clearly inter-related; each is concerned with trying to understand what enables schools to function well and how to continue to do so, or to improve on this.

A definition of school effectiveness proposed by Stoll and Fink (1996), underlines this. Their definition includes four aspects:

- promoting progress for all pupils beyond what might be expected given initial attainment and pupil background factors
- ensuring that all pupils attain the highest standards possible
- enhancing all aspects of pupils' development and achievement, and
- continuing to improve, year on year.

One of the areas that both the school improvement literature and the school effectiveness literature point to as essential for establishing and maintaining effective schools, is that of the department. In Chapter 2 we noted the now recognised neglect of the needs of middle managers for CPD. This need represents a change in focus to acknowledge the mutli-layered nature of school improvement to include departmental and team levels as well as the whole school and classroom levels. In particular the study of departments has grown during the 1990s so that researchers such as Harris (1998), Sammons *et al.* (1997), and Fitz-Gibbon (1991) have revealed some characteristics of effective – and ineffective – departments. Harris (1999) summarises these as follows. Effective departments appear to display the following characteristics:

- A climate for change or improvement, the development of which is an essential prerequisite for effective departmental change; without it practices will be modified rather than changed
- Clear and shared vision; this includes frequent departmental meeting at which all members are involved in shaping policy
- Collegiate and co-operative styles of management by the head of department, where that person is also seen as a 'leading professional',

i.e. someone who is viewed by other staff in the department as an expert practitioner

- A high degree of organisation of collectively agreed teaching and learning, including detailed schemes of work accessible to and used by all staff in the department, which reflect the departmental vision of good practice
- The management of resources to the advantage of the total department and all pupils
- The use of mechanisms for monitoring and evaluating progress of individual pupils both within and between departments
- The existence and active use of protocols for the organisation of teaching and learning
- Careful and active attention to the use of appropriate assessment systems and their accompanying record keeping, including attention to the feedback of assessment outcomes to pupils.

Despite overlapping concerns between school improvement and effectiveness, however, as Gray et al. (1999) have noted, it has proved difficult to merge the two traditions. In addition, they note that the majority of the research on school improvement has focused on the processes of improvement, rather than their outcomes. Similarly, studies of school effectiveness have tended to take 'snapshots' of schools at one point in time. Thus the dimension of change over time is frequently missing.

However there is now a growing recognition of the need to bring school effectiveness and school improvement closer together and to link the processes of effectiveness and improvement with their outcomes for pupil achievement, and the life of the overall school community (Gray et al., 1996; MacBeath and Mortimore, 1994). Although as Gray et al. (1999) point out, the process of melding the traditions has gone further in the USA than in the UK, there is in evidence in the UK of a distinct new way of focusing on the issues in both, in a combined way. These are characterised, as Gray et al. (1999) suggest, by the following features:

- Projects are increasingly adopting mixed methodologies for investigation, adopting instruments which seem appropriate to the questions being asked and the problems under investigation.
- Pedagogy and classroom practice are increasingly targeted for investigation.
- The attention is shifting away from what makes a school 'good' to the processes by which a school can be made to be good.
- There is simultaneous interest in both the processes of schools and their outcomes (mainly in terms of pupil achievement).

- There is increasing recognition of the need to chart school development over the medium and longer term.

*What is your experience of school improvement and school effectiveness? Which part of the spectrum of improvement and effectiveness, has your experience been most connected with? How could your own investigation of CPD work you have undertaken, contribute to either in the context of your own institution?*

---

### Summary of Chapter 4

- In this chapter we have explored the pupil's perspective on professional development and argued that pupil involvement in or at least awareness of their teachers' development is essential for meaningful relationships in the school.
- We have argued that IIP provides a tool for supporting the development of a learning organisation, as well as helping to address elements of the school inspection framework.
- We have explored the findings of classroom effectiveness researchers. We have noted a range of factors which seem to be important, in the areas of curriculum grouping procedures and teacher behaviour, noting also that having a good grasp of subject knowledge, understanding how children learn and having good classroom management skills form an important part of these areas.
- We have explored the findings of some major school, classroom and departmental effectiveness studies including the main (and classic) UK studies of school effectiveness, noting the centrality of relationships and of valuing each member of the school's community in an effective school.
- We have explored the relationship between school effectiveness and school improvement, noting the important role of middle managers which is highlighted by school improvement studies.
- We have explored some of the shifts in focus and methodologies which are currently bringing the two approaches, school improvement and school effectiveness, closer together.
- We have adopted a human relations approach to school effectiveness and improvement.

# Chapter 5

# Evaluation and professional development

## THE CONTEXT OF EVALUATION

The growth of interest in professional development, staff review, appraisal, development planning, school effectiveness and school improvement over recent years has been paralleled by increasing emphasis on evaluation in education. Essentially, evaluation is about ascertaining value and worth. It is not so much about checking that what you planned to do has happened, but about whether or not what happens is worthwhile. Evaluation typically involves asking questions, gathering information, drawing conclusions and making a report, containing recommendations for future action. The questions asked are likely to relate to the purposes underlying the topic for evaluation. Information to answer them can be gathered in a variety of ways, for example through questionnaires, interviews or observation. In drawing conclusions from this information, it will be necessary to employ clear criteria or standards of judgement. Usually these conclusions will be included in some kind of report, designed either to improve what has been evaluated or to justify its cost and quality. As well as enabling us to make judgements, evaluation can also provide description of process. This is the basis of the 'illuminative' tradition in evaluation. The main approach to evaluation used in this book however is evaluation as judgement. In the context of increasingly 'technicist' policy level definitions of pedagogy and effectiveness, as discussed in Chapter 1, the tradition of evaluation as judgement is more in keeping with the wider context in which most UK teachers work.

## THE PURPOSE OF EVALUATION

As with school review, development planning and appraisal, evaluation has been subject to debate as to whether or not it should be primarily concerned with accountability or developmental purposes. Evaluation for purposes of accountability will tend to focus on satisfying the demands of those providing funding on whether or not resources have been used effectively and whether they should continue to be used in a particular way. The audience for the evaluation will tend to be those who have funded for example a project, as opposed to those who have been involved in running it. Evaluation for developmental purposes, however, will tend to include a stronger formative element and is more likely to be woven into a project or change. The audience for the evaluation will primarily be those involved in the implementation of the change. The focus in the developmental approach is on using evaluation to improve practice rather than to satisfy external demands for information.

There is, of course, a danger of polarising issues in this way and often a compromise is struck, whereby the needs of different audiences are addressed by the same evaluation. Nevertheless, as with appraisal, attempts to combine developmental and accountability purposes can lead to tensions. In an article published by ILEA's Research and Statistics Branch in 1990, Desmond Nuttall reviewed and discussed seven different purposes of evaluation, which we find a useful framework in the context of evaluation for professional development. He makes the point that the evaluation of professional development tends to focus around the course or in-service experience needs, rather than on individual staff development needs, the needs of the pupils in schools and colleges, or expressed school needs. He suggests that approaching professional development with a wider set of purposes would help address the main aims of staff development more directly. The seven purposes he suggests are:

### Evaluation to provide accountability

He points out that this is the most widely accepted purpose for evaluation, although the question of to whom accountability is to be provided is often not asked or answered. Accountability must, Nuttall suggests, be 'two-way': in other words, the in-service work should have been demonstrably useful to both pupils (particularly if their learning has been disrupted for their teacher to undertake the professional development) and also to teachers. This includes the extent to which educational provision and practice in school has been affected, as well as the extent to which individual teachers' and pupils' needs have been met. Other aspects of accountability will include resourcing. An in-service experience may of course also be accountable to a funding source, such as the school or LEA, or a national source such as the Department For Education, or the Teacher Training Agency. One way of describing the sources of accountability is as stakeholders, although this Blairite term is not used by Nuttall.

*Evaluation for course improvement*

The aim here is to 'do it better next time round' – regardless of whether the in-service experience was a course or some other form of professional development. Evaluation questions might include questions to do with pace, content, format, approaches used, venue, participants' expectations and needs. Nuttall notes that sometimes this is actually built into the professional development experience itself.

*Evaluation to provide better public relations and good practice*

Here the aim is to identify, build on and disseminate strengths in the professional development, through the evaluation process. Nuttall suggests that where this is the aim, communicating the outcomes of the evaluation are particularly important, and that the audience for this information will typically be a gate keeping caucus, such as senior staff in a school, or the governors or parents. This kind of dissemination is traditionally done in the form of a written report.

*Evaluation to provide information for policy, planning and decision making*

Nuttall defines this purpose of evaluation being to provide the source of data which enables decision makers and resourcing agencies to prioritise funding for in-service work. Again, then, establishing a clear means of communication with decision makers is essential here. Nuttall also points out that it may be as important for managers or decision makers to know whose needs are not being met, as well as whose are.

*Evaluation as a means of 'needs diagnosis'*

This is about using evaluation to help participants in professional development target their next learning and development needs. Appropriate planning for a school must involve some element of this kind of evaluation, as well as, Nuttall suggests, leaving room for some needs to be defined externally, for example by LEA advisory staff, or, we might add, since it was not in existence when Nuttall wrote this piece, by an OFSTED inspection team.

*Evaluation for exploration, to further understanding*

This purpose is about widening the evaluation focus to include more than the initial objectives of the in-service work. This kind of evaluation would involve, Nuttall suggests, discussion and consultation with a wider group. In curriculum development, for example, he suggests it would involve attending to pupils' or students' views and attitudes, and possibly require referral to parents and employers.

### Evaluation as a learning process

Involving the participants in professional development in their own evaluation rocess contributes to the implementation of their learning, suggests Nuttall. He proposes that reflection, review and evaluation can be used as learning processes within the in-service work, and thus evaluation can be embedded within the INSET process itself.

Most important of all, though, in evaluating professional development, is its authenticity. As Nuttall puts it:

> Staff cannot afford to undertake evaluation as a 'paper' exercise. ... Without the real power and commitment to be found in improving quality, evaluation can seem to a hard-pressed staff to be merely an unwelcome additional administrative burden. Effective evaluation offers an alternative to that.

### Framing and re-framing

Essentially, the evaluation of professional development activity enables teachers to examine their practice and the development of it through a 'frame' which enables interpretation against certain criteria. By applying the criteria, practice can be developed and thus 're-framed'.

## EVALUATION INDICATORS

Often in the past, the evaluation of INSET courses has been rather haphazard and not gone beyond measures of participant satisfaction. The favoured method of evaluation – the end-of-course questionnaire – has often failed to get beyond 'what did you like and dislike about the day?' Needless to say, designing an evaluation strategy to get at the impact of a course on pupil learning is difficult and the difficulty is increased when what is to be evaluated is a more complex staff development activity. Certainly the pressures of specific government grants for professional development have increased the pressure to evaluate its effectiveness in relation to pupil learning. In particular they have helped to popularise the notions of needs analysis, setting clear objectives for training and creating an expectation that evaluation is part of all INSET courses. Yet the 'how did you like the course' approach remains common. It is perhaps worth adding that evaluation of broader forms of professional development activity has been even more cursory.

As far as the evaluation of INSET courses or wider forms of professional development is concerned, it is possible to identify a number of areas for evaluation to consider:

- teacher satisfaction
- impact on teachers' knowledge, attitudes and skills
- impact on teachers' practice or personal growth
- impact on teachers' careers or roles
- impact on school or team culture
- impact on pupils' learning
- impact on school or team management and organisation.

and, of course, short- and long-term impact – which might cover any of the above. Each of these ways in which in-service work may have impact represents a different 'stakeholder' in the professional development; something we will return to later.

There are also the inter-relationships between potential areas of impact of professional development. In other words, through influencing teachers' knowledge, skills and attitudes, there may be an impact on the teachers' practice, on the school itself (which may in turn influence the individual teacher's practice) and, where there is a strategy for disseminating what has been learned to other colleagues, then their practice too may be affected. Though impacting on the individual teacher, the school itself and other teachers, pupils' learning may be affected. Clearly, some of the influences may be short-lived. Evaluation of INSET has often not tackled the issue of impact on practice, particularly at classroom level. INSET too has often not included help and support for teachers in disseminating what they have learned.

## Stakeholders in evaluating professional development

As indicated above in the exposition of Nuttall's work on the purposes of evaluation, the stakeholders in professional development are those who have some kind of interest or 'stake' in it. So, for example, in much professional development pupils will be stakeholders, the participants will be, the source of funding (if any) will be, the school governors will be, and so on. The way in which you choose to evaluate professional development may depend in part on who the stakeholders are and what their expectations of the professional development may be (actual or perceived). We explore stakeholders further in Chapter 6.

## Appraisal and evaluating professional development

It is precisely in the areas of the evaluation of INSET courses and of wider forms of professional development that the introduction of appraisal has something to offer. Appraisal and the evaluation of all forms of professional development are linked and indeed may be indistinguishable. That is, evaluation of the individual teacher, and the evaluation of INSET/professional development undertaken by them should form part of the appraisal process. Other dimensions of evaluation, which are less central to the appraisal process, include the evaluation of the curriculum. How, then, do appraisal and the evaluation of professional development mesh?

In the first place, appraisal can help at the needs analysis stage and in securing a better match between the needs of an individual with the in-service activity undertaken. Secondly, the review meeting in the second year of the appraisal cycle is seen as a time for evaluating work on the targets agreed at the previous appraisal interview. Where professional development activities have been undertaken as part of the work on targets, then these two are seen as matters for evaluation. What appraisal also provides at the observation stage is an opportunity for teachers to receive feedback on attempted changes in practice. This provides one opportunity to address the issue of the impact of professional development on a teacher's practice and on pupils. (Note: Observation is not an essential part of most review/appraisal schemes in Scotland).

Appraisal is, essentially, a formalised context for evaluation. It provides a way of considering needs, development activity, data about the match of the two, and subsequent action. In particular it presents an emphasis on data collection and provides a context for change, at the level of individuals; someone needs an overview of the collective effect. On the other hand, evaluation adds to appraisal the concern for data. Thus, if the concern is with a teacher's classroom practice, data from that practice is essential. We come to this next, under evaluation methodology, in Chapter 6.

*Reflect back over your own professional development. How was it evaluated (if at all) and by whom? What do you think the purpose of the evaluation was, and how far did it address the impacts listed above? How closely was it tied in to appraisal?*

## Processes and outcomes

Evaluation of professional development may focus on the processes involved in the experience, or on the outcomes of it, or some combination of these. The balance between the processes and outcomes will in part depend on which stakeholders influence the evaluation.

For example, a senior teacher evaluating her own role as a mentor of a student doing initial teacher training course might be most concerned with the processes involved in her own learning and in the ways she was facilitating the student. She might perceive the interactions with the student to be key since a part of the role of mentor is to offer support, counselling and guidance. She might be less interested in knowing what the outcomes of the professional development were at a later stage, than how the student was finding the mentor–student relationship in the present. The stakeholders in this professional development would mainly be the senior teacher, the student and the pupils the student was working with, and to a lesser extent the provider of professional support to the senior teacher (probably the university in which the initial teacher training course was based).

On the other hand, a primary teacher who had undertaken a course for subject co-ordinators in the primary school might be more interested in looking at the outcomes of it. Here the stakeholders would be the head and governors of the school who had allocated the funding, other colleagues for whom this teacher would be a source of expertise in a particular subject, the children throughout the school and the teacher who had undertaken the course.

It is important to be really clear before starting to evaluate professional development, what it is you are looking at: processes or outcomes. We explore this distinction a little further in Chapter 6.

---

## Task 9

Choose some substantial and 'live' (still relevant) professional development you have undertaken, either as participant or as provider, to evaluate. Note down:

- its purpose, location, length, methods and intended level(s) of impact.
- whether you intend to evaluate for development or for accountability, or for one of the purposes defined by Nuttall (1990).
- how far you think at this stage you will want to follow up the processes it involved, and how far you will want to follow up the outcomes.
- how this particular professional development is 'live'.

---

### EXAMPLES OF FOCI WHICH OTHER TEACHERS HAVE CHOSEN TO EVALUATE

Later in the book, we will be introducing some of the tools you will need in order to evaluate; this will include narrowing down the questions you want to ask, and the criteria by which you will judge any data you collect in answer to them.

But for now, you may find it helpful to know what other students of the course on which this book is based have chosen in previous years; here are two examples:

- A languages teacher in a sixth–form college chose a teacher placement as the professional development she brought to the course. It had involved an orientation day at the local professional development centre, an introductory visit to the supermarket chain, spending time with the staff development co-ordinator in her college, and reflecting on how this placement would connect with her past achievements. She spent two days at the supermarket itself and two days at the depot. The methods involved included receiving coaching, self-directed study and personal reflection, collaborative learning, teacher placement and attending an off-site course, having an on-site working meeting and also job shadowing during her placement.

  For her project, she focused on the job shadowing element of her placement, and how that part had helped her develop
  (a)   the curriculum and
  (b)   her career.

- A senior teacher in a secondary school had undertaken an LEA course on becoming an effective tutor or mentor. It had involved preparation reading, five core days of training, and tasks to complete in school between those days. The methods included self-directed study, an off-site course, action research, personal reflection, collaborative learning and on-the-job coaching. The course was aimed at helping mentors, or teacher tutors, to improve their own job performance skills. She chose as her focus the final day of the course, which had involved role-playing, collaborative learning and action planning. She wanted to look at the outcomes from that day.

**Summary of Chapter 5**

This chapter has been concerned with the evaluation of professional development.

- It has been argued that the evaluation of professional development should go beyond immediate satisfaction and consider subsequent impact on teachers, pupils and schools. It should enable teachers to both frame and then reframe, their practice.
- The role of appraisal/review in potentially reconciling and meeting school and personal development needs has been explored.
- You have been encouraged to select a narrow focus of professional development to evaluate and we have distinguished between focusing on processes and outcomes.

# Part II

# Evaluating professional development

# Introduction

Throughout Chapters 1– 5, reference has been made to the tensions that surround professional development. These were seen, on the one hand, in terms of the tension between school, team and individual needs for professional development. They were also seen in terms of providing professional development in response to both external and internal pressures of accountability. A key task in the management of in-service training involves the resolution of such tensions; a key concern for the individual teacher is how far his or her own professional development needs are addressed alongside those arising from school or team priorities or national GEST (grants for education support and training) priority areas.

As a result of reading through Chapters 1–5, you should have reflected on your own professional development experience in terms of the ideas presented in the text and clarified your own position on professional development. The work you have done in studying these chapters provides a context for the way you use Chapters 6, 7, 8 and 9. You will need to keep in view your own position on what constitutes effective professional development as you develop an understanding of the techniques and issues of evaluation during your study of these next three chapters.

Chapters 6, 7, 8 and 9, then, focus on the evaluation of professional development. In working though them, you should:

- develop your understanding of evaluation in general and of evaluation techniques in particular;
- become acquainted with issues involved in data collection, handling and analysis;
- explore a number of central evaluation issues, such as validity, reliability, criteria and ethics;
- apply the lessons you learn by undertaking a small-scale evaluation of an aspect of your professional development experience.

You'll find that these four chapters have a different 'flavour' from Chapters 1–5 – and that overall Part II has more of the feel of a handbook on evaluation. This is so you can build up your expertise as an evaluator. We also provide some student case-study material, examples of evaluation pro formas and other materials, and in places stop to reflect on issues in evaluation. These four chapters should help you in carrying out the techniques in practice, and to support you in building up your own position on how evaluation fits into professional development in your own career context.

Part II of the book is organised as follows:

*Chapter 6*   This offers practical discussion of how to plan the evaluation of professional development. It explores the methodology of evaluation and focuses on how to plan a small project to evaluate professional development. It considers the focus and purpose of such an evaluation as well as how to ensure reliability and validity in the study. It explores evaluation roles, stakeholder roles and the development of explicit, binding ground rules for the evaluation.

*Chapter 7*   In this chapter we offer guidance on specific methods of collecting data for the evaluation of professional development, with analysis of the strengths and weaknesses of each method. We focus mainly on illuminative, ethnographic methods, since given the realities of school life you are unlikely to be able to undertake a large, statistically based quantitative study of effects of the CPD you have chosen to focus on. The chapter explores the extent to which any particular method might yield the information you require, some of the ethics and ground rules of each method and implications for time and resources. We explore the combination of more than one data collection method and more than one source of evidence, together with methods for ensuring validity and reliability and touch on some of the implications of different methods of collecting data, for its analysis.

*Chapter 8*   Here we explore the development and application of criteria for the evaluation of professional development, from a personal and also an institutional perspective. It is intended to support you in identifying and applying your own criteria. We re-visit the notions of process and outcomes, exploring the asking of evaluation questions which may relate to either of these. We also re-visit the influence and stances of stakeholders in the questions that are asked.

*Chapter 9*   We explore ways of handling and analysing data, whether quantitative or qualitative, and consider formative and summative perspectives on the reporting of evaluation findings.

## Summary of the outcomes

If you have carried out the tasks embedded in it at the end of Part II, you should have:

- explored the theory and practice of the evaluation of professional development, in both the collection and the analysis of data;
- drawn up a range of findings about some specific professional development, for reporting;
- explored ways of reporting your findings and recommendations.

## Chapter 6

# Evaluation methodology
## Planning your data collection

### INTRODUCTION

In this chapter, we aim to give some background to the methodology of evaluation. Building on earlier chapters, it includes discussion of and practical suggestions for:

- planning a small project to evaluate professional development
- the focus of your evaluation
- the purpose of your evaluation
- creating a reliable and valid evaluation
- evaluation roles
- stakeholder roles.

Together with Chapter 7, which looks at a range of different evaluation methods, it should enable you to collect data on a chosen focus of professional development.

### PLANNING AN EVALUATION PROJECT

#### Definitions

An important first step is to be clear on the nature of evaluation. Aspinwall *et al.* (1992) provide the following definition which is reasonably neutral and representative:

> evaluation means placing a value on things … it involves making judgements about the worth of an activity through systematically and openly collecting and analysing information about it and relating this to explicit objectives, criteria and values.

In practice, once a subject for evaluation has been chosen, evaluation typically involves the following processes:

- asking questions
- gathering information
- forming conclusions about … programmes and their implementation in order to make recommendations as a basis for decision-making.

(Hall and Oldroyd, 1991)

This last phrase brings us to a point of difference between those writing on evaluation.

There has been a fair amount of disagreement on how evaluation should be conducted and what it is for. Some of those writing about evaluation emphasise its value for purposes of development, while others see it in terms of accountability. Developmental evaluation is primarily about improving performance while accountability evaluation is about proving the value or worth of something, in order to justify performance to others. The key issue is whether the decisions that are taken as a result of an evaluation are designed to improve the professional development that is evaluated or to do with its repetition, continuance or funding.

It is also useful to make a distinction between formative and summative evaluation: formative evaluation is carried out during an activity to help it evolve effectively, and summative evaluation is carried out after the activity to judge its value and effectiveness. Developmental evaluation is, therefore, likely to contain a strong formative element.

The approach that you take will have implications for your role and stance as the evaluator. In the developmental approach, the evaluator tends to be a teacher, a guide or a critical friend; in the accountability approach, the evaluator tends to be the arbiter, judge or professional expert.

A further distinction in evaluation is between qualitative and quantitative approaches. In the qualitative approach, the emphasis is on the collection and analysis of descriptive data. There is often a concern to bring out the unique features of subjective, individual experience. In quantitative evaluation, the emphasis is on the collection of large amounts of data that can be measured or counted and analysed through the application of statistical tests. The concern is often with achieving results that can be generalised. It is possible, however, to combine qualitative and quantitative approaches in a single evaluation and to avoid taking a polarised position.

Finally, different writers on evaluation have taken different positions on the issue of values in evaluation. Some see evaluation as largely 'closed', where the questions and criteria are all determined before the evaluation starts, and where it is not seen as important or relevant to identify and investigate unintended outcomes. Others adopt a more 'open' approach which there is an opportunity to identify and investigate unintended outcomes, meaning that new questions and criteria are incorporated into the evaluation process as it develops.

*What is your own preferred definition of evaluation? How far does it tally with what is written here? What will your preferred approach to evaluation mean in practice for what professional development you evaluate on this course and how you do it? Jot down your thoughts in your notebook.*

The view we are developing in this book is that the evaluation should be properly planned and integrated into professional development, that it should be based on clear and explicit criteria, and that it should lead to improvement and not be an end in itself.

In other words, evaluation is seen as making judgements about the worth of an activity in order to bring about improvements in its practice.

## PITFALLS IN EVALUATION

As the time scale is often very compressed you will probably find that you need to make some compromises in evaluating a specific focus of professional development, perhaps by narrowing your initial focus, or by considering what parts of the professional development it will be feasible to focus on (process or outcomes or both?), or by considering what purposes this evaluation will reasonably be able to fulfil.

To help you make the most of the time you have, we would like you to read through the following list of common hazards in evaluation, put together by a team of experienced evaluators (Aspinwall *et al.*, 1992). They identify what can happen when evaluation is not planned or managed properly:

- Fragmented evaluation or pockets of enquiry about which little or nothing is known in the wider institution.
- Inappropriate evaluation, often set up in a hurry in response to a request from senior management for evidence of some kind.
- Mis-timed evaluation, which occurs too early in a process for there to be any chance of positive findings or too late to fulfil a formative function.
- Unanticipated outcomes of evaluation where, for example, findings indicate that changes are required in the wider system and not just the area under review. It is comparatively rare for such findings to be acted upon.
- Evaluation which seems to grow exponentially, where the task gets out of hand through the collection of unmanageable amounts of data or the pursuit of an issue in more and more depth.
- Evaluation overload, where staff feel bombarded with questionnaires or other intrusions which may be unco-ordinated to the point of different people asking the same or similar questions.

- Irrelevant evaluation, imposed by insensitive outsiders (or insiders) where this is seen to be over-demanding and pursuing interests that are perceived as contrary to those of the school or college (or other groups within them).
- Threatening evaluation, where the activity is imposed and suspected to be part of an internal or external need for control.
- Unfocused evaluation, where, in the rush to know something about a particular area, we neglect to establish more precisely the nature of the information we require.

*If you have any prior experience of evaluation, consider whether you have encountered any of the problems identified by Aspinwall et al. Were any solutions found to overcome any of them? Jot down your thoughts in your notebook.*

*Now consider your own planned evaluation. Using Aspinwall et al.'s list, highlight any pitfalls which you think your own evaluation could be affected by. How you could avoid each problem? Write your solutions in your notebook.*

## GETTING STARTED

If your evaluation is to achieve the desired results and to be carried out effectively, you need to have an overall strategy or plan before starting. It will also help you to avoid some of the pitfalls Aspinwall *et al.* describe!

You will need to work through the following questions in order to plan your evaluation.

*As you read each of these questions, you may find it useful to note down your responses to each in your notebook as the basis of a preliminary plan.*

### What is the focus of your evaluation?

You already began to consider this in Chapter 5. You may find it helpful to look back at the section on choosing a focus in Chapter 5, and in particular your response to Task 8 where you made a first attempt to choose a narrow focus of professional development to collect some data on. Bearing in mind Aspinwall *et al.*'s pitfalls and the view of evaluation you are developing, what refinements could you make to your focus?

### What are the purposes of your evaluation?

Consider how far the following purposes apply in your evaluation:

- learning more about the evaluation of professional development;

- considering how effective and worthwhile your professional development experience has been;
- making suggestions for improvements to the way the professional development experience was organised;
- helping you identify your own future professional development needs.
- other purposes (such as one or more of those described by Nuttall (1990) as introduced in Chapter 5).

You will need to take steps to ensure that others involved in the evaluation understand your purposes and find them acceptable.

### What questions are to be addressed?

Once you have decided upon the main purposes of your evaluation, you will need to clarify the questions that arise from these. For example, you may be a provider, who is evaluating some school-based professional development in order to get suggestions from colleagues about how to organise this kind of professional development in the future – so questions might include what they each expected, how appropriate the methods, length, location and focus were – and how much impact it has had on the levels intended. You might also want to ask what other outcomes/impacts have come from it – which may not have been intended!

### What information will be needed to answer your evaluation questions, and how will it be collected?

There is a danger in evaluation of acquiring too much information. Concentrate on information that is essential to providing answers to your key evaluation questions. Then think about ways of collecting this information such as using questionnaires, interviews, group discussion or observation and referring to logs, diaries or other documents. Think also about who to approach for information – pupils, teachers, tutors and so on. Consider what information is already available: as Rogers and Badham write, of school evaluation: 'before rushing into designing questionnaires, interview schedules and classroom observation checklists, scan existing sources of information such as attendance registers, room/equipment usage logs, published statistics and other data collected recently by your school' (1992, p.7). In evaluation of professional development, the existing data may be different, but the principle of looking for what data already exists still stands.

Consider how to relate other people's views to your own reflections; how can you draw on other people's perceptions to check the validity of your investigation (i.e. whether or not your data is telling you about what you hoped to investigate)? The reliability of your findings is likely to be increased by using more than one method or source but beware of information overload!

### How can you ensure your findings are credible?

Using more than one source of information and more than one data collection method and being systematic and careful in your evaluation will help to ensure that your findings are credible. It is also important to keep a record of what you do so that others can see how you arrive at your conclusions.

### Who will be involved in your evaluation?

You will probably be carrying out the evaluation yourself but you will need to decide who else will be involved in planning the evaluation, contributing information and learning about the results.

### What are the ground rules for your evaluation?

In carrying out your evaluation, you will need a strategy for obtaining clearance, maintaining confidentiality and for who has access to information. You will need to decide on what basis you are operating and to make this clear to those whom you approach.

### Who, if anyone, will receive a copy of your evaluation findings, and what use do you intend the findings should be put to?

What kinds of outcomes do you envisage for your evaluation? These may include a verbal report at a staff or team meeting, a written report for colleagues or governors, discussion with pupils, personal notes, an entry in your own record of professional development, or evidence for appraisal. Clarify who you will inform of your findings, how and for what purpose. Check how committed other people are to acting upon the implications of your findings and think about ways of gaining their commitment and involving them in the process.

### What are the time, workload and other resource implications of your evaluation?

As we have already acknowledged, you are unlikely to have time, or the need, to carry out an elaborate, time-consuming evaluation. The aim is to be pragmatic and realistic in working to achieve worthwhile results. In

| Stage of evaluation | When to be done | Time needed (estimate) | Time needed (actual) | Those involved | Resources/ support needed | Other comments |
|---|---|---|---|---|---|---|
| **Planning**<br>Overall plan<br>Clarifying purposes<br>Identifying who is involved<br>Identifying key questions<br>Identifying criteria<br>Clarifying ground rules | | | | | | |
| **Data collection**<br>Questionnaires<br>Interviews<br>Observation<br>Documents<br>Other | | | | | | |
| **Data analysis** | | | | | | |
| **Reporting**<br>Formative<br>Summative | | | | | | |
| **Other features** | | | | | | |
| **Summative assignment** (first part) | | | | | | |

Figure 6  Planning your evaluation

addition to thinking about your own time, think about how you are going to gain the commitment of others to spend time in your evaluation.

This last question is written as a short reminder of the need to balance the demands of validity and economy in evaluation. The validity of your findings will be enhanced if you use more than one source of data and combine different methods of data collection. Nevertheless, there is the danger of being swamped by data you haven't time to analyse, collecting data you don't need or putting people off by asking too much of them, when you approach them for information. You also need to think about the scale of your evaluation and match this with what you are evaluating. For example, if you were evaluating your school's annual professional development programme, a more elaborate evaluation would be required than if you were going to evaluate a single closure day. With these general comments in mind, you might like to reflect on what you wrote in your notebook about the time and resource demands on your own evaluation. You might find Figure 6 a helpful tool now, for planning the way you hope to spend your time on your evaluation.

Following it (Figure 7) is a plan created by a student of the Open University course on which the book is based; he is a deputy head of a primary school. He was evaluating the impact of a deputy head's management course he had attended on his management role in school.

---

## Task 10

Use the planning questions above and your notes responding to them, to think further about the professional development you are going to evaluate.

Add to your notes, in light of any further thoughts you may have had. Remember that in answering the planning questions you may well find there are some you cannot yet make enough sense of to answer fully. At this stage simply make provisional answers to them.

---

Creating an outline evaluation plan should have helped you to re-visit and further clarify your views on the accountability and developmental models of evaluation and to decide which model you are adopting in your project. You should be clear as to whether you are undertaking a formative or summative evaluation project.

You should also have been thinking about your questions, the kinds of information you will be looking for, and some of the ways you could manage the project. You will perhaps have thought how your approach will mesh with the culture of your institution or the values and interest of others who it may involve.

We will now look in a bit more depth at some of the planning questions.

## EVALUATION FOCUS: PROCESS OR OUTCOME?

You should by now have a preliminary focus for your evaluation. In Chapter 5, we made a distinction between evaluation focused on the *process* of professional development and evaluation focused on the *outcomes* of professional development. In refining your focus, you may find it helpful to look at the following two examples, loosely based on the work of teachers who studied the course on which this book is based. We will be using these two throughout Chapters 6, 7, 8 and 9 to illustrate the methodology of evaluation.

---

### Case Study 1 – Process evaluation

A teacher who had studied part-time for a master's degree (MSc) at a local university, evaluated her own and other students' responses to the process of study which it involved, including the teaching methodology. It was a summative evaluation.

### Case Study 2 – Outcomes evaluation

An appraisal co-ordinator in a large secondary school with 75 full-time staff, evaluated the impact of the introduction of appraisal on her colleagues. It was a formative evaluation.

---

To enable you to collect data, you need to ensure you have narrowed down the part of your professional development which you will concentrate on, for example you might choose a single professional development event, a professional development programme, or the management or provision of professional development. You might want to focus on a course of some type as in Case Study 1, or you may prefer to evaluate an aspect of professional development which is more closely integrated into your practice, such as monitoring, action research, or appraisal as in Case Study 2. The following list indicates a variety of professional development opportunities, and may help you to decide upon your precise focus. The check list, based on one developed by Bradley (1991) is not exhaustive (for example, it does not include ICT-based opportunities), but does illustrate a wide range of professional development opportunities, from which you might choose to select for your own project.

   In practice, it can be tempting to try and include more aspects of your professional development to evaluate than you can actually manage to collect and analyse data for. Turning to our two case studies, this is how they might have narrowed their data collection:

| Stage of evaluation | When to be done | Time needed (estimate) | Time needed (actual) | Those involved | Resources/ support needed | Other comments |
|---|---|---|---|---|---|---|
| **Planning** | | | | | | |
| Overall plan | 6.1.94 | 1 hour | 1 hour | Me, tutor | FTMA01 | |
| Clarifying purposes | 6.1.94 | 1 hour | 1 hour | Me, tutor | FTMA01 | |
| Identifying who is involved | 12.1.94 | 0.5 hour | 0.5 hour | Me | | |
| Identifying key questions | 6.1.94 | 1 hour | 1 hour | Me, tutor | FTMA01 | |
| Identifying criteria | 6.1.94 | 1 hour | 1 hour | Me, tutor | FTMA01 | |
| Clarifying ground rules | 27.1.94 | 0.5 hour | 0.5 hour | Tutorial group | pp.14, 15 my notes | Also p.13904 |
| **Data collection** | | | | | | |
| Questionnaires | 27.1.94 | 1.5 weeks | 1.5 weeks | T. staff | NQTs questionnaire | Talk to purpose |
| Interviews | 21 & 23.2.94 | 0.5 hour each | 0.5 hour ± 5 mins | | | |
| **Data analysis** | Week of 14.2.94 | 1 week | 1 week | Me | p.14 my notes | |
| **Reporting** | | | | | | |
| Formative | 21 & 23.2.94 | 10 mins | 5 mins | Me + 3 staff | | |
| Summative | Sept 94 | 0.5 hour | Unknown | Staff meeting | Notes of STMA02 | Keep to main finding |
| **STMA02** (first part) | Week of 14.2.94 | 1 week | 1.5 weeks | Me | Data and notes | |

Figure 7 Evaluation plan

*1 MSc process evaluation*   Teaching and learning methods used during the one week of the course (university-based seminar, guided reading and self-study).

*2 Appraisal outcome evaluation*   The appraisal interview (incorporating in it all other required evidence and including the evaluation of targets and achievements).

Inevitably, the distinction between process and outcome evaluation is blurred, as you may have been thinking as you read the appraisal case study. This project could easily slip into a process-focused one, if the emphasis on data collection is to do with how the process went, rather than the *effects* or *outcomes* of that process. To collect data on the outcomes then, does *not* necessarily mean taking no account of the process. It will help you to keep clear about your intentions or the purpose of your evaluation, to which we turn next.

## THE PURPOSES OF YOUR EVALUATION

This section is designed to help you reflect further on the purposes of your evaluation and to help you refine your preliminary thoughts. We highlight a wider range of possible purposes for evaluation. As you read through this section, reflect on how far these purposes apply for your own evaluation.

We have already discussed the broad distinction that is often made between evaluation for development and evaluation for accountability. You may, at this point. find it helpful to refer back to the list of possible purposes of evaluation, identified by Nuttall *et al.* (1990), which we explored in Chapter 5. The purposes identified were:

- evaluation to provide accountability
- evaluation for improvement of professional development
- evaluation to promote better public relations and good practice
- evaluation to provide information for policy, planning and decision-making
- evaluation as a means of 'needs diagnosis'
- evaluation for exploration, to further understanding
- evaluation as a learning process.

- Coaching by a colleague with a particular expertise
- Temporary membership of 'task force' or working party
- Projects which have been custom-designed
- Rotation of job/task/role
- Standing-in
- Informal seminars/workshops/discussion groups (internal)
- Being tutored by peers
- Tutoring of peers
- Visits
- Sitting in as observer on committees and other meetings
- Work on local task groups, etc.
- Training/supporting staff who have less experience
- 'Open learning' and 'distance learning' packages
- Representing the school in the wider community
- Giving formal/informal presentations
- Organising formal events
- Guided reading
- In-house courses – participation/planning/delivery
- External courses – participation/planning/delivery
- Paired observation; working with a 'critical other'
- Team teaching
- Action research
- Mentoring
- Monitoring students, new teachers or other colleagues

*Figure 8* Some professional development opportunities.

There is, too, the purpose of evaluation as a means of learning about evaluation – a purpose which many students who studied the course on which this book is based have identified! The following examples, based on the two case studies introduced in the section on evaluation focus, should help you in thinking about your own project.

1 *MSc process evaluation*   Purposes were mixed – it involved an attempt to provide some data for accountability; the student had been fortunate to have the support of her school and LEA, and so wanted to explore how worthwhile the process of learning had been for herself. It also involved evaluation for development in that she hoped the feedback from herself and some students in the evaluation might inform the way the university constructed that course in the future. She also used it as a form of needs identification in identifying what she saw as her next professional development needs. Finally, she was evaluating in order to learn about evaluation.

2 *Appraisal outcomes evaluation*    Again, there were a number of purposes. She used it for improvement of the appraisal process. Second, she wanted to develop good practice and promote public relations in developing the school's practice by involving all staff and by making recommendations at the appropriate levels. Third, she used it to explore understanding (her own and her colleagues) of the potential of appraisal. Finally, it provided information to her school on policy making and planning for appraisal.

In carrying out your evaluation, you are likely to be aiming to fulfil more than one of these purposes. You may also be both learning about how to evaluate and learning about your own professional development.

*Consider how far the purposes listed here apply in your evaluation, whether you have any other purposes and what the implications of your purposes are. Jot down your ideas near to your original notes on the purpose of your evaluation in your notebook.*

## CREDIBILITY

A number of common evaluation issues are related to ensuring that the findings of an evaluation are credible. These are:

- reliability
- validity, and
- sampling.

We begin this section by considering each, and then go on to discuss systematic approaches to handling information, which provide a means of accommodating these issues. The use of such systematic approaches will ensure that evaluation is carried out in an acceptable way, that the findings are usable and relevant and that other people can have confidence in the process and its outcomes.

## Reliability

Reliability is the idea that another evaluator, or the same evaluator on another occasion, should come up with the same results. There are two dimensions of reliability:

- inter-judge reliability – which is about whether two evaluators studying the same event come up with the same conclusions;
- intra-judge reliability – which is about the consistency of the same evaluator's findings about the same things on different occasions.

You should consider which is more appropriate for your project. Three techniques can be helpful in enhancing the reliability of conclusions: following a case study protocol, using an audit trail and using a systematic approach to data analysis. Firstly, the case study protocol; basically, the protocol for this (Yin, 1984) is a plan containing the procedures and general rules to be followed and the instruments to be used. The protocol, like your evaluation plan, would contain an overview of the evaluation (or case study), that is, objectives, key issues and essential background. It would also contain field procedures including data collection methods, evaluation questions and a guide for the report (e.g. who it is for, and what form it will take).

The important point is that, because the protocol, or plan, is written down, others can see how an evaluator has worked and reached his/her conclusions. A similar approach is that of an audit trail, an idea taken from the work of Schwandt and Halpern (1988). Basically, the evaluator keeps a careful record of what they do, how data are collected and analysed and how conclusions are reached. The record includes a note of methods used to control error and eliminate bias. This record of the evaluation is then available for someone else to audit, in much the same way as a financial auditor might audit the school accounts. A spin-off of this approach is that it can help keep the evaluation well organised and on track.

A third strategy for enhancing reliability is to be systematic about data collection and analysis. What is important here is not so much a specific data analysis model as to have an explicit and open approach to data analysis, one that involves systematic analysis and cross-checking rather than intuition.

In evaluating an aspect of your professional development, you are likely to be concerned with a 'one-off' event, and thus reliability may be difficult. Validity is more important to achieve if you are to have confidence in your findings.

## Validity

Validity is about whether or not the evaluator has recorded, or measured, what was intended. Three techniques in particular will enhance the validity of your evaluation. These are:

1   Use more than one source of evidence and or more than one data collection technique (triangulation).
2   Get those who provide you with data to comment on your interpretations (respondent validation).
3   Be aware of your own impact on the evaluation, monitor this carefully, and make this part of your report (reflexivity).

Before you consider how you can make your evaluation reliable and valid, it may be helpful to look at one of our case studies.

---

### MSc evaluation

As there was just one evaluator, with a very limited time-span, this student was unable to achieve inter-judge or intra-judge reliability in practice for this project. However, she kept an audit trail of the evaluation. so that somebody else could follow the same process as her should that become possible – or she could repeat the same study herself at some other time, although given the overall time-frame which the evaluation focused on, this would be much less appropriate.

To enhance the validity of her project, she asked her respondents to comment on the data she received (respondent validation). Ideally, she would also have used more than one data collection technique; questionnaires or documentary evidence being the other methods appropriate for her focus.

---

*Make some notes in your notebook on how you can make your evaluation valid and reliable; and where it is weak in either. If it is weak on reliability or validity (or both) what are the implications?*

## Sampling

All data collection involves selecting information from the totality of an event. At the two extremes are two dangers: it is possible to collect too little data from too narrow a range of sources to be sure your conclusions are generalisable or it is possible to get swamped by too much data. The question then is how much data is enough data? The answer to some extent will relate to the purposes of your evaluation. There will also come a point when fresh data serves only to confirm your findings although given the time-constraints on you for this project, you are unlikely to face this problem! What is important is to have a rationale for how you go about selecting data.

McCormick and James (1983) identify a number of ways of sampling in quantitative and qualitative evaluation. These are summarised below and will help you develop a rationale for selecting appropriate data:

*Quantitative evaluation*

- random selection: choosing a sample completely by random, for example by taking names out of a hat;
- stratified sampling: dividing a group into sub-groups, according to key characteristics, such as gender or location, and selecting randomly from each sub-group;

Note: Quantitative evaluation normally involves a large sample – and can take longer to carry out than qualitative evaluation;

*Qualitative evaluation*

- theoretical sampling: selecting data according to its capacity to inform theory, that is, looking for fresh data to confirm, refine or falsify emerging hypotheses;
- progressive focusing: successively refining research categories as the relevance of particular issues becomes clearer;
- convenience or opportunistic sampling: starting with the most available people and continuing until you are sure that patterns of response are clearly emerging;
- deliberate or purposive sampling: deciding that a particular group or individual is appropriate for your purpose. For example, you might decide to interview members of an existing group, containing a cross-section of staff.

Sampling might relate to people, time or subject content. As with other aspects of the methodology of an evaluation, your approach to sampling needs to be explicit and open to scrutiny. In so far as your evaluation focus is narrow and the time available to you limited, we would advocate that you adopt a qualitative approach. The approach you adopt in sampling will dictate the ways in which you can analyse your data. We consider this in Chapter 8.

The two main case studies we have been describing throughout Part II of the book have involved contrasting sampling, as you may have noted. The MSc project involved qualitative sampling and was 'deliberate' in that the student selected a particular group, that is, the other students on the MSc course, to collect data from.

The appraisal evaluation involved quantitative evaluation, i.e. a large sample, and in fact she chose to include all the potential respondents in the evaluation, that is, all teaching staff, rather than taking a random or stratified sample of them.

*Who are you going to approach for data in your evaluation? What approach will you use? Will it involve sampling? If so, what approach to sampling will you take?*

---

## Task 11

As you worked through this chapter, you were presented with a number of optional tasks, asking you to think about your own approach to evaluation, and the possible pitfalls in undertaking one of your own.

You were then given opportunities to reflect on specific planning questions relating to your own evaluation: its focus and purpose(s), the questions it will address, what information you will need and how you might collect it, how you might make your evaluation credible, who will be involved, what ground rules might be appropriate, and who the audience of any findings will be.

Reflect on the questions which we considered in depth, and finalise your thoughts and plans for:

- the focus of your evaluation: will it look at the process or outcomes of professional development?
- the purposes of your evaluation: which of Nuttall's purposes will it address, or will it address other purposes? (You may find it useful to look back at your notes for Task 3 for this part).
- how will you ensure your evaluation is valid, and reliable?
- whom will you approach for data, and what kind of sampling will it involve?

## ROLES IN EVALUATION

The purpose to which the evaluation will be put will have implications for the role of the evaluator. In an evaluation for development purposes, the evaluator's role is that of teacher, guide and critical friend, whereas in an evaluation for accountability it is that of arbiter, judge or professional expert. In any evaluation, those involved will form an opinion about the evaluator and their relationship with them. It is also possible to look at the role of the evaluator in terms of the skills and qualities needed by an evaluator, the position of the evaluator in relation to the subject of the evaluation and the perspectives an evaluator can bring. We now discuss each of these issues in turn.

### Skills

An evaluator needs to be systematic in collecting, analysing and presenting data. Rudduck (in Dean, 1991) gives a useful summary of the skills and qualities required:

- some research skills
- knowledge of the education system
- capacity to relate to people readily
- skills of listening and observation
- reliability in producing a report on time
- credibility in the eyes of participants.

*How far do you feel you possess the skills and qualities summarised above? How are you going to build on your strengths in carrying out your evaluation? You may find it helpful to make some notes in your notebook.*

In the section on credibility we introduced McCormick and James' (1983) notion of reflexivity as an important attribute for an evaluator. In other words, to be effective an evaluator needs to be self-aware and monitor his or her own reactions and his or her interactions with others. An evaluator also needs to gain the confidence of, and allay the suspicions of, those involved in the evaluation. This depends on the openness of the evaluator and their willingness to discuss and explain the evaluation, as well as upon the relationship of the evaluator to the respondents.

### Position in relation to subjects of evaluation

It is possible to think of evaluators as either 'internal' or 'external'. Internal evaluators have the advantages of familiarity with context, possibly also of credibility and of ready access. They may be more motivated towards the use of the evaluation to bring about development. Internal evaluators need, however, to be mindful of the pitfalls of participant evaluation, namely of being too subjective and not sufficiently detached. External evaluators have the potential advantages of greater objectivity, possibly of credibility and also of being perceived as neutral. They may be required where the purpose of the evaluation is to do with accountability and where an independent view is called for. External evaluators may, however, not be so aware of context and also find the logistics of the evaluation harder. In the end, there is a place for both internal and external evaluation. You need to decide what is appropriate for you, whilst being aware of the potential pitfalls of whatever approach you adopt.

## Perspectives of the evaluator

MacDonald (1976) sees the evaluator as a political figure and differentiates between bureaucratic, autocratic and democratic evaluation. In the bureaucratic model, the evaluator is charged with finding evidence to answer the questions and test the criteria of those sponsoring the evaluation. In the autocratic model, the evaluator is seen as the expert bringing to bear criteria, which arise from their expertise. Democratic evaluation, however, involves the evaluator in identifying and recognising the full range of value positions of all interested parties.

Wideen (1986) distinguishes between the following possibilities, arguing for an eclectic approach to evaluation using a combination of the various possible roles:

- the descriptive role
- the role of communicator
- the judgement role
- the decision-making role
- the role of facilitator
- the role of provocateur.

If we apply MacDonald's political interpretation to these, we can view the descriptive and communicator evaluation roles as belonging to the bureaucratic model of evaluation, the judgement and decision-making roles as belonging to the autocratic model, and the facilitator and provocateur roles as belonging to the democratic model.

Looking at our two main case studies for Part II of the book, we see that the evaluators took on different roles in each. In the MSc evaluation, the evaluator took on descriptive and communicator roles, adopting a bureaucratic model of evaluation. She was carrying out the evaluation in order to report back to her school and LEA, who had supported her on the MSc course.

In the appraisal case study, the evaluator took on the roles of facilitator and provocateur; she was keen to find out the perspectives of each of her colleagues, whatever their views might be, to take the school forward in implementing appraisal. In MacDonald's terms, then, she adopted a democratic model of evaluation.

To help you decide on the model that you will adopt for your own evaluation, think back to your original purpose. You may also find it helpful to consider who else will be involved at the planning, implementation and follow-up stages. Read the following set of questions, adapted from Aspinwall *et al.* (1992), and consider what your responses to each might be:

1    Who has been involved in determining the focus of this evaluation?
2    Who has been involved in planning it?
3    Who has been or should be involved in clarifying the purpose of it?
4    Who has been or should be involved in determining the questions to be addressed and the criteria by which they will be judged?
5    Who should ideally be involved in collecting the data, producing and reporting the results?
6    Who will or should be involved in determining and implementing action?

You may find it helpful to create a diagram, like the one in Figure 9, from the MSc evaluation project. We will explore the final question in more depth in Chapter 10; but for now, your responses to each of Aspinwall *et al.*'s questions should have helped you to clarify who will be involved in your own evaluation, when, and why.

## THE ROLES TO BE PLAYED BY DIFFERENT STAKEHOLDERS

You will also need to consider the role of other people who may be the subjects of, or the receivers of, the evaluation and to what extent your purposes are shared and understood by them. How far is it down to you to identify a purpose or set of purposes and how far will the purposes be determined or influenced by others? Aspinwall *et al.* (1992) point out that 'at an early stage in planning an evaluation, it is helpful to spend time considering the perspectives of those who have some kind of stake in the development.' They refer to those with a stake in a development that is being evaluated as stakeholders and define them as 'any group or individual who is affected by, or can affect, the future of a development.' They

I've realised that some of the roles are indirect, as shown on the diagram. The importance of my school and LEA and the university department made me realise that I'd taken on the bureaucratic model of evaluation.

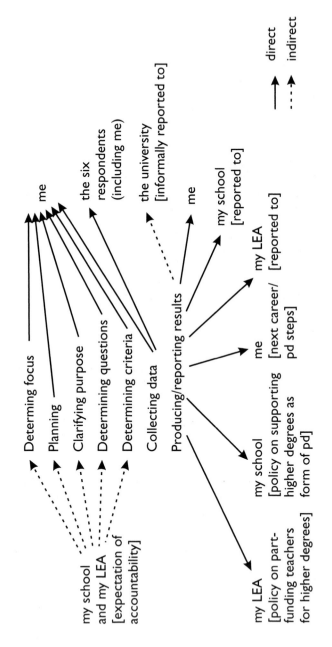

*Figure 9* MSc evaluation: role diagram

note that it is possible to think in terms of both present and future stake-holders and suggest stakeholders might include:

- students (pupils)
- teachers
- parents
- employers
- LEA or education authority
- governors
- Training and Enterprise Councils (or Local Enterprise Companies in Scotland).

In addition we might add Centres for Professional Development, or the Department for Education and the Secretary of State.

Each of these can be listed and their expectations tabulated; for example, if we take the appraisal case study:

*Table 4* Expectations of stakeholders – appraisal case study

| Name of person | Expectations |
| --- | --- |
| Senior management team and professional development group | A summarised analysis of evaluation together with recommendations for discussion and adjustment. |
| Governors' staffing committee | A summarised analysis together with recommendations for discussion and consultation. |
| Whole staff | A summarised analysis together with recommendations for discussion within specially set up consultation teams. Ultimately a revised appraisal handbook. |
| Head teacher | A set of recommendations which have the support of all teaching staff, for further developing appraisal in the school. |

In this example, you can also see the process that meeting these expectations involved. Working out who the stakeholders are will help you to plan how to meet their expectations.

## Task 12

Create a chart of the stakeholders in your evaluation, and their expectations. How can you go about meeting these?

## GROUND RULES IN EVALUATION

We now go on to consider ethics or ground rules, and explore the vital issues of obtaining clearance and maintaining appropriate standards of confidentiality in evaluation.

In this section, we come to the question of ethics in evaluation and consider some of the moral issues involved. All evaluation involves questions of clearance, accuracy, confidentiality, anonymity and openness.

Do not assume that because you have decided to carry out an evaluation project, everyone else who this will involve and impact on will see it in the same way. In fact, the more connected your evaluation is with a permanent system, such as a school (as opposed to a temporary system, such as a project), the more delicate the ethical issues are likely to be. As an 'insider' evaluator, you are unlikely to be, or to be seen as, a complete expert in evaluation; you may have vested interests in, or commitments to, aspects of the system you are evaluating, and you have an existing and continuing role in connection to other individuals in the system.

One guiding principle is to remember the maxim that 'knowledge is, often, perceived to be power'. The act of collecting knowledge can potentially put you in a powerful position, or be perceived thus by colleagues and respondents. It is vital that you consider carefully the politics of the social structures and relationships in the institutions where you will collect your evaluation data, and which will be impacted by the outcomes. One way of sensitising yourself to the possible perceptions and perspectives of others involved in or impacted by your project is to draw a diagram of it, using the questions adapted from Aspinwall which we introduced in the section on evaluation roles, to consider each stage. Figure 10 represents part of the diagram drawn for the MSc case study.

You will see that a number of key issues are exposed through the diagram. For example, the student perceives:

- Jake, her head teacher, has power and authority over her, and has the power to withhold future support for similar professional development. She feels her role in relation to him is compliant. He would probably expect to have an influence in determining the focus of her project.
- Doug, her head of department, has authority over her, and also the power to withhold goodwill and support for future professional development of this kind. He would also probably expect to have an influence in determining the focus of her project. She does not indicate what she feels her relationship to him is like in terms of compliance, withholding or any other qualities. Perhaps then the most appropriate way of involving Doug would need to be carefully considered.
- Harriet, Pauline and Bob, her fellow students, are in a mutual relation-

I took the key people involved at this first stage, to explore power, authority and sensitivity of each, in relation to me and each other.

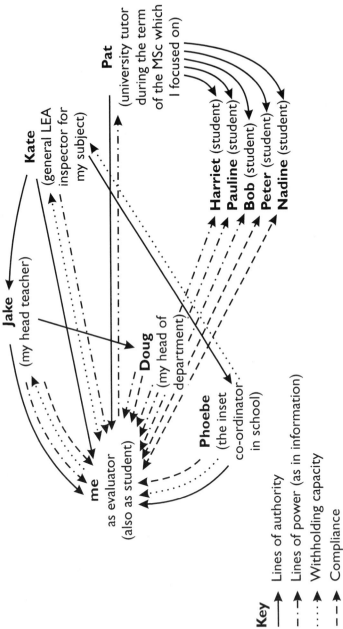

Figure 10 MSc Evaluation: sensitivity diagram for the first stage

ship of power with her, in their capacity to provide or withhold information; perhaps they will need an opportunity therefore to understand (rather than shape) her intended focus.
- Peter and Nadine, also fellow students, on the other hand, may potentially withhold from the project. Perhaps there is a much greater need to try and find aspects of the project which would motivate them – involving them in defining the purpose is an informal way and might be a beginning.

How involved the stakeholders are or want to be, and their perceived impact of your evaluation project, if any, on them, will be influenced to some extent by how overt and open your evaluation is; particularly your methods of data collection, and also who has access to what information.

For your project, you should think about how you can apply the following basic principles; they should be made explicit and binding in your project:

1  Ensure all relevant people/authorities have been consulted, and that you have obtained the necessary permission and approval for your evaluation project.
2  Encourage stakeholders to help shape the project.
3  Negotiate with all those affected (not everyone will want to be directly involved – your work must take account of the perspectives, responsibilities and wishes of others).
4  Report all progress; keep the project visible, and remain open to suggestions (colleagues must have the opportunity to lodge any protests to you).
5  Before observing or recording colleagues, obtain explicit authorisation.
6  Before examining or copying any documentation, obtain explicit authorisation.
7  Allow those people whose work and opinions you describe to challenge your accounts on grounds of accuracy, relevance and fairness.
8  Before quoting from transcripts, audio recordings, etc., obtain explicit authorisation.
9  Remember that different audiences demand different kinds of reports on your evaluation. What is appropriate for a personally focused report, or one associated with a course of study, may not be appropriate for a report to a staff meeting or a newsletter to parents! You should, though, retain the right to report your project. Provided all those involved are satisfied with the accuracy, fairness and relevance of accounts referring to them, the project report/s should not be subject to veto, or to prohibitions of confidentiality. Ownership belongs to the participants in the project, but, ultimately, to you.
10  Accept responsibility for maintaining confidentiality.

## Task 13

Re-read the ten principles above. Consider how to apply them in your own evaluation, or imagine yourself in the following situations:

1   A colleague has asked if she can carry out observations in your classroom as part of her work for a higher degree;

2   You have agreed to lead a school-based professional development day.

What would you want to be agreed before (1)? How would you like your work to be evaluated in (2)? What ethical code would you wish to be applied in each situation?

## Summary of Chapter 6

In this chapter, we have discussed issues in planning and implementing an evaluation of professional development, in particular. The following are key considerations:

- Evaluation involves asking questions, gathering information, forming conclusions and making recommendations to aid the making of decisions.
- A key distinction in terms of the purposes of evaluation is between evaluation for development and evaluation for accountability.
- In this book, we see evaluation as making judgements about the worth of an activity in order to bring about improvements in practice.
- We discussed the possible purposes of evaluation, and highlighted the importance of considering both your own expectations of the evaluation and those of others.
- Ways in which the validity, reliability and sampling can be approached to enhance the credibility of the evaluation;
- The main skills and qualities needed by an evaluator, such as being systematic, having effective communication skills, being self-aware and possessing appropriate interpersonal skills;
- The connection between evaluation purpose and evaluation role; and
- The possible roles for other people in an evaluation at the planning, implementation and follow up stages.
- We explored the need to sensitise yourself to the needs and perspectives of the different stakeholders in your evaluation of professional development.
- We recommended the adoption of an explicitly, negotiated and binding set of principles.

# Chapter 7

# Methods of evaluating professional development

This practical chapter is designed to enable you to select appropriate methods for evaluating specific professional development in your own context.

The point has already been made, but can stand repetition, that it is important to plan an evaluation carefully as a whole before plunging for one evaluation method or another.

It is essential to recognise that no matter how efficiently a method is carried out, its effectiveness is dependent on how well you plan its introduction and follow-up. Aspinwall *et al.* (1992) suggest that 'there is always a danger that evaluation which focuses on technique rather than context may have negative consequences, rather like the proverbial technically successful operation during which the patient died'.

A wide range of techniques, or methods, are available for you to consider with this caution in mind – questionnaires, interviews, observation and analysis of documents, for example. Each method has strengths and weaknesses, depending upon the situation in which it is used. It is important, therefore, in selecting a method to bear in mind:

- what are the strengths and weaknesses of the method?
- will the method provide the information that you need?
- will the method be acceptable to those involved?
- are the time and resource implications of the method acceptable?
- have you the time and the means to carry out the analysis of the data you are planning to collect?

It is also important to consider the context in which you are working and to match the level of evaluation to the scale and importance of what is being evaluated. You need to consider what other evaluation activities are being carried out and peoples' previous experience of evaluation, for example. It is necessary to avoid 'overload' and essential not to ask the same or similar questions to those that have been asked by others. You will need to remember what kind of balance you are trying to strike between process and outcome questions, also. It is likely that different methods will be appropriate for different parts of the professional development that you are evaluating – this may be another opportunity to narrow down which is feasible!

We now look at each of the main evaluation methods in turn in order to help you refine your approach to data collection:

- questionnaires
- interviews
- observation
- analysis of documents
- diaries.

Given the realities of school life, you are unlikely to be able to undertake a large project. In light of this, consider carefully which method will suit your needs best. You will probably need to think about collecting illuminative, ethnographic data rather than large-scale survey data; qualitative rather than quantitative.

You should read the section later in this chapter on ground rules, and Chapter 7 on criteria, before you actually start to collect data.

## QUESTIONNAIRES

Questionnaires are the most commonly used evaluation method, although the typical 'end of course questionnaire' has its limitations. Evaluation by 'correspondence' is relatively quick and can cover large numbers of people. It gives good indicators of participant satisfaction, though detailed questionnaires which invite item-by-item criticism need a complementary section on general response to the activity if balance is to be maintained. These approaches do not tell us about impact on performance or school practice though they can elicit some opinions about changes in attitude. We have to be careful, however, not to confuse opinion with fact. Several studies have shown us that the perceptions of individuals are not borne out by colleagues or pupils. The structured free-response questionnaire is quite good at exploring attitudes and the before-and-after letter is particularly good at highlighting changes which retrospective questionnaires miss because teachers have forgotten where they started.

However, it is possible to use questionnaires in a variety of ways and in this section we describe some different possible forms and uses.

One distinction that can be made is in terms of scale. At one end of the spectrum are large-scale survey questionnaires, often designed to be delivered and returned by post; at the other end come structured questionnaires designed to enable more 'open' answers, and often designed to be administered face to face. It is possible to think of both types in terms of:

- degree of structure
- type of questions, and
- timing.

In terms of structure, at one end of the continuum are highly structured or 'closed' questionnaires or rapid assessment forms, which require the respondent to tick boxes or circle a response. Sometimes in this type of questionnaire, the respondent is asked to rate an activity on a scale; for example, 'How well structured did you find session 1?'

| Very well structured | Quite well structured | No strong views | Poorly structured | Structure totally unhelpful |
|---|---|---|---|---|
| 1 | 2 | 3 | 4 | 5 |

Sometimes, too, highly structured questionnaires use the technique of asking questions which require a yes/no answer.

Another approach is to go for semi-structured or semi-open questionnaires, in which the questions are structured but the responses are not; the respondent is able to respond freely to the specific points raised by the questionnaire. Often a combination of open and closed questions is used, for example, 'How useful did you find the workshop?'

| Very useful indeed | | | | Not at all useful |
|---|---|---|---|---|
| 1 | 2 | 3 | 4 | 5 |

Please say why:

At the other end of the spectrum is the unstructured or open-ended questionnaire, in which the respondent is invited to write a continuous piece of prose or 'essay'. Sometimes, this type of questionnaire can take the form of a letter to course members, written before and after a course or event, asking them to write back to the evaluator outlining what they expect from a course or what they got from it.

Questionnaires depend for their success on careful design and presentation. A useful point to consider is the use of different types of questions. Open questions, reflective questions, closed questions and prompts all have their place. To be avoided are multiple, over complex, loaded and leading questions. Attention also needs to be given to clarity and choice of language, question sequence and layout. The aim should be to write questions in a clear, intelligible style, avoiding unnecessary jargon and to take the respondent forward in a logical manner. You may find the following guide, adapted from Cohen and Manion (1989), useful (and possibly amusing) in designing your own questionnaire or interview schedule:

---

### 'Avoid' Questions

1   Avoid *leading* questions, that is, questions which are worded (or their response categories presented) in such a way as to suggest to respondents that there is only one acceptable answer. For example:

Do you prefer abstract, academic-type courses, or down-to-earth, practical courses that have some pay-off in your day-to-day teaching?

2   Avoid *highbrow* questions even with sophisticated respondents. For example:

What particular aspects of the current positivistic/interpretative debate would you like to see reflected in a course of developmental psychology aimed at a teacher audience?

Where the sample being surveyed is representative of the whole adult population, misunderstandings of what the investigator takes to be clear, unambiguous language are commonplace.

3   Avoid *complex* questions. For example:

Would you prefer a short, non-award bearing course (3, 4 or 5 sessions) with part-day release (e.g. Wednesday afternoons) and one evening per week attendance with financial reimbursement for travel, or a longer, non-award bearing course (6, 7 or 8 sessions) with full-day release, or the whole course designed on part-day release without evening attendance?

4   Avoid *irritating* questions or instructions. For example:

Have you ever attended an in-service course of any kind during your entire teaching career? If you are over 40, and have never attended an in-service course, put one tick in the box marked NEVER and another in the box marked OLD.

5   Avoid *questions that use negatives.* For example:

How strongly do you feel that no teacher should enrol on the in-service, award-bearing course who has not completed at least two years full-time teaching?

---

*Figure 11* A guide to designing a questionnaire or interview schedule

Cohen and Manion also warn that open-ended questions may not necessarily bring a clear response and can take up too much of the respondent's time. They can also generate a lot of data for analysis. Nevertheless open questions can be useful in allowing you to explore someone's views.

In practice, it is helpful to include structured and less structured sections in a questionnaire and to design one with a mixture of closed or rapid response and open questions. Closed questions provide responses that can be analysed quickly and get at key information. Open questions are less constraining on respondents and encourage a greater variety of responses.

This brings us to the issue of timing. In theory, questionnaires can be issued before, during or after a professional development activity. If a sequence of questionnaires is issued, then it is possible to compare responses over time. For example, the expectations of a course to be found in response to a pre-course questionnaire can be compared with what participants actually felt the course achieved in response to an in-course questionnaire and what they actually reported they did as a result of the course in response to a questionnaire issued at some time after the course.

### Summary

Some of the strengths and weaknesses, then, of questionnaires:

- They are easy and quick to administer and can readily be issued to large groups.
- They are flexible; they can be designed in a variety of ways and issued at different points in time.
- The time needed to design and analyse a questionnaire can easily be under-estimated.
- The more open-ended the questionnaire, the easier to construct. The more open-ended the questionnaire, the greater the time for analysis.
- An overly long or complex questionnaire can put respondents off while a questionnaire made up of too many closed questions can cause frustration by constraining what respondents can say.
- Gaining an acceptable response rate (say 50 per cent or more) can make considerable demands in terms of presentation and chasing up.

In view of these points, it may be useful to think in terms of a short questionnaire being used to provide a rough map of the territory to be evaluated. Such a questionnaire would typically generate a number of points for further investigation by other approaches to data collection.

Name: ...................................................    School: ................................

# EVALUATION SHEET

## NATIONAL CURRICULUM TRAINING – SECONDARY SCIENCE

|  | Agree | Agree strongly | Disagree | Disagree strongly |
|---|---|---|---|---|
| The objectives of the day were identified and made sufficiently clear |  |  |  |  |
| The stated objectives were adequately achieved within the time constraint |  |  |  |  |
| The stated objectives were appropriate to my current needs in respect of National Curriculum training |  |  |  |  |
| The day adequately prepared me to introduce my department to the needs of the National Curriculum for the coming year |  |  |  |  |

|  | Good | Satisfactory | Poor |
|---|---|---|---|
| To what extent was the general planning of the day satisfactory? |  |  |  |
| To what extent were the venue and domestic arrangements satisfactory? |  |  |  |

*Figure 12*  Rapid response questionnaire, based on one from the Hertfordshire LEA science advisory team

Included below are a number of questionnaires that have been used in the evaluation of professional development, which illustrate some possibilities for questionnaire design.

Figure 12 combines a rapid assessment section which takes the form of rating scales with a section inviting comments. Such a questionnaire can be useful in indicating strong responses one way or the other and to identify aspects for further investigation. When such questionnaires are used on a routine basis it allows comparative information to show how particular activities or sessions within them are working. They are also easy to

---

# EVALUATION OF PROFESSIONAL DEVELOPMENT

Professional Development Event: ...................................

Dates: ..............................

1. What did you intend to achieve by attending this professional development event?


2. Did you find it useful in achieving these objectives? (And how?)


3. How could the content have been made more valuable for you?


4. How might the sessions have been better managed?


5. What kind of follow-up would be useful for you?


[If you are interested in follow-up sessions of any kind, please give your name, school address and telephone number in block capitals.]

---

Thank you for taking the time to fill out this sheet; it helps us to improve the quality of future professional development events.

---

Return this sheet to: ....................................By (date): ........................

---

*Figure 13* Open-ended evaluation questionnaire

'decode' on a very large scale, since they lend themselves to a numerical score indicating how many people adopted which stance on each question asked. However, questionnaires of this kind have the disadvantage of giving little information as to why each respondent gives each view.

Figure 13 provides a contrasting style of questionnaire, arranged in the form of a series of open questions.

Clearly, one of the advantages of the open-ended approach is that the respondents can give much more of their own expectations, hopes and perspectives on the professional development. Indeed, their responses may include areas which the questions you asked did not directly address and so open new areas for evaluating. One of the disadvantages however is that, given the individuality of each response, the job of summarising and categorising responses is far more complex.

You may find it useful to examine the role of questionnaires in one of our case study examples.

---

### Appraisal evaluation project

As there were seventy-five members of staff involved, this student decided to use a short questionnaire as her main data-collection method. Since she was interested in finding out how positive or negative the appraisal experience had been for each member of staff, she began with a closed question, asking each respondent whether they had found the process generally more positive than negative. All of the questions which then followed were open, offering respondents the opportunity to give as personal response as possible, to questions such as 'how would you change the processes to improve the scheme?' and 'for which specific aspects of appraisal would training have been of benefit?'

Because she was looking at outcomes, and evaluating the scheme at the end of its first cycle, the questionnaire was given to all members of staff after the experience.

---

Analysing the questionnaires involved this case study teacher in categorising responses to the open-ended questions; we will look at this method of analysis in Chapter 9, on analysing data.


## INTERVIEWS

Interviewing can give us deeper knowledge of attitudes, as it allows us to probe, to follow-up and to check our perceptions with the responder in a way that questionnaires cannot. However, it is a costly procedure in terms of time and is likely to be done only on a sampling basis and for very important issues. A participant observer, who takes part in the whole process as a participant but looks at it through the eyes of an evaluator, is a useful alternative. This is particularly so if the observer has time to talk to other participants about their perceptions.

As with questionnaires these vary in terms of:

- degree of structure
- type of questions, and
- timing.

Taking structure first, interviews can be placed along a continuum with structured interviews at one end and unstructured interviews at the other. In a structured interview, the questions are set out in a precise manner and the interviewer has little or no discretion in terms of departing from the fixed interview schedule. The aim is to standardise data gathering and to facilitate analysis. The drawback is that the opportunity to find out about unexpected outcomes or views that don't fit the schedule is lost. In effect, interviews of this type are rather like oral questionnaires. As such, the presence of the interviewer may help to encourage a response but also allows follow-up; for example, to find out why the interviewee gave a particular response. At the other end of the continuum comes unstructured interviews. In these, the interviewer follows the lead given by the interviewee and aims to be non-directive. This approach can be very effective in encouraging interviewees to respond freely and does not restrict or constrain their responses. It can, however, generate a vast and varied amount of data to analyse and can lead to areas being missed out in some interviews, which appear as important in others. The interviewer is then left unclear as to whether their omission reflects their lack of importance in the eyes of some interviewees or simply lack of time or direction.

In order to achieve a balance between the extremes, a number of evaluators use semi-structured or focused interviews. In a semi-structured interview, the interview schedule takes the form of a mixture of closed and open questions and often contains suggested probes or follow-up questions. Often, there is a catch-all 'Is there anything else you want to tell us?'

A focused interview is one where the interviewer has some general topics, but aims to use these as prompts to explore the interviewee's perceptions and subjective experience. It is a type of semi-structured interview but one with a particular orientation.

Cohen and Manion (1989) describe focused interviews in this way: 'The distinctive feature of the focused interview is the prior analysis by the researcher of the situation in which subjects have been involved.'

Structure for the interview can be arrived at by, for example,

- exploring the agendas of the stakeholders (e.g. your own; the interviewee's; the institution's; the head of department's; etc.)
- exploring the interviewee's feelings about the professional development in relation to their learning preference.
- exploring the interviewee's feelings about the professional development in relation to their job role.
- referring to other data (such as the interviewee's response to a questionnaire).

Figure 14, developed in the Evaluation of School Teacher Appraisal Pilot Study, shows how open questions can be linked to prompts for following up initial responses. Note the final all-purpose 'Is there anything else you want to tell us?' The instrument combines a question guide with reminders to the interviewer.

The issues of type of question and timing are the same as with questionnaires, except that it is easier to explain an unclear question in a face-to-face interview. As with questionnaires, interviews depend on the appropriate use of questions and a logical sequence of inquiry.

In general, interviews, particularly those with at least some open questions and freedom for the interviewer to use his or her discretion, have a number of advantages over questionnaires. They allow questions to be clarified and explained and allow for issues to be explored in depth by means of probes and follow-up questions. Also, the process of being interviewed can have a valuable psychological effect on the interviewee, making them feel valued for their involvement in an activity or project. Conversely, results may be affected by the interviewer's personality and style or status. Recording what is said is also a potential difficulty. Note-taking can be obtrusive or difficult to keep up with sufficient speed. The use of a tape recorder can also be off-putting and can lead to a demand for time to transcribe later. Transcribing a one-hour tape can take up to ten hours, although, of course, a summary might be made in a shorter time. Perhaps a good compromise is to take handwritten notes, but to have drawn up a recording schedule in advance on which *abbvtons, key wds* and *sht-hnd, lg-hd* can be inserted. You can record as a back-up in case you need precise words.

Another potential drawback of interviewing is time. Indeed the student who evaluated appraisal in her school had insufficient time to carry out interviews, although interviewing a small cross-section of staff would have added validity to her project. One way of making the most economical use of time is to go for group interviews or discussions. In the context of the evaluation of professional development, this might take the form of 'an end of professional development review'. Group interviews, as well as saving time, can be less threatening and can be useful at the beginning of an evaluation to identify areas for exploration. They can also help an evaluator refine their key evaluation questions and begin to uncover the criteria implicit in these. The drawback of a group discussion is that people can take the lead from each other and that certain individuals with strong positive or negative views can dominate. Group discussions can be harder to manage than individual interviews. One way of overcoming these difficulties is to use a nominal group technique. Individuals are asked to note down their own views, then to share and compare these with a partner's. Each pair then goes through a similar process with another pair and then

*Interview schedule for use with teachers after appraisal*

*Reminders*

1   Please clarify whether your interviewee was an appraiser or appraisee. If they were both, ask questions from both points of view.

2   The following general questions are linked to the seven topics chosen for our reports. They are followed by prompts based on the relevant *aides-mémoire*, to enable detailed follow-up in the interview, should time permit.

*Questions*

1   *How do you feel about the appraisal process?*
    – what do you feel you gained?
    – were there any drawbacks?
    – what changes, if any, would you want in the process next time round?

2   *Can you tell me how the following went?*
    (a) *Preparation*
    – initial review discussion
    – length, agenda
    – self-appraisal
    – how done/scope/support for/time taken/shared
    – other preparation
    – collection of second opinion/scope and time taken
    (b) *Classroom observation*
    – amount/emphasis/position in cycle/techniques used/who does it/nature of preparation and feedback criteria
    (c) *Appraisal interview/target setting*
    – organisation of interview
    – who involved, when, how long?
    – preparation
    – what data were used?
    – interview structure
    – agenda, agreed statement (nature/access/use)
    – type of targets set
    – follow-up action to monitor/enable targets

3   *Looking back, how well do you feel the training you had prepared you for appraisal?*
    – how far did training prepare you for each stage of the process?
    – balance of awareness raising/information giving and skills development
    – mode of training/trainers/activities/time and timing

4   *What impact has appraisal had (a) on you, (b) on your school?*
    – Look for data relating to change in induction of new teachers/changes in ways teachers participate in INSET/new or modified roles/career development/help with performance difficulties/use of appraisal information in references

5   *How has the appraisal process been organised?*
    – rolling programme? length of process?
    – hours taken? co-ordination of process?

6   *What use, if any, has been made of supply cover?*

7   *What links, if any, have there been between whole-school review and appraisal?*

8   *Is there anything else you want to tell us?*

*Figure 14* Example of an interview schedule used in the evaluation of the School Teacher Appraisal Pilot Study

the full group come together. At each stage, people are asked to identify areas of agreement and disagreement and to negotiate what they see as joint priority issues. This approach can be used in reviewing a professional development activity, where colleagues are asked to identify positive and negative features of the experience or to reflect on what they will do as a result of it. However, because the technique itself relies on group pressure, it can alter and affect views rather than simply helping to identify them.

Another issue for those carrying out interviews or using questionnaires, is the need to explain to respondents the purposes of the inquiry. While in the case of a questionnaire, this might be done in a covering letter or introductory paragraph, in the case of an interview it will need to be done through the interviewer's opening comments. These may prompt questions and care is needed to ensure that this part of the process does not go on so long as to squeeze the main agenda. On the other hand, if the interviewee is left unsure or anxious, then responses may be very guarded. An interview requires a 'settling-in procedure' to help the interviewee feel at ease.

You may find it useful to look at how interviews were used in one of the case studies:

## MSc process evaluation

Because the numbers of people involved were small, this student decided to interview the five other teachers in her MSc group, using a semi-structured interview schedule to find out the answers to her questions which we outlined under the section on 'evaluation questions'. The interview method enabled her to follow up and clarify the responses to gain a fuller understanding of why each respondent felt the way they did about that week of the course.

## OBSERVATION

Observation is a valuable evaluation method and one that is at the heart of ethnographic or illuminative studies. In terms of the evaluation of professional development, it is possible to think of both the observation of a professional development experience itself or of the observation of a teacher before and after such an experience to investigate changes in practice. It is also possible to think of observation and feedback or post-observation analysis as an approach to the professional development. For example, it could be linked to the 'practice and coaching' stages of the Joyce and

Showers model for INSET (Joyce and Showers, 1980) or be part of the cycle of action research for mentoring.

In observation, there are a number of choices to be made. The following sets out the range of possibilities:

*Choices in observation*

| | |
|---|---|
| *Who observes?* | self/a colleague/a line manager or senior colleague/an outsider |
| *What is the level?* | pupil(s)/teacher/teacher/pupil interaction/subject general (wide-angle lens)/specific (zoom lens) |
| *Style?* | participant/'fly on the wall' systematic/open |
| *Source of criteria?* | individual/school/external explicit/implicit predetermined/emergent |

The possible permutations of approach are great. In effect, there is no one all-purpose best approach. Rather, you need to select the best approach for your particular situation or purpose. The following discussion is designed to help clarify the basis on which the choice of an appropriate method can be made.

The first issue raised was the question of who observes. The options listed were self-observation, observation by a colleague or line manager and observation by an outsider, for example an inspector. Self-observation and observation by a colleague feature in action research. The ideas of the teacher as a researcher in his or her own classroom developed by Stenhouse and Schon's notion of the reflective practitioner have influenced this type of approach. Teachers undertaking the observation of their own practice in a systematic way have used a variety of methods: audio-tape and video recording, diaries, field notes and log books. Audio-recording and audio-visual data are of course selective, depending on the position of microphone and cameras. They do, however, enable both the observer and teacher to 'replay' the lesson during a feedback discussion or to check on what occurred, for later analysis. Sometimes they check their own data with data from other sources, for example pupils or a colleague observer. It may be possible to work with a colleague in a process of paired observation where each of you works together with a shared purpose. This can be particularly effective where you are endeavouring to extend your repertoire of teaching or training skills. It is possible to set objectives and give direct feedback to each other. Observation where two individuals are also working together in some way is sometimes called 'participant observation'.

Cohen and Manion (1989) review the strengths and weaknesses of participant observation. On the positive side, they see it enabling the observation of 'ongoing behaviour as it occurs'. In other words, 'it is possible to develop a more intimate and informal relationship with those being observed and they are less likely to react in an artificial way.' On the other hand, Cohen and Manion refer to the dangers of subjectivity and imprecision. They ask: 'How do we know that the observer does not lose his perspective and become blind to the peculiarities that he is supposed to be investigating?' A participant observer needs to be alert to threats to the validity of his/her findings and can do so by focusing on what happens (description) rather than make judgements, while observing and by triangulating data (see the section on credibility).

Participant observation is particularly appropriate in the evaluation of professional development and INSET. It might be used in a number of ways. For example, you could observe your own classroom before and after a professional development activity in order to monitor changes in practice. Another approach would be to observe a professional development activity as you experience it. For example, you could keep a record of your observations during a professional development activity, or ask another participant to keep a similar record.

The use of other people as observers again has strengths and weaknesses. Other people, particularly if they come from outside, may be less subjective, but on the other hand they may lack contextual knowledge, and can be more threatening and as a result create an artificial situation. In addition the involvement of others is more difficult to arrange. Nevertheless another observer can provide a very helpful extra pair of eyes, especially when their views are compared with those of participants. This type of approach is, of course, a feature of appraisal schemes, with the most successful schemes in terms of their use of observation being those where it is handled in a collaborative way and the observer and teacher are able to identify and jointly evaluate specific aspects of teaching and learning.

Another issue in observation is the matter of level. A number of examples were given: pupil(s), teacher, teacher–pupil interaction and subject. These would apply particularly to classroom observation. If other things are being observed, for example management or pastoral work or professional development activities, then the choice of level is wider. It would be possible in a course, for example, to focus on content, delivery, participants' reactions, activities and so on. Level can also be looked at in terms of whether the observation is general or specific, in other words the degree to which the observer narrows down what he/she observes. A general or wide-angle lens approach might take the form of the observer attempting to record a narrative of the event, whereas a specific or zoom lens approach would lead the observer to narrow down to investigating one or two selective categories. Both approaches have their place. The general approach can be a useful means of identifying specific areas to look at in a future observation: in other words it can generate a hypothesis to investigate further. It can also be helpful in terms of getting people used to observation. However, a selective approach can be more manageable and be used to focus on specific areas for development.

Another area of choice in observation is style. Reference has already been made to the style of participant observation, where the observer participates in the activities of the classroom or situation in some way (usually filling an existing role to allow for their transient status). Someone observing their own classroom or course is by definition a participant observer. It is also possible to participate when observing someone else's lesson. The alternative approach is the 'fly on the wall' approach, in which the observer aims to be as unobtrusive as possible and to minimise the impact of their presence. It is possible also to vary the style used within the span of a single observation, joining in for some of the time and standing aside at other times. Joining in, at least for some of the time, can be more natural and can lead to good quality data and help understanding of what is going on if, for example, it involves talking to those present. On the other hand, too much joining in can lead the observer to losing sight of what they are there to observe. The 'fly on the wall' approach, while useful in terms of aiding the observer's concentration, can be more threatening and artificial, particularly where observation between colleagues is concerned.

There is also the contrast between structured and unstructured or open observation. Structured observation involves the use of structured observation schedules, that can be analysed in a quantitative way. On the other hand unstructured methods of observation are qualitative and in their purest form involve the observer in writing field notes or a narrative account of what is observed which takes their shape from the event and are descriptive. There is a long-standing debate between exponents of these approaches but there have been recent moves to some sort of reconciliation and towards an eclectic position.

It follows that different approaches to record what is observed follow from the basic approach, depending upon whether it is structured or systematic. Evertson and Holley (in Millman, 1981) distinguish between a number of types of written recording instruments; (1) frequency/count systems, which take the form of ascribing what is observed during regular scans of an event into a pre-determined category or putting down a tally or other sign or symbol against a category each time it occurs; (2) rating systems, in which the observer rates the presence or absence or effectiveness of particular features of the event on a scale; (3) narrative systems of a more or less structured nature ranging from attempts to write a transcript of the event to taking notes under selected headings.

By way of contrast to pencil and paper methods of recording are video and audio recording. Both can be valuable although potentially threatening or obtrusive. Both can provide valuable data for later (and time consuming) analysis but are selective depending upon what the microphone picks up and where the camera points. Nevertheless, particularly with video recordings, they can provide a very powerful and illuminating record.

In deciding on which approach to recording to use, it is necessary to decide whether to invent, adapt or adopt an instrument. The aim should be to produce a simple and usable instrument and to test this and refine it in preparation for its proper use. It is important to remember that you will be looking at an event through the instruments or medium you use and will, therefore, need to get used to the instrument. Some approaches to observation depend on a higher degree of interpretation or inference by the observer than others. Complex instruments and those involving greater inference and interpretation usually require the most practice.

Table 5 contains a set of instructions which one of our Open University students gave to a colleague who had agreed to observe her in her role as mentor to a licensed teacher. She asked her colleague to collect data during a tutorial with the licensed teacher on:

• her listening and questioning skills
• the nature of her feedback
• whether she helped the licensed teacher in lesson preparation, language teaching and classroom teaching.

She set a range of criteria from her evaluation questions, and asked the observer to make a tally of each time she interrupted the licensed teacher. The diagram that follows is adapted from her final assignment.

You will see her instructions for the observer contain a range of open and closed options; the more open the option, the more difficult the observer's job was!

In fact the task her observer undertook was additionally complex, as disentangling several criteria during observation is not easy.

If you choose descriptive observation, you will, like our pilot student, need to work out what your observer should look for to show the presence of your selected criteria during the observation. This approach does not necessarily preclude the later identification of additional criteria or the refinement of initial ones, if the observation yields unexpected outcomes. What is important is that your criteria are articulated and made explicit to all involved in the process if appropriate, and certainly to your observer! Poor evaluation, like poor appraisal, is characterised by the use of implicit criteria or even prejudices. Wragg (1987), writing about classroom

Table 5 Example of evaluation questions for descriptive observation

| Questions | Criteria | What my observer should look for |
|---|---|---|
| 1. Am I helping Paulette in the areas of lesson preparation, language teaching and classroom management? | Value-judgement: I should be helping Paulette in all three areas. | What kinds of help I am giving Paulette by: (a) covering these areas in the tutorial? (b) setting up observations for her? (c) giving her feedback on her competence? |
| 2. Am I establishing and developing confidence, and raising morale? | Value-judgement: I should be helping Paulette establish and develop confidence, and I should be boosting her morale. | How confident is Paulette in our tutorial and how am I supporting this? (verbal/non-verbal) |
| 3. Am I giving Paulette individual attention and hearing what she says? | Value-judgement: It is essential that I listen to Paulette and hear her concerns. | In our one-to-one tutorial: (a) how much do I paraphrase and summarise what Paulette says? (b) is her talking space protected? (i.e. I do not interrupt her) (c) do I make constructive use of silence? (d) what kinds of positive body language do I use? |
| 4. Do I use a range of questions where appropriate? e.g. – open – closed – exploratory – probing – reflective | Value-judgement: It is important that my questioning technique enables Paulette's concerns to come out and that I help her to move forward by reflecting on her actions. | Look for evidence of an appropriate range of questions – note them down if you can! |

observation, warns of the dangers of compensation and projection. In the case of projection, the observer sees a lesson in terms of what they would do and in the case of compensation is excessively harsh, when they see that colleague guilty of one of their own deficiencies. These are but examples of the problems that can occur, when judgements are made without reference to explicit criteria. It is also important, whatever approach is taken to the generation of criteria, to reach clear agreement before an observation on what is to be observed and to what purpose.

Some of the possibilities are:

### Open recording

Here the aim is to create an observation/recording schedule which categorises in advance types of observations, and which enables you to record factual and descriptive information. For example, you might use open recording for observing a colleague's communication skills during a team meeting (obviously with their permission). The schedule might look something like this:

*Communication skills*

- Leadership
- Clarity
- Influencing others
- Feedback to others
- Presentation (voice, eye contact, body language, etc.)

The advantages of open recording are:

- the schedule is simple to construct
- it is adaptable
- it allows choice of headings for focus.

The main disadvantage is that it is easy fo fill in an open recording schedule judgementally rather than factually.

### Tally systems

Here, you record the number of times a particular event happens. If we take the example of observing a colleague in a meeting, you might begin to construct a tally recording system as follows:

| Category of communication | Tally |
|---|---|
| Silent agreement | |
| Silent disagreement | |
| Questions to group (open) | |
| Questions to group (closed) | |
| Questions another individual (open) | |
| Questions another individual (closed) | |
| … and so on. | |

The main advantages of tally systems are that they are quick, reliable, factual and adaptable. The disadvantages are that it may potentially give a narrow view of whatever is being observed, depending on which categories are used.

### Keeping a time-log

This is a form of time-based recording. It involves developing your own version of time-sampling and note-taking in order to log what is happening at any one time, for example using this kind of format:

| Time | Event |
|---|---|
| | |
| | |
| | |
| | |

The advantages of keeping a time log are that it is objective, and reliable. On the other hand, they can become complex, they can present a narrow view of what is being observed, and unless repeatedly used, will give a particular view of 'today'.

### Prompting questions

Here you create a recording schedule containing 'prompting' questions, to remind you what to look for. The following example was created by one of the authors to observe a university seminar session:

Observation of seminar on: ..................... Date ...................

Tutor being observed: ........................................................

*Curriculum*

Look for the following:

- What activities are taking place in this seminar?
- Who has selected the content of this seminar – tutor or students?
- How is the content related to student experience/ knowledge?

---

*Teaching*

Look for the following:

- What is the nature of the relationship between tutor and students?
- What opportunities are there for students to demonstrate leadership/to take on a teaching role?
- What standards of expectation are evident?
- How is the tutor accessing students?

---

Talk

Look for the following:

- What is the nature of talk, and between who is it (tutor/student, or student/student, etc.)?
- Who initiates discussion?
- Comment on student participation in discussion.

    ...    and so on.

---

The advantages of using prompting questions are that questions help to clarify the observer's role and the method is adaptable. Disadvantages are that the method can lead to judgemental observation and there is a danger of creating too many questions.

### Classroom mapping

The focus of this kind of recording is learner or participant involvement/integration. The idea here is to draw a sketch of the space being observed, indicating where each participant is sitting or working. A code is used to record on the diagram the kind of involvement each pupil has in the learning experience, over a period of time. Thus a code might look something like this:

1    Answers a question voluntarily.
2    Volunteers a comment or view.

3   Answers a question when asked.
4   Make a disruptive comment.
5   Initiates collaboration with other learners.
6   Resists collaboration with others.

Advantages of mapping are that it is adaptable, flexible and can involve all individuals assuming the seating/working arrangement remains static. On the other hand, of course, not all learning environments are set out in the same way. In active learning environments, where learners move around, you may need to restrict your observational focus to one or two people – but could record movement as well as quality of engagement.

*Consider the five example forms of recording described here. Which, if any, would you be able to adapt for use in the evaluation of your own professional development focus?*

## Clinical supervision

Of particular help in the context of observation are the ideas of clinical supervision (see, for example, Goldhammer *et al.*, 1980; Acheson and Gall, 1980; Cogan, 1973). Essentially, although differing in detail, these authors describe a process involving a pre-observation conference, observation and follow-up. In the pre-observation meeting, the observer and observed plan the observation by identifying areas to focus on and associated criteria. The aim is then to use the observation to gather data that can be presented to the observed and a follow-up meeting as the basis of bringing about development and improvement. The approach tends to be specific and focused and is characterised by a philosophy of collaboration, ethical behaviour and collegiality. It is an approach that has been influential in the development of appraisal and provides a neat planning framework for the use of observation in evaluation.

Applying clinical supervision to evaluation results in a cycle of planning, observing and feedback, which then feeds on into planning.

*Think about whether to use observation in your evaluation. If you decide that this is an appropriate method, develop an observation strategy, using the ideas provided here, remembering to follow clear, ethical ground rules. Keep a note of your reasons for using this method and for the design you use, in your notebook.*

*Carry out the observation(s),and analyse the results. (You should read the section on analysing your data first). Consider whether you need to follow up your observation(s) with further inquiry using another method.*

*Keep your notes and analysis in your notebook.*

## ANALYSIS OF DOCUMENTS

A variety of documents is usually produced in the course of a professional development experience. These might include planning notes, course programmes, handouts, course work and notes arising from activities. They may include both teachers' and pupils' work. These documents form a record of the activity that can be used in an evaluation. The advantage is that they can be used at leisure. They may also provide a historical and ongoing record of an event. Such documents can yield unexpected information and provide useful indicators of areas for further inquiry.

The analysis of data will be dealt with further in the next section, on credibility, but it is appropriate to make one or two comments about the analysis of documents here, that are particular to this form of data. Bell (1987) suggests a number of questions about a document:

- What kind of document is it? A statute? A policy paper? A set of minutes? A letter from a long correspondence? How many copies are there?
- What does it actually say? Are the terms used employed in the same way as you would use them?
- Who produced it? What was its purpose? Did the author aim to inform, command, remind (as in a memorandum) or to have some other effect on the reader?
- When and in what circumstances was it produced?
- Is it typical or exceptional of its type?
- Is it complete? Has it been edited or altered?

You could also carry out what McCormick and James (1983) call 'content analysis', which they suggest can be useful in the analysis of documents, interview transcripts and open-ended questionnaires. Essentially, this involves reading the documents to identify key themes or issues, and establishing these as research categories, a point we develop further in Chapter 9, on handling data.

It is important for the evaluator to be clear on the distinction between what is in a document and the analytic categories and assumptions he/she brings to it. It is also important to be clear on how far particular documents are confidential. Given such clarity, the use of documents in evaluation can be a helpful early source of ideas and points to investigate and can also complement other methods of data gathering.

*Think about the professional development which you are going to evaluate. Assemble any documentary data you have relating to it. This may include transcripts of interviews, notes you have made and completed questionnaires as well as readings, course programmes, notes, handouts, etc.*

*Read through the documents you have and make a list of the key themes and issues.*

*Identify on your list those themes (categories) which you feel are clearly established and those that you need to verify through the collection of further data. Write down ideas for what sort of data you need and how you might get it.*

*Be careful to follow clear ethical ground rules in your use of documents.*


## DIARIES

In the context of the evaluation of professional development, it is possible for someone involved in professional development to keep their own diary or to get other people to keep one. (It is probably best to think in terms of teachers, rather than pupils, keeping a diary for analysis). Diaries can be kept over a shorter or longer period and vary in terms of reactions. Similar in intent are logs and item cards. In a diary, it is left to the diarist when, what and how much to record. The use of a log provides a timeline to structure what is written. Item cards are card index cards, on each of which a key and distinct evaluation issue, category or question is written by way of a heading. The cards are kept to hand and filled in as appropriate with a note and time of a key event. All these approaches can be carried out by a participant evaluator as well as being used by others. They can also be kept up during an event or written up straight afterwards.

These approaches allow an ongoing record to be kept and can provide access to what cannot be observed. For example, in the evaluation of the school teacher appraisal pilot study, the evaluators felt that it would be inappropriate to observe classroom observations or appraisal interviews. The completion of diaries by some of those involved in appraisal was seen as a useful means of gaining access to immediate reactions to the appraisal process. For deepening understanding of an issue, diaries can be good: the price is that they can yield a good deal of rather disparate data for analysis and can be difficult to generalise from.

Several different types of entry can be made in a diary; factual/recordings of the sequence of events, and recordings which capture both events and also thoughts or feelings directly related to these. Diary entries can also capture events and thoughts and feelings which these trigger, but which may not be directly related to the events. Finally, diary entries can be used to try and understand outcomes from events.

You may find it useful to look at the following extract from a diary kept by a student who studied the course on which this book is based; she was concerned to reduce the fragmentation of her time as part of the outcomes of a management course. She is deputy head teacher of a large secondary school in Scotland.

To monitor her time management she kept a diary over two days. This is her entry for one of those days.

### Wednesday

8.30   Arrive in office. File a few of the items which I read last night. Mailsort as usual. Today's 'action' includes letter from Drugs Education Unit in response to my request for outside expert to help with three pupils whom we know to have been involved in trying to sell cannabis, letter from parent requesting child's absence for holiday, complaint from colleague that there's a problem with our behavioural support unit as teacher is sometimes not available to take individual referrals, etc.

*Forward this to head teacher for meeting this afternoon. Hope for a speedy response to colleague.*

8.40   SMT meeting. Discuss possible agenda items for meeting later today.

8.55   Assembly (S4). Consider issue of individual's need to make up his/her own mind on issues and not 'follow the crowd'. Demonstrate this in a light-hearted way with volunteers from the year group.

9.10   Teach.

10.10  Back in office to deal with some of the mail plus referrals from colleagues. Take call from parent explaining pupil's absence, call from Exam Board regarding business item from last Panel meeting (which I chair), memo from colleague whom I am currently reviewing regarding proposed date for the final interview.

*This is another standard 'gap fill' form which I have devised to ensure that form teacher and guidance teacher also receive this message.*

10.30  Draft a letter to associated primary schools setting out proposed schedule of liaison visits for next term (requested at the last cluster head teachers' meeting). Will need to consult several colleagues to agree dates for visits to our nine associated schools.

10.45  Interview pupil who had two referrals yesterday. Discuss problems – essentially difficulties relating to other pupils in the class so I'll need to see them too. Seems in a reasonably positive mood when he leaves agreeing to apologise to a teacher in whose class he had misbehaved (albeit provoked by someone else) and is reassured the provoker will also be seen. This pupil has caused us considerable difficulties over the years but has recently been doing very well. I try to encourage the positive.

11.10 Coffee in the staff room. Manage to chat to several colleagues e.g. about forthcoming drama production, a poster campaign and personal issues.

11.25 Teach until lunch time.

1.00 Back in office checking next batch of mail and eating sandwich.
Return a few calls re drugs information session, cover problem for Special Needs candidates in next week's exams and request for clarification from the Exam Board about the future provision for Special Needs pupils. (Dictate this and several other letters).

1.45 House staff meeting (Erskine House). Discuss current problems including strategy for briefing all staff on the needs of a newly diagnosed diabetic child. Deliberate on the 'case load' which is almost exclusively male and promise to pass round Angela Phillip's new book *The Trouble with Boys*.

*I keep a polypocket for each House and update the information on a weekly basis. I also leave myself non-urgent memos in the pouch to pass on to House staff at our next meeting.*

2.20 Join head teacher to review timetable for next session (a new responsibility I've been given as our Depute is seconded).

2.55 SMT meeting. Agenda includes my item on the deployment of the behavioural support teacher, plans for the election of a committee to manage our Devolved School budget, discussion of Minute of Stress management group and their request for INSET on time management.

4.00 Return to timetable but end up taking it home at 4.30.

*Consider whether or not a diary or log could be used in your evaluation. Think about how you would organise it yourself and whether anyone else could be asked to keep one. If you do decide to use this approach, keep a note of your reasons, what you do and your analysis in your notebook. Remember also to follow a set of ground rules.*

## Task 14

**Return to your outline evaluation plan (Task 10). Consider whether, in the light of reading this chapter, you wish to re-work your evaluation plan, and in the light of your responses to Tasks 11, 12 and 13.**

## Summary of Chapter 7

In this chapter we considered a variety of approaches to data collection in evaluation, which are of interest in the context of the evaluation of professional development.

In selecting a method, we stressed the need to remember:

- the strengths and weaknesses of the method
- whether the method will yield the information required
- the acceptability of the method
- time and resources

It is also useful at the data-collection stage to:

- combine more than one method of collecting data and more than one source of evidence
- keep a careful record or archive of the data that you collect
- keep a clear record of the procedures you use and of the chain of evidence that you collect.

These last points are related to ensuring the validity and reliability of your findings in an evaluation. They are also designed to facilitate the analysis of your data.

It will be clear from reading this chapter that in choosing one or more methods you will be seeking to balance two ends of a data-collecting continuum. At one end there are methods such as brief rapid response forms that produce data that are easy to collect and analyse but which may conceal more than they reveal. At the other end is the collection of in-depth and highly illuminative evidence, which takes longer to analyse. It is important to clarify the kind of information you really need and how you can use different kinds of data in a complementary way.

# Chapter 8

# Developing and applying criteria

This chapter explores the development and application of criteria for evaluating the quality and value of CPD undertaken from an institutional perspective and a personal perspective. It is intended to support you in identifying and applying your own criteria.

First, let us re-visit evaluation questions, because it is these which provide the source of the evaluation criteria.

In Chapter 6, we began to consider what questions evaluation can address. This section offers some guidance on refining the questions that you might wish to find answers to, in evaluating your own professional development. Joyce and Showers (1988) provide a useful model for planning the evaluation of professional development. It draws attention to the number of areas or roles that may need to be considered. These include:

- teachers' knowledge, skills, growth, etc;
- the school and system's leadership, general climate, governance processes and connection to the community;
- the staff development programme's goals, the process and content of the training itself, and implementation;
- cognitive and affective outcomes for pupils.

The Joyce and Showers model serves as a reminder of the points made about the possible levels of impact of professional development in Chapter 1. In effect, it is important to be clear in planning your evaluation of a professional development experience on what can be investigated, and which are the processes and which are the outcomes of the professional development. You may find it helpful to consider your own planned focus using this model. Which do you think are the areas or roles which your evaluation will encompass – teachers, staff development programmes, school/systems or with pupils, or some combination of these? What kind of questions will you want to ask of each?

You may find our case studies helpful in seeing how to apply Joyce and Showers' model: Again, you can see from these examples how the process/outcome distinction is not always clear-cut. Because the purpose of the first case study was to explore the processes of the professional

1  *MSc. process evaluation* – involved investigating:
   - *Teachers' perceptions* of their knowledge and understanding of the topic under study that week, and their personal intellectual growth during that time in relation to their own goals. Questions included how much each teacher felt they had understood that week, how they would describe the personal/intellectual growth which they underwent and to what extent that week of the course had met their goals.
   - *The course:* the goals for that week and the learning processes used to achieve them. Questions included what were the course goals and what were each teacher's perceptions of the appropriateness of the learning processes used that week to achieve them

2  *Appraisal outcomes evaluation* – involved investigating:
   - *Teachers' perceptions* of their appraisal interview, the extent to which they met their targets and the extent to which their professional development needs were addressed. Questions included how each teacher felt their appraisal interview went and why, whether they had met their appraisal targets and why, and whether their own professional development needs were adequately addressed through the interview.
   - *The programme of appraisal:* the goals set for the appraisal interview (an amalgam of legal requirements and the school's policy on implementing these), and the process the appraisal interview involved. Questions included what were the goals for the appraisal interview, and what process did each interview involve in practice.
   - *The school's climate of values and beliefs about appraisal and its systems for implementing* it (including leadership structures). Questions included how each teacher felt about appraisal and about the formal structures/mechanisms set up in the school for implementing it.

development, the areas targeted for questions were to do with the teaching and learning processes. Although the second case study aimed to look at the effect or outcomes of appraisal implementation, the questions needed to target aspects of the process itself to help build up a picture of the wide range of outcomes of appraisal implementation.

You may also have commented to yourself on the range of questions asked in each of these case studies; in thinking through what questions you want to ask, you may find it's necessary to sort out which are the main ones and stick to them, otherwise your project could easily become unmanageable! Your choice of questions may also be steered by national standards identified for the CPD you have undertaken, depending on your professional context.

Any attempt to predict the outcomes of your evaluation is likely to be influenced by who you think the stakeholders are in the professional development and in the evaluation, as explored in Chapters 5 and 6. Your questions will need to take account of the differing perspectives and to give individuals opportunities to be as open as possible in their responses to you.

To sum up so far then, we have suggested that in the evaluation of professional development, your questions should relate to either the *process* (what happened during the professional development, for example, methods used), or the *outcome* (what happened afterward – such as impact on individual staff, teams, school and pupils).

We have encouraged you to ask questions in relation to appropriate areas, such as:

- teachers' practice
- the school as an institution
- the pupils' learning
- any relevant national standards associated with these; and
- the professional development experience itself and other professional development activity.

We have also emphasised the importance of being sensitive to the perspective of the stakeholders. Finally, it is important to identify a manageable and clear set of questions to structure your evaluation.

In the next part of the chapter we consider the criteria which will shape the

---

## Task 15

Look again at what you wrote in your notebook in answer to the question 'What questions are to be addressed in your evaluation?' Refine your questions using Joyce and Showers' model, if this seems appropriate to you. You may want to go back to some of your earlier notes, too, such as those to Tasks 10, 11, 12 and 13 in Chapter 6 and Task 14 in Chapter 7.

---

way you collect and analyse your data in order to answer your evaluation questions.

## CRITERIA IN EVALUATION

In order to judge the answers to your evaluation questions, you will need to develop criteria or standards of judgement. In other words, it will be necessary to decide on criteria for effective staff development in terms of matters such as design, delivery impact and cost.

Help in identifying appropriate questions to address and possible criteria in an evaluation of staff development is provided in the extracts below. The first from Bradley (1991), suggests questions to be asked about the various stages in the in-service activity, starting with preparation for it and ending with the resulting impact in school. Bradley's list of questions contains implicit criteria, which we have indicated in italics.

### Preparation

Was the process of identification of need accurate? Was there consensus about the needs among all the people concerned? Did the school do the necessary preparatory work:

- to enable the teachers taking part to obtain maximum benefit?
- to enable other staff to benefit from their experience?

*Preparation criteria: accuracy of needs identification, extent of consensus, extent of preparation to enable maximum benefit for participants and wider staff.*

### Planning the activities

Did those who planned the activities have skills in the design of INSET activities? Were the goals for each activity clearly defined? When change in attitude, teaching style or other fundamental factor was desired, was this made clear or was it hidden behind a façade of content allowing participants to miss the point of the exercise? Were the goals shared by the participants in the activity? Was the methodology appropriate to the goals? Was it appropriate for adult learners?

*Planning criteria: adequacy of INSET design skills, clarity of goals for each activity, explicitness of intention in change attitudes, extent of shared goals.*

### Execution of activities

Did the participants recognise the purpose and value of constituent parts of the activities? Did the participants in fact share common purposes and goals or were there 'hidden curricula' which impeded group coherence?

Did the participants enjoy the process? Did they find it of value to themselves professionally? Did they feel it equipped them to help their colleagues?

*Execution criteria: degree of recognition of purpose and value of activities by participants, extent of truly shared common purposes/goals by participants, degree of participant enjoyment, professional value for participants, contribution to participants; capacity to help colleagues.*

## Impact

Was the school willing to change? Did the school make use of the participants' experience? Did the INSET activity result in a change? Was the change effective and in line with the needs and the priorities of the school?

*Impact criteria: willingness of school to change, amount of use by school of participants' experience, degree of change resulting from INSET activity, effectiveness and relevance of change to needs/priorities of school.*

Bradley's first three areas: preparation; planning the activities; and execution of activities, are concerned with the process of professional development; impact on the other hand is concerned with its outcome. You may find this a helpful way of pinpointing exactly what your own criteria relate to.

Bradley's criteria promote a view of evaluation which countenances:

- the importance of a longer-term, process view of CPD as a part of the continuing education of teachers;
- a needs-based, consumer-centred approach to CPD, involving targeting and increased negotiation between providers and teachers.

In choosing criteria for evaluating professional development, we make a value judgement about what is important. Bradley's implicit criteria involve matching the professional development with fitness for purpose; i.e. considering whether specific needs at different stages of the process, were met.

Your choice of criteria will reflect your personal position on professional development. For example, a primary teacher who had undertaken a teacher placement and whose questions were focused on how far her own practice and that of the other staff was influenced by it, might choose criteria relating to her own skill in disseminating, structure and 'space' for developing a staff response, measures of staff interest and motivation, degree of staff involvement and extent of influence on the curriculum and learning. These criteria suggest she sees professional development as being directly related to children's learning, and there is an implication that she views the professional development experience of one staff member as having automatic relevance to other teachers. Had the same teacher, however, identified a different set of questions, for example, relating to her own career progression, the criteria for measuring these would have been different and the underlying view of professional development would be emphasising the role of professional development in helping individual professionals to develop in career terms.

It is important to acknowledge that, whatever criteria you select, you are likely to be measuring the *perceived worth* of the professional development, and that the 'measure' you use will thus be subjective judgement. One way of pinpointing and using criteria in your project is to work out what value judgements underlie your questions. Underneath the question 'how did each teacher feel about appraisal?' for example, in Case Study 2, is the implicit value-judgement 'every teacher's view is valued', thus all the responses would be interpreted in terms of how much each person felt they were acknowledged in the process of appraisal.Once you have made your value judgement clear, you can decide how to judge the responses you get. Let's take a look at the case study on the MSc process, to see how this works.

---

### MSc process evaluation

As it focused on the teaching and learning process, the questions and their underpinning criteria are related to Bradley's 'execution of activities' stage of professional development.

| Questions | Criteria |
| --- | --- |
| How much did each teacher feel they had understood that week? | *Value judgement underlying question:* Teachers should have understood all that they learned that week. |

Responses to this question are quite likely to be on a continuum, for example:

---

I understood nothing at all                                    I understood all of it

---

Now that we have made clear the value judgement which lay behind the question, we can see that any responses which come out on the left hand side of the continuum will be of particular interest.

## Task 16

In your notebook, plan out your own criteria, showing how they underpin each of your questions. You need to consider how your criteria will influence the way you judge the data that you collect. Jot down your ideas in your notebook.

If you need to refine the part of the process or outcome you are asking questions about, you may find Bradley's model helpful (preparation, planning, execution, impact).

If you have not already done so, you should now begin to collect your evaluation data.

---

### Summary of Chapter 8

We have been exploring questions and criteria for evaluating the processes and outcomes of professional development. We have discussed and explored:

- asking evaluation questions which relate to either the process or the outcomes of the CPD; for this we drew on Joyce and Showers' (1988) work;
- some of the range of issues in professional development about which questions can be asked;
- the influence of stakeholders' perceptions of the evaluation on choosing and defining questions;
- the use of Bradley's (1991) framework in identifying which part of the process or outcomes your criteria will relate to;
- the way criteria underpin questions, and also reflect your personal position on professional development, and
- one way in which you can use your criteria to help you 'judge' the data you collect.

# Chapter 9

# Evaluation methodology

## Handling data

You will find that you can be more confident about the findings of your evaluation if you are well organised. It is also important not to get over-whelmed by the data. Developing a systematic framework for collecting, handling and analysing data will help you achieve these aims and ensure that your findings are valid.

### QUALITATIVE EVALUATION

You will find it useful to think of a framework for handling data in a quali-tative evaluation as consisting of four stages:

1 collection of data/identification of categories;
2 validation of categories;
3 interpretation of categories;
4 presentation of theory/conclusions/recommendations – action.

At stage 1, you will be collecting data from a range of sources, immersing yourself in the data and beginning to identify recurrent themes, issues and categories.

You will then need to sort the data according to these categories. This might involve counting up how many times something occurs, noting patterns or themes, and trying to find groups and sub-groups of issues. You can identify categories or themes by writing symbols in the margin; some people produce a card for each theme and then transcribe relevant bits of the data on to the card using a code or symbol. As you sort your data, you will find you can group the responses and start to refine and dif-ferentiate the categories they fall into. You should try to relate the grouped or categorised responses back to your original questions and the criteria you decided to judge them by. You will probably find that categorising the data throws out unexpected groupings as well as expected ones, and also that some of the groupings reflect aspects of your own position on profes-sional development. These interactive and ongoing processes of reducing

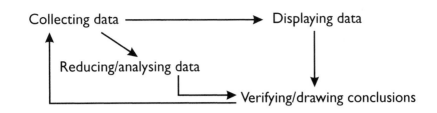

*Figure 15* Components of data analysis

or summarising the data and displaying it will help you to analyse it. This process of analysis is illustrated in Figure 15.

At stage 2, your emphasis will be on the *validation* of the hypotheses and categories identified in stage 1. Two ways of validating your data which you may find particularly useful are *saturation* and *triangulation*. Saturation is the term used to describe the point reached when you judge that a sufficient proportion of responses fall into each category. The exact number of responses this actually involves will depend on the size of your sample. If, as you work through your responses, you decide that the responses in a particular category are very few, you may decide to abandon that category, or modify it. In the case of a very small sample, though, as in our MSc evaluation case study, you may judge that even one response in a particular category is sufficient.

Triangulation, on the other hand, involves contrasting different points of view. There are a number of dimensions to triangulation:

- time triangulation: involves comparing data from the same people at different points in time or collecting data from different groups at the same point in time;
- space triangulation: involves comparing data from different cultures or sub-cultures;
- combined levels triangulation: involves comparing analysis at different levels, i.e. individual, group and organisational, cultural or societal;
- theoretical triangulation: involves testing competing theories against the data;
- investigator triangulation: involves using more than one evaluator;
- methodological triangulation: makes use of the same method of data collection on different occasions or different methods on the same object of study.                        (Adapted from Cohen and Manion, 1989)

Whether you choose saturation or triangulation or both, you will be using the method to check that the categories of data are still convincing.

At stage 3, your emphasis will be on *interpretation*. The aim is to fit a valid category into a frame of reference or theory, usually related to your evaluation questions and the criteria underlying them. Hopkins (1989) refers to two useful techniques at this stage – the search for rival explanations and testing for negative cases. In the former, the aim is to look for data to support alternative or rival explanations of the same thing. Lack of data to support an alternative explanation helps to support the original proposition. Searching for negative cases involves looking through the data for contradictory evidence. You may find either or both useful in analysing your own data. The process which we have described so far involves using and developing 'grounded theory', i.e. linking the analysis of data to wider theory.

At stage 4, *conclusions are presented, recommendations are made and appropriate action follows*. This stage might involve the production of a formative or summative evaluation report or an alternative method of presenting your findings.

## THE ANALYSIS OF QUANTITATIVE DATA

Quantitative data principally results from research methods which involve measuring or counting. So, for example, observation schedules, interview schedules, test scores, rating scales, will all yield quantitative data, although where the raw data has been recorded by means of ticks, crosses, etc., it will need to be converted into numbers before it can be used. In a similar way, qualitative data can be converted into quantitative data. Essentially this involves defining categories of data, and assigning instances to each category.

In analysing and presenting quantitative data, there are certain conventions which must be observed; what follows is a simplified discussion of the principle issues.

### Variables

Variables are the elements of the study which vary. So, for example, the length of the in-service work and its location are variables. Variables can be measured or described in two different kinds of ways. Discrete variables, such as the location of in-service work, are so called because each location is completely separate from the next (e.g. the staffroom, the local university, your study area at home). Continuous variables, such as the length of the professional development work, are so called because they are measured or described on a continuous scale. You probably know how long a particular session of development work lasted, to the nearest ten minutes, but what about to the nearest minute? The nearest second?

Clearly, the kind of data that you collect will influence the ways you can analyse it.

## Categories

A category is simply a way of grouping information. For example, a questionnaire which asks colleagues to rate a particular experience as 'very useful', 'quite useful', 'no particular view' not useful' 'not at all useful' would contain five categories for describing the data. Unlike variables, which can be continuous or discrete, categories are always discrete, in other words recognisably separate from one another.

The point of categorising is to separate out different kinds of response from one another. For example, in an observation schedule looking at interactions during a staff meeting, you may have three main categories of interaction, where you distinguish between classroom teachers and staff who have management posts (such as the deputy head and the head): 'teacher/teacher', 'teacher/manager', 'manager/manager'. You might also choose to distinguish between male and female speakers by means of ticks and crosses for recording on your schedule.

Clearly, the categories which you have chosen will influence the way you analyse the data you then collect.

## Using numerical totals and calculations

As noted earlier, quantitative data is usually in a numerical form, because it involves measuring or counting. Raw quantitative data can rarely be interpreted without some form of mathematical intervention, such as totalling the number of responses in each category. Calculating the percentage of each kind of response can provide interesting and accessible information. To take the example given above of categories of interaction in a staff meeting, you might total the amount of responses in each category, and then compare them as percentages with the whole. Saying that 64 per cent of the interactions were teacher/teacher, rather than saying 86 out of 134 interactions were teacher/teacher, is more accessible.

Percentages also enable you to make direct comparisons of discrete data from unequally sized groups. Using the above example, you might have an overall gender imbalance present during the meeting. Knowing what percentage of interactions were undertaken by the women and what percentage were undertaken by the men, would provide interesting data when compared with the overall percentage gender balance.

Similarly it can be useful to calculate the average, or mean. Again using the example of the staff meeting, if you had unequal numbers of men and women and also had uneven data on their interactions, you could confirm the extent to which one gender dominated (or didn't) by calculating the mean number of interactions per person overall (in other words, to divide the total number of interactions by the total number of staff participating in the meeting), and then compare it with the means for each gender.

## Presenting quantitative data

The standard forms of presentation for quantitative data include tables, graphs, bar and pie charts and histograms. Tables that summarise raw data can be useful aids to interpretation and analysis. Points to remember about tables however are that they should not contain too much information, and that they should be clearly labelled and appropriately titled, so as to convey precisely what information they contain.

Pie charts, bar charts, histograms and graphs can convey information more succinctly and powerfully than tables in some circumstances. To take these one by one:

### Bar charts

Bar charts represent categories in columns, and are usually used to demonstrate the differences between two or more discrete categories. Conseqently, the bars of a bar chart should not touch, and the horizontal axis of the bar chart should represent a discrete category.

### Pie charts

Pie charts represent categories in 'slices'; the size of the slice is determined by expressing the data in percentages. Thus, if one category contains 25 per cent of the total number of cases, its angle will be one quarter of 360 degrees, in other words, 90 degrees. It is important to indicate the total number of cases on which the pie chart is based. Where the data contained within two or more pie charts is being compared, the size of the circle representing the pies must be proportional to the total number of cases.

### Histograms

As with bar charts, histograms represent data in columns. The main difference between the two is that in a histogram the columns of data actually touch whereas in a bar chart they are separate. The reason for this is that histograms represent continuous data; the horizontal scale on the histogram representing a continuous variable, such as a time interval, or age group.

*Graphs*

Graphs can be used to plot continuous data, and are useful for representing relationships between continuous variables. Both axes of a graph represent continuous variables and thus show change. Typically, the horizontal axis represents the passage of time in some form.

Discrete category data should be conveyed through pie charts and bar charts, whereas continuous data should be communicated in histograms.

If you are using quantitative evaluation methods, you may find it useful to refer to one of the following books which address statistical analytical techniques in greater depth:

Graham, A. (1990), *Investigating Statistics: a beginner's guide,* London, Hodder & Stoughton

Rowntree, D. (1981), *Statistics Without Tears: a primer for non-mathematicians,* New York, Charles Scribner & Sons

---

## Task 17

**First, consider what kinds of data analysis will help you to make sense of your own evaluation data. Then, begin to analyse your data.**
**As you analyse your data, consider:**

- **the links between the data you have collected and the initial needs identification and therefore reasons for undertaking the in-service work, whether at a personal or an institutional level.**
- **the links between the data and your evaluation purpose, questions and criteria.**
- **the relationship between your data and your personal position on professional development.**
- **(if appropriate) the relationship between your data and your personal position on appraisal.**

---

## REPORTING OUTCOMES OF THE EVALUATION OF PROFESSIONAL DEVELOPMENT

You will be reporting on your evaluation in your summative assignment. You may also need to communicate your findings to colleagues or other people. You might do this through a written report or some other means, such as a verbal presentation. You should consider whether to keep the reporting you do in your summative assignment separate from any report to colleagues or other people, as it may not be possible to combine the two processes to meet the needs of the different audiences. Also, if you are to use your evaluation data you will need to find ways of using the 'politics' of your workplace to enable you to present and take action on your findings. We will explore some of the 'politics' of doing this in Chapter 10.

In this final section of Chapter 9, we focus on the issue of reporting the findings of your evaluation to colleagues or to others you work with, who may have an interest in your findings.

There are two types of reporting in evaluation:

- formative feedback or reporting, during the evaluation process, and
- summative reporting after the process ends.

At both these stages you should remember the ground rules of the evaluation and guarantees to confidentiality and anonymity. If necessary turn back now to the section on ground rules in evaluation and your notes on it. If time allows, you should try to go through the formative reporting stage as well as the summative one.

The following suggestions for formative feedback are based on the ideas of Aspinwall *et al.* (1992):

- circulating notes, brief reports or memoranda on the evaluation to interested parties or displaying them;
- keeping an open evaluation diary, in which those involved in the evaluation write regular updates about the evaluation data/outcomes;
- regular, brief and well-structured agenda items at staff meetings or specific meetings for review and exchange of information, which are themselves recorded and become part of the evaluation data base; informal contact;
- involving a range of people in analysis and writing up.

It is important to remember that formative feedback can help improve what is being evaluated as it happens. Remember, too, that formative feedback can generate new evaluation questions. Both of these possibilities are more likely to occur when attempts are made to share the findings of the evaluation and to involve people in it. Sensitivity in presenting information may also be necessary. In some circumstances, it may be appropriate to present your data to a particular group and involve them in drawing conclusions.

Summative reporting can also be written, or verbal, or both. You will need to decide what is appropriate for your own project. A key need, as in formative feedback, is to keep summaries of data and factual information separate from interpretation. It is then open to a reader to check how a conclusion was reached. It is not usually necessary to include raw data in the body of the report, except in the form of extracts, which act as illustrative examples of a point being made. It may, however, be desirable to include raw data, at least in summarised or reduced form, as a set of appendices. Indeed, for your summative assignment you are expected to demonstrate the evidence which you used to reach your conclusions. It may also be desirable to identify possible areas for further inquiry or where the data you collected turned out to be insufficient to answer any of your evaluation questions. Beyond this the shape and substance of the report will relate to the particular evaluation purpose which you identified (see Chapter 6).

Essentially, the purposes of reporting will relate to the general purposes of the evaluation and it is important to return to these at the reporting stage.

Oldroyd and Hall (1988) give the following advice on writing reports, which serves as a conclusion to this section:

> Effective reports need to focus on what the specified audience really needs to know. There is little point in asking busy professionals to spend time producing documents that have no practical use. Good quality evaluation reports depend on clear evaluation questions, authentic information rather than impressions and clear conclusions based on explicit criteria and linked to specific recommendations. The more concise and clear they are, the more likely they are to be read and to influence decision making.

In other words, the acid test on an evaluation, including its report, is whether it brings about learning and whether it leads to appropriate action or development. Of course, such action may depend on factors, such as resourcing, training or time, which are outside your control as an evaluator, but which it is your task to highlight as necessary through recommendations.

## Task 18

1  In the light of this section and what you wrote earlier in your notebook in response to the question 'Who, if anyone, will receive a copy of your evaluation report and what use will be made of it?', consider how you will report on your own evaluation.

2  As part of the previous task, you may have begun to analyse your data. Once you have carried out an initial analysis of your early data, consider making a formative report. Once you have collected any necessary additional data, take time to complete your analysis of the data and make a final report, if this is part of your plan. (Refer back to the section on data analysis if necessary).

## Summary of Chapter 9

Throughout this chapter, we have suggested ways of ensuring that the process is reliable and valid. These have included the use of multiple sources of data, and systematic handling of data. We have suggested an overall approach in which your methodology is explicit and open.

The following key points were made:

- Data needs to be processed in an organised and systematic way.
- The analysis of qualitative data can be carried out in four stages:
  - collecting data and studying it closely to identify issues and hypotheses
  - confirming the validity of these issues and hypotheses
  - interpreting findings
  - presenting conclusions.
- A variety of techniques can be used to enhance the validity of the findings of a qualitative evaluation. These include saturation, triangulation, searching for rival explanations and testing for negative cases.
- The analysis of quantitative data will involve using numerical methods, and will involve key variables and categories.
- We explored some of the ways raw quantitative data can be manipulated and analysed.
- We looked at a variety of ways of presenting quantitative data
- We explored ways of reporting the evaluation.

Part III

# Planning future professional development

# Introduction

## PLANNING FUTURE PROFESSIONAL DEVELOPMENT

In Part I, we explored some of the tensions that surround professional development. These were described, on the one hand, in terms of the tension between school, team and individual needs for professional development. They were also described as providing professional development in response to both external and internal pressures. In Part II, the focus was on the evaluation of professional development and a guide was provided to help you evaluate a specific segment of your own professional development.

Part III will focus on supporting you in making professional development plans. We encourage you to reflect first on whether the needs addressed by the professional development you evaluated were met; whether additional needs or follow-up needs in that area of professional development arose; whether other areas for professional development were suggested or have become apparent. It offers opportunities for you to reflect on what you have discovered makes for effective professional development, your own preferred style of learning, the appropriateness of the methods used in the professional development which you have experienced. Also, how far what you undertake as professional development fits into the broader context of your own personal, professional and career development, and the priorities of your school, department and team as well as the wider national context. We discuss the following issues, from both a personal and an institutional perspective:

- views of 'professionalism' and of career development;
- stakeholders in further professional development, including pupils;
- the nature of change in education, strategies for change, implications of change, blockages to change and the politics of change;
- personal factors in development, including previous experiences of professional development, career and job requirements, and individual development needs;
- personal growth and professional learning;
- individual learning preferences;

- the appropriateness of teaching and learning methods to desired outcomes;
- the institutional context for professional development, and mechanisms, such as appraisal and school development planning, which can help in identifying, harmonising and prioritising school, department, team and individual professional development needs;
- re-visiting school effectiveness discussions, and school culture;
- a look to the wider future surrounding continuing professional development.

Part III is organised as follows:

*Chapter 10*　In this chapter, we look at making professional development plans based on evaluation evidence. We look at the questions which can be asked following the evaluation of professional development; the extent to which various needs were met; and whether other areas for professional development were suggested or have become apparent.

We explore short-, medium- and long-term planning for professional development, in the context of change and intensification in education. Topics discussed include the chaotic and endemic nature of change in postmodern times, the role of schools within this and the impact of change upon their functioning and strategies for change, including the role of knowledge creation in change. Blockages to change, the politics of change, and emotional and intuitive responses to change are each addressed, supported where appropriate by examples.

*Chapter 11*　This chapter explores a range of personal circumstances which have a bearing on personal development, including previous experiences of professional development, career and job requirements and individual development needs. We explore personal learning as a professional through autobiography and subjective experience as alternatives to technicist models of CPD. We discuss briefly a range of documented practitioner stances on the nature of their role and professional development in this policy context, ranging through those who feel empowered and those who feel deprofessionalised. We explore aspects of personal growth and CPD and discuss the changing notion of the career in education and the increasingly prevalent role of mentoring during various career stages. The chapter draws on Appendix 1, which is a critical piece based on Robertson's work which looks at gender issues in education stemming from the models of Joyce and Showers.

*Chapter 12*　This chapter explores further the learning of the individual teacher, and sets this into the context of the institution. It aims to support further reflection on the types of opportunity available for professional development, preferred learning style(s), and purposes in professional development. To enable the planning of next steps in the school context, we re-visit teacher appraisal/review, some of the ideas in the school effectiveness and school improvement literature, and the wider policy context these are set in. We consider some strategies for providing increased opportunities for professional development, and its dissemination, in the process of creating and maintaining schools which are learning organisations.

*Chapter 13*   This final chapter attempts to identify trends for the continuing professional development of teachers and schools in the initial part of the twenty-first century, taking account of the potential roles of ICT as well as shifts in policy initiatives and the potential of professional bodies in England such as the General Teaching Council and National College for School Leadership.

---

## Summary of outcomes

If you have carried out the tasks embedded in it, at the end of Part III you should have:

- developed a clear set of conclusions from the evaluation of some focused continuing professional development;
- explored a range of personal circumstances which have a bearing on professional development, including gender issues;
- developed a plan for professional development in the short, medium and long term, from a personal and/or an institutional perspective, taking account of the nature of change, blockages to change and the politics of change;
- some notion of your own expectations of trends in continuing professional development for teachers and schools in the future.

# Chapter 10

# Using professional development evaluation to identify future CPD

*Consider your evaluation outcomes, and review what you have learned about your future professional development needs as either participant or provider. What do you think others may have learned from the evaluation?*

In addressing this question, you may have found yourself considering whether:

- the needs addressed by the professional development you evaluated were met;
- additional needs or follow-up needs in that area of professional development arose;
- other areas of professional development were suggested;
- what you learned about what makes for effective professional development;
- what you learned about your own preferred style of learning;
- the appropriateness of the methods used in your professional development to the intended purpose;
- how far what you did fitted into the broader context of your own personal, professional and career development and the priorities of your school, department and teams as well as the broader policy/government-led priorities to which you have to respond.

What you learned about your future professional development needs as a result of your evaluation provides some of the information which you will need to take into account when planning your future professional development. Your future plans will also need to take into account:

- views of 'professionalism' – your own, your institution's and those of policy makers;
- the implications of the involvement of yourself or your institution in change, including the politics of change;
- personal factors, such as previous experience of CPD, career and job requirements, and individual development needs;
- your individual learning preferences;

- finding teaching and learning methods appropriate for the outcomes you desire;
- mechanisms, such as appraisal, development planning and school improvement strategies, which can help in identifying, harmonising and prioritising national priorities, school, department, team and individual professional development needs.

The combination of these factors will influence the context for your future professional development. The context also depends on two other more general elements. First, there are a number of practical issues, such as the accessibility of suitable opportunities and the availability of adequate resources, support and time. To a large extent, these are likely to be influenced by national and both local or school priorities for development. Second, there is the more fundamental issue of the value of any professional development that is done. In this context, value might be thought of in terms of how well the experience fulfils the original purpose (whether this relates to national, local, regional, school, pupil, department or team needs, or individual job, career, professional or personal needs, satisfaction or growth). Value could also be thought of in terms of how well a professional development experience develops the potential of an individual for future personal or professional development or contributes to a developmental or learning culture in a school.

These issues are summarised in Figure 16 on page 173. You may find it helpful now to look back at any notes you may have made from Chapter 1 about 'levels of impact', particularly if you completed the reflection point on the levels of impact which you hoped your chosen professional development had had.

Planning forward on any of the levels which are relevant to you will also involve being clear about your own time-horizons, and who will be involved, which may depend in part on your role in school. Planning for the short term, if you are classroom-based, could mean planning for the next week, half-term or term; it may involve yourself , your pupils and perhaps other colleagues. Whereas planning for the short term if you have a management role, such as being head teacher, could mean planning for the next year or two years and is more likely to involve yourself, a large number of pupils and a range of staff including non-teaching staff.

## Task 19

Write in your notebook your own outline plan for future professional development. Distinguish between short-, medium- and long-term plans (defining what these mean for you) and take into account, as far as possible, the needs of your school, any team(s)/departments you belong to and yourself. In the case of your own needs, try to separate needs that are job related, career or professional or personal. Figure 17 on page 174, which is in the form of a matrix, provides headings to consider as you develop your plan. You should aim to address as many of these headings as you can in your plan, but need not necessarily present it as a matrix.

To enable you to complete this task you will need to refer

- to the work you did in connection with Chapter 3 in identifying needs (especially for Task 6);
- to what you learnt from the evaluation you undertook (if this is appropriate and relevant);
- to Figure 16 opposite, which provides a checklist of factors to take into account and highlights areas about which you may need to obtain more information.

---

Whatever your role, however, the plans which you make will be subject to external scrutiny of some kind.

So far, then, you have probably begun thinking about the various factors that might influence your future professional development, such as:

- your previous professional development
- your understanding of the nature and purposes of professionalism and professional development
- what you learnt from your evaluation of professional development;
- appraisal and development planning
- your own development needs
- your preferred learning style
- the needs of your school and department(s) or team(s)
- the appropriate form of professional development to meet each particular need.

You may also have prepared an outline plan for your future professional development.

The rest of Chapter 10 and also Chapter 11 will help you become aware of which aspects of your plan could be refined. We look first at change in education, then (in Chapter 11) at personal dimensions of planning professional development, and then (in Chapter 12) at the institutional context for professional development.

The next section then, is concerned with the nature of change in

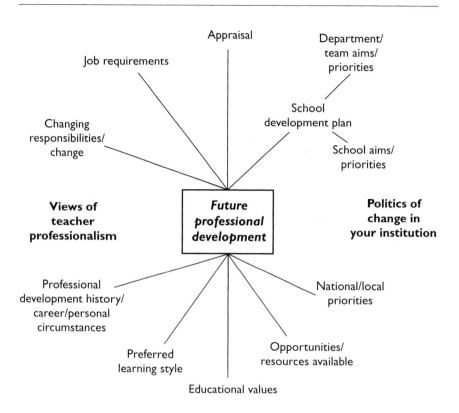

*Figure 16* Factors affecting the planning of professional development

education and is designed to help you refine your ideas on the impact of change on professional development.

## CHANGE IN EDUCATION

Over recent years, the British education system and those of other countries have been characterised by continuous, rapid and multiple change. Change is a complex process and this complexity tends to be underestimated by those responsible for introducing it. Change can also occur at a variety of levels, from individual to organisational. Alongside the changes themselves, there has grown up what is now an extensive literature on the theory and practice of change. Within this body of literature, there has been a shift from earlier concerns with why change often fails and how to ensure the successful implementation of single changes, to a concern with managing the implementation of multiple change and describing ways of

| Level / Time Horizon | School | Team/ Deparment | Individual – Job related | Individual – Career related | Individual – Professional | Individual – Personal | Pupils |
|---|---|---|---|---|---|---|---|
| Short | | | | | | | |
| Medium | | | | | | | |
| Long | | | | | | | |

Figure 17  A matrix to assist planning professional development

developing a school culture, that is conducive to enabling individual growth and to handling multiple change effectively.

In this section, we review the key lessons from the literature on change in education. It is designed to help you think about how your own professional development can help you handle change and how your outline professional development plan can be refined to take account of factors making for successful change. It is organised into the following subsections:

- the nature of change
- strategies for change
- blockages to change
- the politics of change, and
- emotional and intuitive responses to change.

## The nature of change

Fullan (1982), arguably the most influential of current writers on change in education, coined the phrase that 'change is a process, not an event' and suggested that 'educational change is technically simple and socially complex,' (Fullan, 1991) with the emphasis very much on the social complexity. He also (ibid.) noted that 'educational change depends on what teachers do and think – it's as simple and as complex as that.'

His comments highlight the way change can be a time-consuming and complex process, which can operate at different levels. For example, change can challenge individuals to develop their attitudes, behaviour and skills. It can also operate at whole school level and have potentially far-reaching implications for the culture and organisation of a school. For Fullan, a crucial factor in bringing about successful change involves providing opportunities for individuals to come to find meaning in the change:

> The real crunch comes in the relationships between .. new programs or policies and the thousands of subjective realities embedded in people's individual and organisational contexts and their personal histories. How these subjective realities are addressed or ignored is crucial for whether potential changes become meaningful at the level of individual use and effectiveness.

Fullan sees change as involving a number of phases:

- initiation, i.e. when the decision to adopt a change is made;
- implementation, i.e. when the change is first put into place;

- continuation or institutionalisation, i.e. whether the change becomes embedded and part and parcel of school life;
- outcome, i.e. the effects, positive and negative, of the change.

Over recent years, as discussed in Chapter 1, there has been an increase in nationally mandated change across the UK. The question at the initiation stage is often not *whether or not* to adopt a required change but how best to take it on board. Change also forms part of what some writers (e.g. Apple, 1986; Day, 2000; Helsby, 2000) refer to as the 'intensification' of work practices in education (and elsewhere), which includes increasing demands together with a rapidly changing environment. This is codified in policy as well as experienced as the everyday by practitioners. For example, the initial planning of the General Teaching Council for England refers to a part of its role being the fostering of what they call the 'thinking professional', i.e. teachers who see themselves as learning and change agents (UCET, 1999).

Writing from a different perspective, Everard and Morris (1990) also describe change as a complex process:

> Few individuals in an organisation appreciate how multidimensional change really is; we tend to espouse a comfortably simplistic notion of it. ... Once we understand that it is the *social system* that withstands change, we begin to realise some of the complexity; for there exist within such systems innumerable relationships, unwritten norms, vested interests and other characteristics that will probably be disturbed by a proposed change ... Change will affect beliefs, assumptions and values and be affected by them. Change will alter the way we are expected to do things. And change will alter the things we need to do with them.

Fullan (1999) and others (such as Stacey, 1996) have suggested that rapid change is inevitable and endemic in current postmodern society, which continuously generates multiple and complex change. Because of this, attempts to manage change cannot assume a stable environment in which to do this, since instability and continued change forms part of the environment for any implementation.

In this context, the process of change can therefore be accompanied by a mixture of feelings, including insecurity, uncertainty, and a sense of becoming de-skilled. Yet on the other hand, it can make people feel vital and motivated. Goddard and Leask (1992) describe the notion of 'the change dip' to illustrate the loss of confidence and de-skilling that can accompany change. In other words, as change is introduced, there is a gradual decreasing of skills, and a need for support to help prevent potential immobilisation. Over time skills gradually increase and potentially outstrip the starting position. The change dip notion points to the need for appropriate support, including in-service training, to help people emerge from the dip. It is also important to acknowledge, as Fullan has suggested (1999), that to an extent every change situation is unique and most are complex. There are no short cuts to living through and learning to adapt to and with, what he calls 'the roller-coaster of complex change' (p. 14).

Not all change is held to be desirable, of course, and some changes stand a better chance of success than others. A number of writers (for example, Fullan and Park, 1981; Miles, 1986) stress that, to be successful, a change must address real needs, be supported by quality materials and training and fit the local setting. And there is now increasing recognition that, as Hargreaves (1994) has put it, 'Teachers are not just technical learners. They are social learners too' (p. 11).

Fullan (1999), drawing on evolutionary theory and also complexity (or chaos) theory, suggests, drawing on Ridley (1996), that the most successful groups in terms of evolutionary survival have been co-operative ones. Building on this idea, Fullan suggests that schools themselves have a role to play as change agents, in contributing to changes in society's morality. As he puts it: 'The ..school is a critical agency in developing the capacity of individuals and communities to pursue higher moral purpose under conditions of great complexity' (p. 12).

A final point concerning the nature of change relates to how far the change itself can change as it is introduced. Sometimes it may be necessary to introduce a change faithfully or with 'fidelity' (Fullan, 1982). On the other hand, it may often be more beneficial if the change itself is developed and if both the change and those using it change together in a process of 'mutual adaptation'. Clearly, however, there may come a point when the change has been so altered as to be unrecognisable. And this, suggests Fullan (1999), may be inevitable in that the creation of knowledge by reference to the internal and external environment is integral to change having a positive force in any organisation. He takes the idea from Nonaka and Takeuchi (1995) who studied successful Japanese countries and who identify knowledge creation by organisations as essential to success. Fullan (1999) explains this as the continuous conversion of tacit knowledge to explicit knowledge, a similar idea to that put forward by Eraut (1994) in his discussion of knowledge creation in educational research. We return to the notion of knowledge creation in the section below.

## Strategies for change

It will be apparent from what we have written so far that successful change depends upon a strategy that recognises the social and psychological processes involved. Three broad strategies for introducing change first described by Bennis *et al.* (1969) are often referred to in the literature. The strategies are described as power-coercive, rational-empirical and normative-re-educative.

The *power-coercive* approach has as its basic assumption that individuals change when formalised authority and power are imposed on them. Viewed through this approach, real change happens through change in laws and regulations, where there are sanctions for non-compliance, and rewards for compliance.

The shortcomings of this approach, Bennis says, are that the use of power and authority often leads to subversive factors or use of countervailing power (such as industrial action), resulting in conflict and hostility.

The *rational-empirical* approach assumes that individuals are rational and change in response to trustworthy information relating to their own self-interest. Viewed through this approach, real change comes about through effective communication about the innovation and its benefits, with practical demonstration of the new technique and provision of the necessary resources.

The shortcomings of this approach however, Bennis notes, include the problem that the real world and people are not purely 'rational'. There are competing values and 'rationalities' which lead to conflict of interest. This view is underlined by Fullan (1999) who suggests that 'The jury must be in by now that rationally constructed reform strategies do not work' (p. 3), his reason being that the wider environment contains too much rapid change to enable such strategies to work.

The *normative-re-educative* approach assumes individuals change when group social pressures realign their beliefs and behaviour. According to this approach, real change happens when significant formal and informal groups are identified and helped to explore the implications of the innovation for themselves, examining and changing hostile attitudes through group discussion and training, developing a 'critical mass' of support for change.

The problems with this approach, Bennis suggests, are that group norms are not easily influenced, and often small groups within an organisation cannot 'go it alone'. Also, even committed groups cannot overcome lack of rewards or shortage of resources.

You will see that the last of Bennis's approaches best accommodates the issues outlined so far in this section and recognises the social and psychological complexity of change. However, it may prove necessary, particularly when attempting to introduce a statutorily mandated change, to combine two or even all three of these strategies. Goddard and Leask (1992) suggest that organisations should analyse mandated changes to work out what is required and what is discretionary. They can then concentrate on implementing the required element and only those aspects of the discretionary elements that address their own needs. This allows for a degree of mutual adaptation and the use of a change strategy, which combines two or possibly three of Bennis *et al*.s' strategies (and also takes account of the co-operative and adaptive aspects of change highlighted in Fullan's (1999) writing discussed in the previous section to this one). As an illustration of how Bennis's strategies have been used in practice, consider, for example, how appraisal was introduced in England and Wales. There was a statutory requirement to introduce appraisal and certain minimum legal requirements, for example the process had to include observation, an interview, an appraisal statement and interview, and a review meeting. This was the power–coercive element. There were then a number of books, guides, manuals and videos, which sought to promote appraisal as a useful process. These often operated at a rational–empiricial level. Finally, a good deal of emphasis was placed on the need for training and preparation for appraisal, which included consultation with staff about how the scheme should be developed and aims to develop ownership of the process. This provided opportunities for a normative–re-educative approach.

In Scotland, education authorities had to seek approval from the Scottish Office for their schemes for staff development over appraisal. These schemes, whilst reflecting local needs, all had certain common features and include, for example, collection of data, an interview and a follow-up meeting in year 2 of the cycle. These schemes could be described as the power–coercive element, but, in most instances operate at a rational–empirical level.

The creation of knowledge and its role in educational change is an area which has received increased attention over recent years (Eraut, 1994; Hargreaves, 1998; Fullan, 1999). Eraut has highlighted the role of unsystematised, chance personal knowledge, (much of which is 'tacit' in Fullan's (1999) terms), in the creation of professional knowledge. He distinguishes between research knowledge and practitioner knowledge. As this book is primarily concerned with practitioners investigating and enhancing their practice, we focus on the latter here. He notes the under-exploitation of the knowledge-development potential of practitioners, suggesting that reasons for this may include the fact that much of teachers' knowledge is particular to a specific incident, and transferred from one case to another by association in an ad hoc rather than systematic way. In addition he suggests that teachers tend to operate as individuals rather than sharing the knowledge they have created. On top of this he notes that the sharing of 'practical knowledge' is tricky because such knowledge involves much interpretation and thus much discussion of meaning, which requires time and inclination, neither of which are in high evidence in the current context. His proposals for forward movement concern a closer partnership between higher education and the professions.

Hargreaves (1998) on the other hand, whilst starting from a similar place to Eraut in that he suggests a radical education agenda is needed whereby the teaching profession must make much larger shifts to meet the challenges of the twenty-first century, has proposed a far more central role for the teaching profession itself. He places teachers at the centre of knowledge creation about pedagogy.

Of the three commentators, Fullan (1999), writing most recently, places knowledge creation by the teachers within the institution as most central to the processes of change. He suggests that the conversion of tacit to explicit knowledge is essential although difficult since tacit knowledge is by its nature elusive, it is also not always useful and it is imperative that useful ideas are retained and shared within the organisation. His emphasis on teachers as part of the school as a whole offers a much more global view of the role of knowledge in change. In his analysis, he suggests that middle managers play a critical role in the formation and sharing of shared knowledge, for their role is to help to develop coherence between tacit and explicit knowledge, bringing together individual, group and overall collective thinking. He also offers a caution about avoiding 'groupthink' in the creation of shared knowledge (in other words, where a closely knit group of people develop a set of assumptions in an uncritical manner so that dissent and conflict are minimised and what emerges is essentially a set of shared prejudices). The workings of the institution in implementing and devising change seem likely to become an increasing focus in coming years, given the continued emphasis on the overall performance of the school as a unit. The processes by which knowledge is created, shared and used seem likely then to come under increasing scrutiny. Barriers to these processes such as the culture of individualism still evident in many institutions (Hargreaves, 1994) and the culture of compliance documented in many primary staffrooms (Nias, 1989) seem likely to form a part of this investigation for development.

*Think about a recent change that has affected you, whether you were responsible for it or not. What strategy was used to implement it? How well did this work? To what extent was new knowledge created and new change triggered by the implementation, how did this occur and what was your own role in this?*

It has been shown in a number of research studies that long-lasting change is unlikely to occur without a period of destabilisation (Fullan, 1991). Yet, it is during such periods that most change fails to make progress beyond very early implementation. When institutional resistance is met, turbulence often emerges and the focus of change leaves the classroom and gets stuck in the processes of those trying to implement change. Eventually progress slows and is abandoned – and another focus is found for working on, sometimes involving other people. Stoll *et al.* (1996) call this 'the cycle of educational failure, the predictable pathology of educational change' (p. 143).

Another key point in creating successful change is the need to provide people with support as they engage upon change. The value of ongoing training and other professional development work cannot be overestimated. Such support will help people come out of the change dip and enable them to acquire new knowledge and to develop new attitudes and skills. You will remember from Chapter 3, however, that according to recent thinking, professional development, which attempts to develop new skills, needs to be experiential and to include opportunities for practice, feedback and coaching (Joyce and Showers, 1980). As change takes place over time, professional development needs to be ongoing and integrated with practice. Crucial too, is the context for professional development.

We have already argued that school and individual development go hand in hand. Indeed, appraisal, school development planning and school improvement have the potential to develop the culture of a school to enable it to become better at handling change. Fundamental to successful change is the creation of a school culture that is conducive to change at both individual and school level, a culture described in Chapter 3 as a learning organisation and as having the following characteristics:

> The Learning School aims to be like learning itself:
> interactive and negotiative;
> creative and problem-solving;
> proactive and responsive;
> participative and collaborative;
> flexible and challenging;
> risk-taking and enterprising;
> evaluative and reflective;
> supportive and developmental.
>
> (Holly and Southworth, 1989)

In Chapter 3 we also introduced the notion of the 'corporate intelligence' demonstrated by schools which are successful in coping with change, a term coined by McMaster (1995) and used by MacGilchrist *et al.* (1997). These inter-related intelligences MacGilchrist *et al.* described as:

| | |
|---|---|
| *contextual intelligence* | the ability of a school to view itself in relation to the world of which it is a part |
| *strategic intelligence* | the capacity to engender clarity about and a shared responsibility toward goals |

| | |
|---|---|
| *Academic intelligence* | placing high value on achievement and scholarship, in both children and teachers |
| *Reflective intelligence* | monitoring and evaluating the school's overall effectiveness |
| *Pedagogical intelligence* | continuous learning by staff about pedagogy |
| *Collegial intelligence* | staff working together to improve classroom practice |
| *Emotional intelligence* | a school's ability to enable the feelings of pupils and staff to be acknowledged |
| *Spiritual intelligence* | valuing all within a school community in the context of a wider, mysterious universe |
| *Ethical intelligence* | recognition of each pupil's rights and the valuing of justice and equality |

They propose a model of the 'intelligent school' which uses each of these interdependent intelligences to maximum effect in classroom practice as well as across the school as a whole.

Implicit in what both sets of authors are saying is the principle of the 'empowered school' put forward by Hargreaves and Hopkins (1991) where the school is 'neither the unwilling victim of externally driven changes nor the innovator who reacts unthinkingly to every fad or whim'. This idea is developed further by Hopkins and Lagerweij (1996) who suggest that whilst maintaining a powerful awareness of the external context, a focus on the internal conditions of the school is essential to keeping efforts toward making changes in a school's functioning. This means placing the scrutiny of classroom factors such as curriculum, pedagogical practices including grouping, assessment processes and so on, at the heart of all attempts to implement change. It means also seeing the school as an organisation rather than as what MacGilchrist *et al.* (1997) have referred to as a 'loose federation of autonomous and unaccountable classrooms in which one teacher is predominantly autonomous and unaccountable to the whole' (p. 113).

## Blockages to change

Given the relative complexity of many changes and the omnipresence of multiple change, it is not surprising that change is often resisted or proves difficult to implement. In the sections above we touched on potential barriers stemming from school culture and knowledge creation.

Hall and Oldroyd (1991) provide two further perspectives on blockages to change. First they identify three types of barrier to change – technical (lack of resources, facilities, time, etc.), value (where teachers' beliefs and attitudes are opposed to the change) and power (where the head teacher is against the change or there is not a 'critical mass' of staff in favour of it). They suggest that these barriers are often encountered in the following order: technical, value, power. The second perspective is the characteristics of settings, change strategies and changes that are likely to lead to resistance to change. Hall and Oldroyd (1991) argue that, in settings where

- morale is low
- change agents (i.e. those advocating or introducing change) are not respected
- there is a track record of failed innovation
- risk-taking is discouraged
- leaders are inflexible in their attitudes
- there is little outside support …

… teachers will be less motivated to support *change strategies* which …

- are unaccompanied by practical training and support on-the-job
- do not adapt to developing circumstances
- do not recognise local needs
- offer no sense of collective 'ownership'
- do not build a 'critical mass' for change.

Neither will they commit themselves to *innovations* which:

- are not seen as beneficial
- cannot be clearly understood
- are at odds with their professional beliefs
- are inadequately resourced.

These points apply particularly to school level change but can also create a climate in which even change at individual level is more difficult.

Everard and Morris (1990) suggest that those introducing change can fail for a number of reasons:

- They can be too rational in their strategy for change and assume that spelling out the logic of where they want to go will motivate others to follow;
- They can be operating at a different level of thought from those affected by the change and fail to take account of how others see things;
- They might rely on their position and power to the neglect of the feelings, ideas, values and experiences of those affected by the change;
- They can fall into the all too easy trap of ascribing problems necessitating change to individuals rather than to methods and systems, and thus cause defensiveness;
- They might be dealing with an insoluble problem.

You might find it helpful to think about how far you feel these points apply to (a) a change introduced generally in your school or institution and (b) a change you yourself have introduced in your own classroom or in your daily work.

One set of reasons why people can be too rational in their strategies for change is that touched on earlier, proposed by Fullan (1999), namely, a lag in expectations, i.e. they expect a more stable environment than they are in fact living with. However, the complexity and pace of change at this point in history is such that it does not lend itself to a rational approach. Another set of reasons stems from people ignoring the *politics* of change and *emotional* or *intuitive* responses to change.

## The politics of change

In every institution, there are networks and hierarchies of power and authority alliances. Some of these are formal and explicit; for example, job titles usually give an indication of which responsibilities and what power and authority the post holder carries, at least in theory. However, much more influential than the mere job title is the myriad of personal factors and alliances which can influence the trust people have in each other at work, their commitment to team decisions and goals, the way decisions are made and carried out, and even the overall ethos of the institution. Being aware of the politics of work is like listening to 'the music behind the words'; just as in a song, the music can have far more impact and effect than the words alone, so it is important to be aware of the political context in which choices are made in your institution.

One way of doing this is to represent your relationships in your institution by means of diagrams, representing the politics of power and influence symbolically. You can represent the flow of information and power, who the 'gatekeepers' to change are, and expose and analyse your own feelings about the current situation in this way. By making the current arrangement explicit you can see where the access points might be for you. To give you an idea of how this can be done, we are including one created by a newly qualified primary teacher wanting to gain experience of teaching a different age group in her school (Figure 18).

The teacher who created this map wrote in her notebook:

> I realised in doing this socio-map that I was getting a lot of support from some other colleagues, in particular from the Deputy Head, Manjula, but that although I was getting support from Jane, the Head Teacher, she was unwilling to consider change in relation to me. But I also realised that she is not the only decision maker, that Manjula is also able to heavily influence decisions like this – and that Anji Y2 teacher, and

Barbara, Chair of Governors, as sources of influence on Jane, are important 'gatekeepers' for me. I need to work on my relationships with Manjula and Anji to persuade Jane. I also need to explore the politics of their relationships further – especially between Jane and Manjula. I also realised that I have a poor relationship with Ricky, the Y6 teacher, in so far as I perceive a conflict of personality and a disinterest from him; it made me aware of some of the issues which could arise if I taught Y5, since I'd need to link with Ricky over children going into his class from mine. Similarly I'd need to work on my relationship with John though I feel there's a willingness there. It also became obvious that I'm not really developing a positive relationship with Betty, the current Y5 teacher, in fact I couldn't work out what the dynamics of our relationship are at all! If I want to swap classes with her I'll need to spend some time on this!

I've realised I have a lot to 'listen to' behind the structures of my school and I have a lot to learn.

Note: Whilst this exemplar uses terminology applicable to England and Wales, the same exercise could equally apply in Scotland, where schools have School Boards. A reception class equivalent in Scotland is a nursery class for pre-school children aged four.

## Emotional or intuitive responses to change

Throughout your life, you are faced with choices about change – the most fundamental of which is whether to see yourself as the victim of change, which 'happens to you', or whether to own your power in choosing. By adopting one attitude or another, you set up a personal framework for perceiving and living with change in your own life. Much of the literature on personal growth and development reflects this view and many writers in this field believe that we all have within us the capacity to allow our emotional or intuitive sides to choose, rather than seeing ourselves as a victim – a ping-pong ball at the mercy of luck, chance, fate, or other external circumstances beyond our control (Edwards, 1993). In a professional context, in the midst of multiple change, it is all too easy to dismiss your intuitive or emotional responses, particularly when the triggers for change are outside your control, even beyond the control of your school or institution. It can seem as though personal choice is a luxury no longer available (if it ever was) in education – and it can seem difficult to see how there is space for an emotional response. This is partly a function of where you perceive the impetus for change originating from; the less you identify with its source, the more you are likely to have a 'disempowered' response.

It can also seem that there is little scope for intuition to drive choices in making change. But, actually, the emotional elements of both opting for

Aim: to plan my next career step (i.e. to change classes in my school from Reception to Y5)

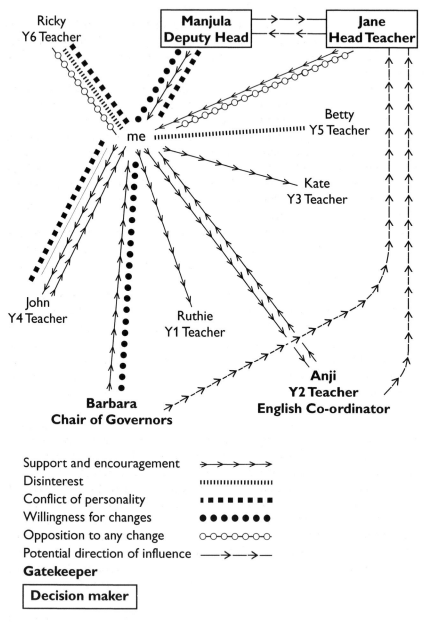

*Figure 18* Socio-map of E634 student: NQT in a primary school

and responding to change are part of the powerful 'music behind the words' we explored within the section on the politics of change, and cannot simply be dismissed. They are real.

One way forward in taking account of emotions and intuition in planning professional development is to allow enough space in the process for these responses, and to find ways of enabling and supporting individuals (including yourself) in choosing and owning changes.

One technique developed by Simon Stanley (1994; unpublished) is to use metaphor and symbolism to analyse changes you would like to implement in light of your relationship with the 'gate keepers' you have identified, and to explore your own and their emotional/intuitive responses (in so far as you can know theirs). In other words, to conjure up images that are driven by your intuitive feelings, but like metaphor, are not a direct representation of the actual situation you are in. The power of using metaphor and symbolism is that it is a non-linear and non-rational way of thinking. By working with and through metaphor you can release and expose different, powerful and often unconscious aspects of your feelings about change. This can provide a starting point for finding space within the change process for each person to 'opt in' emotionally. You may also find it helpful, and quite amusing!

So, for example, an NQT in a primary school who felt the head teacher was 'blocking' her from swapping classes with another teacher, created a visual metaphor of the head teacher as a large, deep-rooted bush. Through exploring her metaphor she realised that the bush was large and looming and yet fragile. Applying the metaphor to her work, it helped her become more aware that any attempt to change the head teacher's behaviour must acknowledge the upheaval to the status quo, and the head teacher's own feeling about it.

Another teacher, a head of department in a comprehensive school, found departmental meetings frustrating in that a teacher in her team appeared to be non-co-operative. She visualised her as a creature, and then explored the characteristics of it. In her visual metaphor, her colleague was an owl. She realised she in fact had a great deal of respect toward her 'owl' colleague, and recognised that the departmental meeting gave her colleague little opportunity to offer her insight and experience.

The following quotation from Fullan (1991) takes the form of a list 'do's and don'ts' about change and draws together the points that have been made in this section. As you read each section, you might like to consider how far it applies to a change you have been involved with.

1  Do not assume that your version of what the change should be is the one that should be implemented. On the contrary, assume that one of the main purposes of the process of implementation is to exchange

your reality of what should be through interaction with implementers and others concerned.

2 Assume that any significant innovation, if it is to result in change, requires individual implementers to work out their own meaning. Clarification is likely to come in large part through practice …

3 Assume that conflict and disagreement are not only inevitable but fundamental to successful change. Since any group of people possesses multiple realities, any collective change attempt will necessarily involve conflict. Smooth implementation is often a sign that not much is really changing …

4 Assume that people need pressure to change (even in directions that they desire), but it will be effective only under conditions that allow them to react, to form their own position, to interact with other implementers, to obtain technical assistance, etc …

5 Assume that effective change takes time. It is a process of 'development in use'. Unrealistic or undefined time lines fail to recognise that implementation occurs developmentally …

6 Do not assume that the reason for lack of implementation is outright rejection of the values embodied in the change, or hard-core resistance to all change. There are a number of possible reasons: value rejection, inadequate resources to support implementation, insufficient time elapsed.

7 Do not expect all or even most people or groups to change. The complexity of change is such that it is impossible to bring about widespread reform in any large social system …

8 Assume that you will need a plan that is based on the above assumptions and that addresses the factors known to affect implementation. Evolutionary planning and problem-coping models based on knowledge of the change process are essential …

9 Assume that no amount of knowledge will ever make it totally clear what action should be taken. Action decisions are a combination of valid knowledge, political considerations, on-the-spot decisions and intuition …

10 Assume that changing the culture of institutions is the real agenda, not implementing single innovations. … Put another way, we should always pay attention to whether the institution is developing or not.

In his most recent thinking (1999) Fullan proposes eight 'lessons' for understanding and living with complex change. As you read these you may like to reflect on how relevant these seem to your own current professional experience.

*Lesson 1: Moral purpose is complex and problematic.* Here Fullan is encouraging schools to be inspired by moral purpose but not naïve about it, for it needs to be supported by the resources and infrastructure provided by the other seven lessons in order to actually achieve it.

*Lesson 2: Theories of change and theories of education need each other.* The basic idea here is that without a current understanding of change and its effects on people and their work, combined with appropriate well-worked out approaches to education, new initiatives will not get off the ground. Fullan emphasises that understanding the wider context is essential to both sets of theories.

*Lesson 3: Conflict and diversity are our friends.* The idea here is that conflict is useful in enabling breakthroughs in turbulent and complex conditions. Fullan emphasises the notion of 'collaborative diversity' meaning that heterogeneous environments are much more likely to produce productive change, as the resistances which are likely to be generated in such an environment are essential ingredients in moving forward. An aspect then of effective change generation and implementation is the formation of relationships with people one may not like or understand (and vice versa). Learning from dissonance and discomfort is, he suggests 'a new requirement for living on the edge of chaos.' (p. 23)

*Lesson 4: Understand the meaning of operating on the edge of chaos.* Here Fullan is emphasising that to operate at the edge of chaos in current conditions means getting used to a degree of uncertainty which means that expecting frequent change, having space within frameworks of a few clear and shared priorities, for adapting, and making time and space for communication within and across groups, is essential.

*Lesson 5: Emotional intelligence is anxiety provoking and anxiety containing.* Here, drawing on the work of Heifetz (1994), Stacey (1996) and Goleman (1995), Fullan is suggesting that not only is anxiety integral to change, but that people who are able to cope with anxiety as one of the spectrum of emotions which they have, are better able to be effective in complex, changing environments.

*Lesson 6: Collaborative cultures are anxiety provoking and anxiety containing.* This is closely related to lesson 5, in that Fullan is suggesting that for collaborative cultures to be effective there needs to be a degree of dissonance, or what Leonard (1995) calls 'creative abrasion'. There is a need for leaders to both foster such dissonance and hold the environment to enable this to happen. His suggestion is that 'vitality springs from experiencing conflict and tension in systems which also incorporate anxiety-containing supportive relationships.' (p. 27)

*Lesson 7: Attack incoherence: connectedness and knowledge creation are critical.* This was discussed earlier in the chapter; Fullan suggests that making meaning in moving from tacit to explicit knowledge in a collaborative way within the system of the school is essential to effective functioning within a change environment. This means the organisation electing to do this and creating mechanisms for developing and integrating knowledge.

*Lesson 8: There is no single solution – craft your own theories and actions by being a critical consumer.* This is an extension of the previous point, i.e. that developing explicit knowledge will be deeply affected by the context of the school itself. As Fullan puts it, 'no one can solve your change problems but yourself' (p. 29).

## Task 20

Review what you wrote in your outline plan for your own professional development in the light of this section, by considering the following questions:

- What changes are you involved in or going to be involved in? What type of professional development might be useful in supporting you with these changes?
- Can you think of ways in which your own future professional development can affect the development of your school or institution and help it to develop as a learning organisation?
- What are the implications of the ideas about change included in this text for your professional development? (You might like to consider such issues as continuity, timing, and methods, for example).
- Are there any changes you need to make to your outline plan?

## Summary of Chapter 10

This chapter has been about planning future professional development. We considered various factors which might influence your future choices, such as what you may have learned from your evaluation of professional development, your own understanding of the nature and purposes of professionalism and professional development, your own development needs and the needs of your department, team or school.

We also explored aspects of change in education, and made the following points:

- we live at a time of continuous and multiple change;
- change is a complex and chaotic process, socially and psychologically, that it involves instability far more now than ever before – and that change inevitably leads to further change;
- institutions which are most successful in coping with change work co-operatively to do so and an important part of this is the creation of professional knowledge within the institution which operates in making tacit knowledge explicit.
- change is influenced by beliefs, assumptions, values, skills and behaviour of individuals on one level and for the organisation, culture and systems of a school on another;
- change often prompts initial feelings of insecurity, which need to be addressed;
- an overly rational approach to change or relying solely on power, position or sanction to produce change is likely to lead to less real change than a strategy that involves a normative–re-educative approach;
- that change implementation often founders in the initial stages;
- professional development needs to be a major part of a successful strategy for change;
- the key to successful change within a school lies in the development of a culture which expects change and which is conducive to evaluating and handling it at whole school level whilst involving individuals actively and promoting individual growth;
- thus that individual and school development go hand in hand and we explored the concepts of the learning school, the empowered school and the intelligent school as models for doing so.

# Chapter 11

# Personal learning as a professional

This chapter considers a range of personal circumstances, which have a bearing on professional development planning. It rests on our belief that the personal circumstances of an individual and his or her professional development are interlinked; a belief we have been exploring particularly in the politics and intuition sections of Chapter 10. This belief is in tune with the ideas and research findings of a number of writers. For example, Joyce and Showers (1988) found that teachers 'who were more active professionally were also more active personally' – an idea which we explore later in the chapter, and also in Appendix 1. In a complementary discussion of contexts for teacher development, Raymond *et al.* (1992) argue that 'the link between personal and professional dispositions makes it important for teachers to have opportunities to examine their own personal commitments, histories, and teaching styles. Discovering and making explicit the roots of their commitment, understanding the personal grounds that underlie their professional work, being clearer about the types of educational contexts that best suit their biographical dispositions – all these kinds of reflections might assist the process of teacher development.' They go on to argue that 'in order to know what we wish to do next …we need to know ourselves, who we are, and how we came to be that way.' In other words, for Raymond *et al.*, planning professional development needs to take account of an individual's 'autobiography', that is based on:

- the context of a teacher's current work
- a description of their current pedagogy and curriculum in use
- reflections on their past personal and professional lives to assist their understanding of present professional thoughts and actions, and
- a projection into their preferred professional futures arising from a personal critical appraisal of the previous three areas.

In exploring this notion of teacher autobiography, we will focus on:

- personal views on the nature of teaching and learning
- personal growth
- professional development and career history
- professional journals.

We will be exploring the links between these points and future professional development will be discussed.

We take the view expressed by sociologist Tony Giddens (1991) that through understanding personal identity and choosing ways to re-invent, develop and re-create it, we create wider change in education and society. A number of writers in education (for example, Dadds, 1997) have noted that professional development, and planning for it, needs to take account of a person's own biography.

This emphasis on biography and autobiography, although widespread in educational practice in North America, parts of Europe and Australasia, is also paralleled by policy measures in all three places which, as discussed in Part I of this book in the context of the UK, appear to contradict or undermine the place of personal history and values in professional life. For the acknowledgement of biography values the practitioner's own involvement in self-study and self-development and stands in apparent contradiction to technicist models of pedagogy and thus of professional development, as argued for example by Day (2000) and by Goodson (1991).

Technicist models, as discussed in Part I, propose teaching as an activity which can be broken into behavioural and other outcomes which are generalisable and repeatable and 'measurable' in teachers' practice. An assumption underlying this perspective appears to be that, given a particular approach to classroom teaching, certain outcomes in children's learning will be an automatic consequence.

Also embedded in the technicist model is an assumption that teaching is not a matter of subjective and professional judgement concerning appropriate moments for interventions of a myriad of kinds. But rather a question of uniform, generalisable behaviours which bear no direct relation to the specific teacher and learners involved in any one situation. Thus, national strategies such as the National Numeracy Strategy and the National Literacy Strategy introduced during the late 1990s, could be described as part of a technicist policy. Other plans, such as those by the DfEE (2000) to introduce a national standards framework for career progression may similarly be seen in this light, as may the standards mapped out by SEED in Scotland with a similar intention.

Writers such as Dadds (1997) argue against the technicist model of pedagogy (and therefore technicist approaches to continuing professional development). Dadds proposes a continuum for CPD, at one end of which are 'delivery models', and at the other the cultivation of self-understanding by the active engagement of the practitioner in their own self-study, in ways which articulate with their experience and knowledge. Her proposal is that CPD which involves self-study and which takes account of individual biography, leads teachers to deep changes in understanding of their professsional practice.

The study of one's own practice can engage at the level of the institutional as well as the personal, as Goodson (1991) has argued. Indeed Goodson places biography and autobiography at the heart of teachers' exploratory interactions between their own actions and the wider institutional and political contexts in which they operate.

## PERSONAL VIEWS ON THE NATURE OF TEACHING AND LEARNING

As a result of formative influences, including teaching experience, teachers develop a personal view about teaching and learning. In part, this might be linked to a philosophical position concerning the purposes of education. For example, education might be seen as about transmitting a culture, developing individual potential, transforming society or serving the needs of society. The view taken will affect someone's view of teaching and may benefit from being challenged through professional development.

Eisner (1985), for example, describes five broad philosophical positions on education. These define education as primarily about:

1  *The development of cognitive processes* i.e. children should be concerned with learning how to learn and be encouraged to exercise and develop their intellectual powers in solving problems;
2  *Academic rationalism* i.e. the major function of the school is to foster the intellectual growth of all students by introducing them to each of the major fields of knowledge and the best work in each field;
3  *Personal relevance* i.e. the aim is to take a child-centred approach and to emphasise the pupil's role in framing their own curriculum;
4  *Social adaptation or social reconstruction* i.e. education should be about either fitting children for the society they have to live in or fitting them to analyse social issues so that they can change and transform society;
5  *Curriculum as technology* i.e. education is about achieving present objectives and using standardised tests to assess these.

Eisner sees schools as adopting one or more of these positions and as often changing their approach from one to another according to what is being done. The point here is that a teacher's basic underlying assumptions about what education is for will form part of the context for both their teaching and their approach to professional development.

The same can be said for teachers' assumptions about how children learn. Broadly speaking, it is possible to categorise theories of learning in the following way:

1   *Learning as growth* i.e. learning is seen as 'the growth of cognitive structures along an internally directed course under the triggering and partially shaping effect of the environment' [Chomsky, 1980]; the key is to provide children with free experience to bring out what is already there and to enable their innate powers to develop. Examples of adherents to this view include Montessori, Rousseau and Froebel.

2   *Learning by association* i.e. on the premise that events occurring together in experience will be represented together in the mind, learning is seen as the acquisition of such associations. For example, we learn common categories (e.g. dog) by associating their key features (e.g. tail, four legs, fur, etc.). Behaviourism takes this notion one step further by adding the principles of positive and negative reinforcement. In other words, for behaviourists the learning of associations can be strengthened by the use of positive reinforcement or rewards, when appropriate behaviour takes place. The best known adherent of behaviourism is Skinner.

3   *Learning as development and construction* i.e. learning is seen to depend on the development of mental structures for organising, sorting and conceptualising the world around us. This development is seen as being aided by providing problems for a child to 'discover' solutions. Adherents of this view of learning include Piaget, the writers of the Plowden Report and Vygotsky.

*Consider which of Eisner's philosophical positions corresponds most closely to your own view of the purposes of education. How far do your views about how children learn fit into the three approaches to learning; learning as growth, learning by association, and learning as development and construction?*

Beliefs about teaching and learning will affect someone's approach to both teaching and professional development and influence what is sometimes referred to as their theory or theories of action. West (1992), referring to the ideas of Argyris and Schon, defines a teacher's espoused theory of action as how a teacher describes what he or she does when teaching in order to produce intended outcomes in appropriate circumstances. A teacher's theory of action would include:

- how they characterise the way they teach a particular subject or area;
- what they feel characterises the way their pupils engage in learning; and
- the attitudes, skills and key concepts they are aiming to develop.

West sees such a theory as 'enabling us to engage in our work, to be able to predict what might happen, and in consequence, control events within our work setting.' However, there can be a mismatch between someone's theory of action and what they actually do in practice, what West describes as 'theory in use'. West sees a role for both self-evaluation and appraisal in highlighting any mismatch and in confirming congruence. Because theories of action can be implicit rather than explicit, there is also a role for appraisal and self-evaluation in helping people to articulate what they are aiming to do.

West introduces the concept of a teaching repertoire to 'encompass the set of skills, devices, methods, strategies, knowledge and understanding which a teacher deploys in the course of promoting quality learning in the range of activities, curriculum areas and subject they teach.' He sees the extension of our teaching repertoire as a career-long goal dependent on a range of developmental factors, such as reflection, experimentation and feedback. He notes that a teacher with an extended repertoire or range of skills, methods and strategies will have an 'extensive theory of action system' or a number of interrelated theories of action. These ideas are useful in the context of this text as they provide a means of conceptualising professional development as involving extending a teacher's repertoire.

West prefers the term teaching repertoire to teaching style, as he feels style has too often been portrayed in rather a crude and simplistic way in the form of polarities, such as 'formal–informal', 'teacher-centred–pupil-centred', or 'traditional–progressive'. Clearly it is important to avoid over-simplification. Useful here are the ideas of Joyce and Weil (1980) who identify a number of models of teaching and argue a case for teachers extending their teaching repertoire by becoming proficient in an increasing number of models; in other words, 'growth in teaching is the increasing mastery of a variety of models of teaching and the ability to use them effectively', a mastery that depends on appropriate professional development. They identify some twenty-two models of teaching, which they classify into four 'families':

1   Information processing models (centre on how pupils handle information, organise data, generate concepts, solve problems and employ verbal and non-verbal signals).
2   Personal models (emphasise learning through feelings and emotions and are concerned with the subjective reality of individual pupils).
3   Social interaction models (give priority to the individual's ability to relate to others and to work productively in groups).
4   Behavioural models (emphasise changing the visible behaviour of the learner, using such principles as reinforcement).

Someone's view of teaching will also tend to be affected by their experience and the type of schools they teach in, as well as the wider context. Day (1991), for example, argues that teachers judge professional learning opportunities according to their learning preferences and attitudes, which he sees as formed largely by events, people and experiences in their learning lives during critical stages in their development, such as early childhood, youth, initial training and previous continuing professional development. He notes that the most common attitudes of teachers to their own learning appeared to be 'self-sufficiency, hard work, conscientiousness, caring, enthusiasm and interdependence' and that their most common ethic was practicality. More recently, Day (2000) has suggested, based on a small-scale study, that the influence of an enforced policy context in England where teachers' professionalism has increasingly been defined externally and in a technicist way, provides forces both for and against 'professionalisation'. In other words, that externally imposed reforms have, whilst holding the potential to 'de-skill' teachers, and to make them feel their professional artistry is being undermined, the potential to reinforce teachers' own stances. This suggestion has been documented in primary schools by Woods (1994) and Troman (1996) and in secondary schools by Helsby (2000) as well as suggested by others such as Ball (1994, 1996) and Hargreaves and Goodson (1996).

*Think about your own views of teaching and learning. What implications do they have for your own professional development? How did you come to develop your views?*

The notion of the impact of a practicality ethic is relatively common in the literature. Huberman (1992), for example, argues that 'essentially teachers are artisans working primarily alone, with a variety of new and cobbled together materials, in a personally designed work environment. They gradually develop a repertoire of instructional skills and strategies, corresponding to a progressively denser, more differentiated and well-integrated set of mental schemata; they come to read the instructional situation better and faster, and to respond to it with a greater variety of tools. They develop this repertoire through a somewhat haphazard process of trial and error …'. As a result, Huberman argues (with others, such as, more recently, Helsby, 2000) that a crucial ingredient in teacher development involves supporting networks of teachers, who can learn from each other or carry out their own individual learning. Those who subscribe to a view of teachers as artisans are likely to stress this and other forms of 'on the job', practical professional development as particularly beneficial. In other words, they are likely to stress the need to integrate training and practice and to provide opportunities for development, which are integrated into peoples' jobs. They are also likely to draw attention to the way teachers develop as a result of unplanned opportunities, that arise in the normal course of work.

Other writers have tried to explore the view of teachers as professionals and the impact of underpinnng views held by both teachers and policy makers on the CPD which teachers become involved with. Hoyle (1980) makes the distinction between restricted and extended professionality. His notion of restricted professionality is similar to Huberman's view of the teacher as artisan. The contrasting concept of the extended professional portrays a view of teaching which has different implications for professional development. Hoyle writes as follows:

> By *restricted* professionality, I mean a professionality which is intuitive, classroom-focused, and based on experience rather than theory. The good restricted professional is sensitive to the development of individual pupils, an inventive teacher and a skilful class-manager. He is unencumbered with theory, is not given to comparing his work with that of others, tends not to perceive his classroom activities in a broader context, and values his classroom autonomy. The *extended professional*, on the other hand, is concerned with locating his classroom teaching in a broader educational context, comparing his work with that of other teachers, evaluating his own work systematically, and collaborating with other teachers. Unlike the restricted professional, he is interested in theory and current educational developments. Hence he reads educational books and journals, becomes involved in various professional activities and is concerned to further his own professional development through in-service work. He sees teaching as a rational activity amenable to improvement on the basis of research and development activities, particularly those involving extended study.

This view of extended professionality leads to an emphasis in professional development on the value of theory and off-site training and development.

Stenhouse (1975) took a rather different view of the characteristics of an extended professional. For him the essential quality of an extended professional is 'a capacity for autonomous professional development through systematic self-study, through the study of the work of other teachers and through the testing of ideas by classroom research procedures.' This view draws attention firmly towards developing theories of teaching through the analysis of practice and using such self-generated theories to inform practice. It gets away from any suggestion of the separation of theory and practice. It lies at the heart of the teacher as researcher and action research traditions and leads to an emphasis in professional development on self-study, action research and peer-assisted learning, processes often to be found, of course, in evaluation. It can be seen as an early view of the kind of professional knowledge-creation that we explored in Chapter 10.

What the extended professional chooses to take up as CPD, has been developed by Higgins and Leat (1997), who note the existence of competing and radically different models of so-called appropriate and effective teacher development, the impact of the move toward competence-based initial teacher education, on CPD, and the consequent squeezing out of approaches involving critical scrutiny of fundamental questions underpinning the purposes of education or pedagogy. Their contention is that, although there may be different strengths and weaknesses to different forms of professional development and the policy context is a powerful influence, nevertheless individual learning preference plays a significant role in what teachers select for themselves.

Personal learning preferences may be influenced by what are sometimes termed 'critical incidents' in a teacher's career. This has been used widely in the research literature, for critical incidents often form a turning point in a person's professional and/or personal life. They often occur at times of strain, endings and beginnings, changes and turning points brought about unexpectedly, or by shock or surprise. Teacher biographies often focus upon these aspects of their professional and personal lives.

In addition, teacher development often occurs through formal or informal mentoring, which we explore later in the chapter.

## PERSONAL GROWTH

Joyce and Showers, as noted above, argue (1988) that teachers who are active professionally are also more active personally. They feel that teachers vary in the degree to which they view their environment, including the environment of professional development opportunities, as an opportunity for satisfying a need for personal growth. Basically, they believe that teachers' enthusiasm for professional development is affected by how actively they engage with their environment and by the state of their conceptual development. Joyce and Showers note that affirmative and active friends and colleagues and a positive social climate can encourage people to engage more actively with their environment than they would do if left to themselves. With this in mind, they distinguish between a number of orientations towards personal growth. People in their various categories are described as follows:

- *gourmet omnivores*: 'mature, high activity people who have learnt to canvass the environment and exploit it successfully ..', they both exploit and enrich 'whatever environment they find themselves in'.
- *passive consumers*: show 'a more or less amiable conformity to the

environment and a high degree of dependence on the immediate social context' and therefore, 'their degree of activity depends greatly on who they are with'.

- *reticent consumers*: are reluctant to interact positively with their environment and can react negatively or with anger and suspicion to those around them.

Joyce and Showers relate these levels to conceptual development and self-concept. They see 'gourmet omnivores' as having the most sophisticated and complex conceptual development. They also see gourmet omnivores as having 'strong self-concepts .. accompanied by self-actualising behaviour, a reaching out toward the environment with confidence that the interaction will be productive'. At the other end of the continuum, they see reticent consumers as having less well developed conceptual frameworks and relatively weak self-concepts and feeling unsure of their surroundings and of their ability to cope. They also begin to tease out some of the implications of these ideas for teacher development, stressing the need to consider carefully the degree of support, interaction, encouragement and energy that will be needed to develop people at different stages of development.

The essential point to emphasise here is that professional development has a major role to play in enabling individual growth and learning and in helping people to realise their potential, defined in the broadest sense. To quote Hopson and Scally (1981), 'growth and development never end.

---

## Task 21

Read Appendix 1, entitled 'The gender debate in professional development'. It is a comparative piece based on the feminist rebuttal and critique by Robertson to the Joyce and Showers position outlined above. Given the influence that Joyce and Showers have had on the theory and practice of professional development both sides of the Atlantic, we provide the reading by way of balance.

1  What do you feel about the ideas of Joyce and Showers on personal growth and levels of activity, bearing in mind Robertson's critique?
2  How far do you feel that your own development as a person is linked with your professional development?

Write your ideas in your notebook. You may find it useful to make a copy of your notes and views to keep in your portfolio.

Self-empowerment is not an end to be achieved but a constant process of becoming'. And personal development both in and out of school is as relevant for the provider of professional development as it is for the consumer of it. Life events such as the birth of a child can affect the way in which a teacher is able to engage with their professional role and the development involved in this. Caring responsibilities, particularly but not exclusively for women, have an impact on what sorts of CPD can be undertaken and how, as Robertson argues. Models which take no account of this may be described as unrealistic and as denying the reality of ways in which teachers' different selves merge in their professional persona. The impact of life outside school on the way in which teachers develop in their professional roles has been documented by Day (2000). Coming from a slightly different slant, Jersild (1995) has emphasised the importance for teachers' successful personal and professional development, of acknowledging and exploring the effects of fear, anxiety, helplessness, meaning and meaninglessness, hostility and loneliness in understanding oneself as a teacher, whatever the sources of these feelings.

In a recent study carried out by the NFER, John Harland suggested that there may be several modes of working as a provider of professional development. These were drawn from a study of the way advisory teachers work with teachers, but the approaches he identifies may be more widely generalisable. He described the following four main modes of working as:

1   *The provisionary mode:* The advisory teacher provides physical resources to support teachers' work in school. This mode can be summarised as 'I'll give you' (Harland, 1990, p.36). As well as having direct practical benefit to teachers, it can give the advisory teacher access to schools, and a starting point for further advisory work with them. However, it has the drawback of implying that the advisory relationship is resource-dependent, which it is not. It also does not address how the resource is used and incorporated into the teachers' repertoire.

2   *The hortative mode:* The advisory teacher communicates verbally, and, less frequently in writing, with teachers, passing on ideas, advice or information, encouraging teachers to apply them in school. This mode can be summarised as 'I'll tell you'. (Harland, 1990, p.36). Harland noted that teachers found this mode most influential through informal conversations rather than formal talks or workshops.

3   *The role-modelling mode:* The advisory teacher demonstrates how a particular area of the curriculum could be taught – often alongside a teacher in their classroom. This mode can be summarised as 'I'll show you'. (Harland, 1990, p.36). Teachers in the Harland study found this

supportive, but particularly if they were freed from their own contribution to the lesson sufficiently to be able to observe the demonstration. One of the drawbacks, though, as Harland points out, is that it can tend to lead to uncritical imitations of the behaviour or teaching style.

4  *The zetetic mode:* The advisory teacher encourages the teacher to critically examine their current practice. This mode can be summarised as 'in order to help you develop your teaching, *I will ask you* what it is you are attempting to achieve, what it is you are doing in your classroom practice, and to what effect' (Harland, 1990, p.37). Harland describes this mode as a 'high-risk strategy', in that the extent to which it was successful in his study was dependent on the personalities involved; as he put it: 'when it works, it can be an inspiring and productive experience for all; when it fails, it can precipitate an aggressive response which leaves the advisory teacher little option but to withdraw from the input altogether'. (Harland, 1990, p.47)

The teachers interviewed in Harland's study described their advisory teachers each using a variety of modes. But it may be that among the factors behind their selections of mode was their own self-concept and stage of growth. If you are a provider, you may find it useful to reflect on Harland's modes; how inclusive do you find them in describing your work?

## PROFESSIONAL DEVELOPMENT AND CAREER HISTORY

We have argued throughout this book that professional development can serve school, team or individual needs and that individual needs can relate to carrying out a job, be it of a more general professional or career nature or to do with personal development. In essence, career concerns can affect professional development in a number of ways. Professional development, say in the form of a course for prospective heads of department or deputy heads, can be thought of as preparing someone for a change of role or as putting them in contention for selection for a new post. It might, for example in the form of job shadowing, be part of a strategy of succession planning undertaken by a school. Alternatively, professional development could take the form of support for those new in post, for example in the shape of an induction programme for new head teachers. It might also have a role to play for those with a number of years' experience in the same post, who feel the need for refreshing their approach. With these general points in mind, it is possible to look at career development in a number of ways. First, career development can be thought of in terms of stages of experience. Second, it can be seen as a series of typical career moves. Third, it can be thought of as a series of typical psychological stages that someone goes through. These ways of looking at career are not necessarily mutually exclusive but can provide helpful insights, when planning professional development. Let us consider each of these three views of career development in turn.

The idea of thinking of a teacher's career in terms of cycles or stages of experience was popularised in the early 1970s by the James Report (James, 1972). Since then it has become common to think of teaching in terms of the three phases of initial training, induction and in-service. Each of these stages can be seen to pose different requirements in terms of teacher development. Day (1991), for example, suggests that teachers have particular needs for professional support to allow them to take stock, gain new perspectives and link theory and practice, at the following points:

1   on entry into teaching (induction phase);
2   on re-entry to teaching after a break (induction phase);
3   preparing for increased responsibility (preparation phase);
4   shortly after assuming increased responsibility (development phase);
5   after a substantial number of years in a similar post (review/audit phase).

You may find it useful to compare the expectations and hopes you have now with those you may have had in the past, in light of changes to linear career opportunities. Indeed, the move toward a more personally directed, multi-faceted and non-linear working life is a pattern of employment across the global economy and not purely characteristic of teaching in the UK. For many professionals, there is a phase of working life sometimes referred to as a 'portfolio career stage', where they work for a range of employers on narrowly defined tasks, which may in themselves be diverse. This is becoming true for teachers as well as workers in other sectors. The changes in working patterns are of course due to a range of factors, and these vary in different sectors of employment and different parts of the world. But the need for flexibility, to have a developing repertoire of transferable skills, and to acknowledge both the likelihood of non-linear career paths and also the necessity of taking responsibility for oneself in responding to career opportunities, is a necessary fact of working life.

Current concerns with defining competences of teaching and learning, as highlighted in Chapter 3, are having an impact on initial training, where there is a shift from the teacher as reflective practitioner approach to more competence based training. Such an approach is also apparent in some of the work being done at the induction stage and the way is open for developing this approach further as a basis for CPD. The argument for the competence approach is sometimes linked to the idea of personal portfolios for teachers, much along the lines of records of achievement for pupils. What remains to be resolved is whether it is possible to develop statements of competence of teaching and learning that can be achieved at a progressively higher level as teachers gain more experience. The alternative is to develop different sets of competence for teachers at each stage of their career.

*How helpful do you find the idea of a career cycle? How would you characterise where you currently are? How could you use this idea to help you to map out and plan professional development, whether for yourself or others?*

A second way of thinking of a teaching career is in terms of a series of possible career moves. It suffers from the drawback of any attempt to map out a typical career: not everyone can or wishes to follow the pattern and as already noted, changing economic circumstances and broader changes in the way education is organised can quickly make such a map appear dated. Indeed, the possibility of a move into LEA (or EA in Scotland) work is no longer a realistic option in an increasing number of LEAs/EAs. This, in turn, creates a situation where previous assumptions about career progression no longer apply. The approach, also, does not necessarily help teachers who do not plan out their career but rather make career moves in response to opportunities as they arise. It is, therefore, offered as a stimulus for thinking rather than a model to be followed uncritically.

Figure 19 is an example from an Open University student who studied the course on which this book is based (Figure 19). She used the career map idea simply to log what happened in her career; this gave her a starting point to consider what she wanted to do next and how to make it happen.

---

### Task 22

Use the career maps as a stimulus for thinking about or discussing with a colleague what your own career cycle or career stage map has looked like, what it might look like in the future, and the professional development you need to help you along your preferred route. Think about whether you want to accept the 'onward and upward' model of career. Perhaps a 'horizontal' route would be equally rewarding.

Consider how best you can create a route which will use your skills and experience as well as being interesting, particularly if you have taken a career break or are a late entrant to teachingTeachers in Scotland will find the career maps in Figures 20 (a) and (b) suggesting career routes for primary and secondary teachers in Scotland, more appropriate.

---

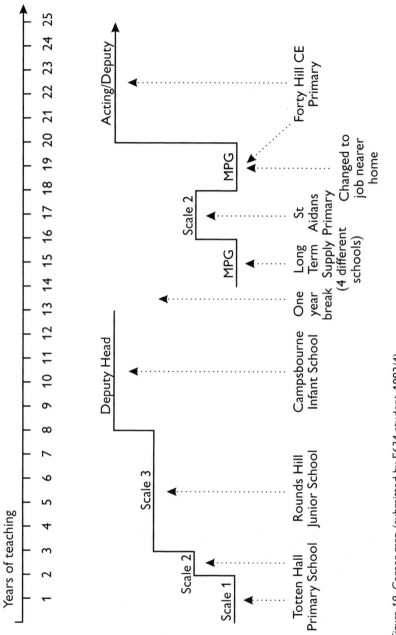

Years of teaching

1 2 3 4 5 6 7 8 9 10 11 12 13 14 15 16 17 18 19 20 21 22 23 24 25

Acting/Deputy

Deputy Head

Scale 3

Scale 2

Scale 1

Totten Hall
Primary School

Rounds Hill
Junior School

Campsbourne
Infant School

One
year
break

MPG

Long
Term
Supply Primary
(4 different
schools)

Scale 2

St
Aidans

MPG

Changed to
job nearer
home

Forty Hill CE
Primary

*Figure 19* Career map (submitted by E634 student, 1993/4)

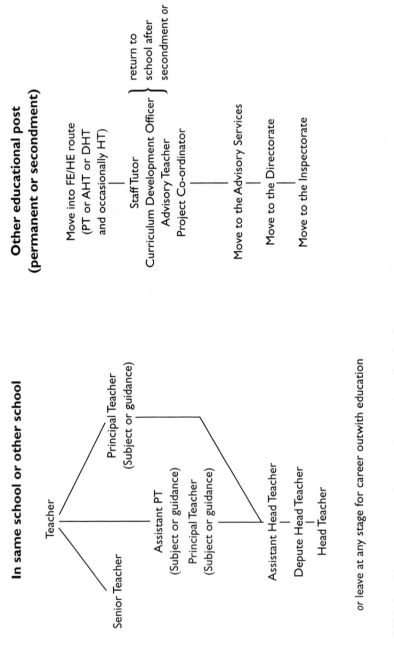

**In same school or other school**

Teacher

Senior Teacher

Principal Teacher
(Subject or guidance)

Assistant PT
(Subject or guidance)

Principal Teacher
(Subject or guidance)

Assistant Head Teacher

Depute Head Teacher

Head Teacher

**Other educational post
(permanent or secondment)**

Move into FE/HE route
(PT or AHT or DHT
and occasionally HT)

Staff Tutor
Curriculum Development Officer
Advisory Teacher
Project Co-ordinator

} return to
school after
secondment or

Move to the Advisory Services

Move to the Directorate

Move to the Inspectorate

*or leave at any stage for career outwith education*

*Figure 20(a)* Possible career routes for secondary teachers (Scotland)
NB This may not represent a national picture, due to changes in local government

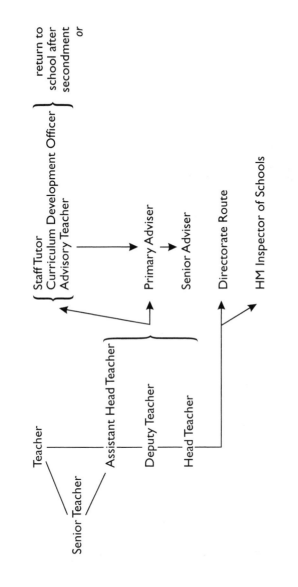

**In same school or other school**

**Other educational post (permanent or secondment)**

Teacher

Senior Teacher

Assistant Head Teacher

Deputy Teacher

Head Teacher

Staff Tutor
Curriculum Development Officer
Advisory Teacher
} return to school after secondment

*or*

Primary Adviser → Senior Adviser

Directorate Route

HM Inspector of Schools

or leave at any stage for career outwith education

*Figure 20(b)*  Possible career routes for primary/nursery teachers (Scotland)

A third way of thinking about a teacher's career to be discussed here is in terms of psychological stages that a teacher goes through. Huberman (1992) attempts to map out possible psychological stages that a teacher can go through. This model works as follows. Basically, on entry to the profession, teachers are likely to be preoccupied with survival and discovery and characterised by initial enthusiasm. There then follows a period of stabilisation, where a teacher decides to remain in teaching and gains in proficiency and competence. This is the time when a teacher becomes socialised into the norms of the profession. The stage of stabilisation can lead into a greater willingness to experiment and extend the professional repertoire and a desire for new challenges. However, there is also the possibility that stabilisation can give way to self-doubt and re-appraisal or that a period of experimentation can lead this way. In other words, there is the possibility of a mid-career crisis of some kind. There can then follow phases of serenity (where people can gradually lose energy but gain in self-confidence and self-acceptance), or conservatism (where people become nostalgic, resistant to change and compare their present situation unfavourably with what existed in the past). Finally, there comes a period of contented or bitter disengagement as other concerns become increasingly important. While this model is to be regarded somewhat tentatively, it does highlight that professional development may have a role in helping teachers to go through successive psychological stages in a smooth and contented way. For example, it could help to provide new challenges for someone who has 'stabilised' in the profession and who, without these challenges, may fall prey to self-doubt.

*How helpful do you find the notion of psychological stages? How far would you accept the stages in the model we have described? What relevance do you feel the model has for you and for your own professional development? Compare your own views, if you can, with those of colleagues.*

## MENTORING

However we characterise career development, the role of mentoring has assumed a central place in induction and staff development over recent years. By this we mean support offered by staff with more experience to staff with less experience, which may range over a great number of activities, or may be more restricted. It is a way of the more experienced passing on knowledge, understanding, abilities and skills, to the less experienced.

Blandford (2000) suggests that teachers (including senior and middle managers) may engage in a range of mentoring relationships, including the mentoring of:

- trainee teachers
- registered teachers
- licensed teachers
- newly qualified teachers joining their teams
- colleagues, in order to support them in new roles.

(Blandford, 2000)

She distinguishes between mentoring roles which have a *vocational focus* (for example, learning about the subject being taught, or ways of thinking about pedagogy, in the case of a newly qualified teacher, or one where the mentee is developing their own goals and implementing them, as in the case of a newly appointed senior or head teacher), and those which have an *interpersonal focus* (for example enabling the mentee to gain insight into how the mentor operates in their professional capacity – here the mentor offers a role modelling and counselling role and also acknowledges successes). She offers a model of shifting mentoring roles over the course of a career and over the course of a professional relationship which begins by involving educating, role modelling, consulting, counselling, networking and gradually moves into becoming a peer and friend, or what we have called in Chapter 6, a 'critical friend'.

The assumption that taking on a mentoring role is a part of the teacher's regular duties, is one which is increasingly prevalent, not just in the UK, as documented by Klette writing about teachers' professional lives in Norway (Klette, 2000). Clearly, the mentor role is a responsible one and as institutions schools have a responsibility to ensure that they too are supported appropriately. At different points in a professional career, a mentoring role will involve different kinds of teaching and learning for the mentor themselves.

## PROFESSIONAL JOURNALS

Over recent years the idea of teachers keeping a record of their own professional and career development has gained in currency. People have spoken variously of professional journals, logs and portfolios and there have been parallels between work on records of achievement for pupils and attempts to find something comparable for teachers. Basically it is about a teacher keeping a record of their own professional development history. This may be a simple, factual, record. On the other hand it is possible to assemble a collection of reflections on teaching, including professional development experiences. It is possible therefore to go for either a record outlining events and activities or aim for a collection of reflections on practice – or a combination.

The more reflective definition is to be found, for example, in Holly (1987), who sees a professional journal as 'a dialogue with oneself, over time' and keeping it as 'a learning process in which you are both the learner and the one who teaches'. The idea depends upon 'reflecting on experiences before or as you write; and then reflecting on the journal entries themselves at some later stage'. Keeping such a journal is a way of undertaking your own professional development by exploring your own action and development as a teacher. Practices such as keeping a journal foster ways of reflecting about professional practice, and can be seen as stemming from the ideas of Schon (1991b) whose work we referred to in Chapter 7. He distinguished in his writing between two forms of reflection: reflection-*on*-action and reflection-*in*-action. Reflection-on-action Schon describes as organised and careful thinking about how you conduct yourself and the decisions you make in your work and is the one which keeping a journal lends itself most readily to. Reflection-*in*-action by contrast refers to the thinking a teacher or practitioner does 'on their feet' whilst doing the job.

In journal keeping, the concept of a personal development plan is sometimes introduced. Such a plan usually sets out an individual's priorities or targets for development, perhaps categorising these according to whether they serve an individual, team or school need. Personal development plans tend to be linked with work on school development planning. In many ways, they appear very similar to appraisal statements but do not have to conform to the constraints of appraisal regulations. In both cases, priorities for development are noted and linked to an action plan for how they are to be achieved. Such plans can become part of a teacher's professional journal.

*You may like to consider how you feel about keeping a professional journal and how far you would like it to be reflective or simply a record of your professional development and future plans. In either case you might also like to consider how far you feel the material you may have produced in working through this book could be the basis of such a journal; indeed the notion of the professional portfolio is a very similar idea and you may well have been developing one alongside your study of the book.*

## Task 23

Review what you wrote in your outline professional development plan in the light of the ideas in this chapter and the linked Appendix 1.

Make any changes you wish to make to your plan, and keep the revised version in your notebook.

---

### Summary of Chapter 11

In this chapter, we have explored a range of personal or biographical dimensions involved in planning professional development and have placed these in the context of technicist models of CPD. We suggested that these latter, whilst holding the capacity to undermine personal dimensions in CPD, may also foster personal stances as 'the other' to policy requirements. The personal/biographical dimensions which we explored were:

- your views about teaching and learning;
- your theory of action;
- the extent of your teaching repertoire;
- your view of professionality;
- the concept of personal growth;
- your professional development and career history and intentions;
- the psychological stage you are at in your career;
- aspects of mentoring which you may be involved in as mentor or mentee at different stages in your career, and
- reflecting on personal dimensions of practice and CPD through the use of a journal or notebook.

# Chapter 12

# Learning individuals, learning schools

In this chapter, we develop our consideration of individual, and professional learning and explore the need to take account of your own preferred learning style, when planning your professional development.

The issue of how teachers learn was raised in Part I of this book. It was suggested that teachers learn:

- as part of their work, for example, by studying their own work and that of other teachers, discussing their work with colleagues, being given a temporary responsibility and getting feedback from pupils,
- by specific provision within their school, for example, by guided reading, seminars, workshops, courses, being part of a working group, being involved in coaching or mentoring and visits to other schools or centres,
- and through external provision, for example through courses, working parties and inter-school discussions including those facilitated by ICT.
                            (Dean, 1985; Bradley, 1989; Blandford, 2000).

Thinking about professional development as encompassing a broad range of planned and naturally occurring opportunities is essential in planning professional development. You will need to reflect on the range of professional development opportunities and think about which are possible for you to undertake and which you find particularly appealing and appropriate as ways of serving your purposes in professional development. If you are responsible for planning the professional development for others, your focus will, ultimately, be a broader one, exploring what opportunities might be available and appropriate and matching these to individual needs. But a good starting point is yourself, and your own professional development.

A number of writers on the psychology of learning provide ideas on the development of criteria for effective learning. Among these writers are Honey and Mumford. They identify four basic learning styles, which are termed activist, reflector, theorist and pragmatist. The idea is that people have a range of preferences for each style of learning, from very low, to very strong. Thus they have preferred or dominant styles of learning but

## Task 24

Reflect on the range of opportunities for professional development and think about which methods you prefer, for your own context – whether your focus is your own professional development or that of others, or both.

Take the list of possibilities above and add to it any other possibilities you can think of. Think about each possibility in terms of:

- how appealing you find it as a learning method
- how appropriate it is to your purposes in professional development
- its availability and practicality.

---

can be encouraged to develop other styles. Honey and Mumford's four basic styles are shown and explained in Figure 21.

### 1 ACTIVISTS

Learn best from opportunities where:

- there are new experiences/problems/opportunities
- they can get engrossed in short 'here and now' activities, e.g. role-playing exercises
- there is excitement/drama/ crisis, and things chop and change with a range of diverse activities to tackle
- they have high visibility (e.g. can chair meetings, lead discussions, give presentations)
- they can generate ideas, without policy or feasibility constraints
- they are thrown in at the deep end with a task they think is difficult
- they work with other people, e.g. in a team
- it is appropriate to 'have a go'.

Learn least from situations where:

- learning involves being passive
- they are asked to stand back and not be involved
- they are required to assimilate, analyse and interpret lots of 'messy' data
- they are required to engage in solitary work by reading, writing, thinking alone
- they are asked to work out beforehand what they will learn, and evaluate it afterward
- there is a lot of repetitive activity (e.g. practising)
- they have precise instructions to follow with little room for manoeuvre
- they have to do a thorough job

### 2 REFLECTORS

Learn best from activities where:

- they are allowed/encouraged to watch/think/chew over activities

Learn least from activities where:

- they are in the limelight

- they can stand back and listen/observe
- they are allowed to think before acting
- they can carry out some painstaking research
- they have the opportunity to review what has happened, or what they have learned
- they are asked to produce carefully considered analyses and reports
- they are helped to exchange views in a structured situation
- they can reach a decision in their own time, without pressure and tight deadlines

- they have to take action without planning
- they have to do something without warning
- they are given insufficient data on which to base a conclusion
- they are given cut and dried instructions of how something should be done
- they are worried by time pressures or rushed from one activity to another
- in the interests of expediency they have to make short cuts or do a superficial job

## 3 THEORISTS

Learn best from activities where:
- what is offered is part of a system, model, concept or theory
- they can explore associations and inter-relationships between ideas, events and situation, methodically
- they have the chance to question and probe the basic assumptions or methodology
- they are intellectually stretched
- they are in structured situations, with a clear purpose
- they can listen or read about ideas and concepts that emphasise rationality or logic
- they can analyse and then generalise
- they are offered interesting ideas and concepts, even if they are not immediately relevant
- they are required to understand and participate in complex situations.

Learn least from activities where:
- they are asked to do something without context or apparent purpose
- they are asked to explore or express feelings or emotions
- activities are unstructured, ambiguous or uncertain (i.e. open-ended)
- they are asked to act without a basis in policy, principle or concept
- they are faced with a mixture of alternative or contradictory techniques or methods, and are not given a chance to explore them in any depth
- they doubt that the subject matter is methodologically sound
- they find the subject matter groundless or shallow
- they feel themselves out of tune with other participants (i.e. when with lots of activists, or people who are less intellectual)

**4 PRAGMATISTS**

Learn best from activities where:
- there is an obvious link between the subject matter and a problem or opportunity on the job
- they are shown practical techniques
- they have a chance to try these out with coaching/feedback from a credible expert (who can do the techniques themselves)
- they are exposed to a role-model they can emulate
- they are given immediate opportunities to implement what they have learned
- they can concentrate on practical issues (e.g. drawing up action plans)

Learn least from activities where:
- the learning is not related to an immediate need they can recognise
- organisers of the learning seem distant from the reality
- there is no clear practice or guidelines on how to do it
- they feel people are not getting anywhere, or going round in circles
- there are political, managerial or personal obstacles to implementation
- there is no apparent reward from the learning activity

*Figure 21* Learning styles

*Source:* Adapted from Honey and Mumford (1986)

Honey and Mumford also point out:

> No single learning style has any overwhelming advantage over any other. They will have their strengths and weaknesses. (Though it is important to be cautious abut labelling strengths and weaknesses since, to some extent it depends on the context within which they are viewed).

> (Honey and Mumford, 1986, p. 40)

They summarise them as follows:

### *Activist*

*Strengths*

Flexible and open minded.
Happy to have a go.
Happy to be exposed to new situations.
Optimistic about anything new and therefore unlikely to resist change.

*Weaknesses*

Tendency to take the immediately obvious action without thinking.
Often take unnecessary risks.

Tendency to do too much themselves and hog the limelight.
Rush into action without sufficient preparation.
Get bored with implementation/consolidation.

### Reflector

*Strengths*

Careful.
Thorough and methodical.
Thoughtful.
Good at listening to others and assimilating information.
Rarely jump to conclusions.

*Weaknesses*

Tendency to hold back from direct participation.
Slow to make up their minds and reach a decision.
Tendency to be too cautious and not take enough risks.
Not assertive – they aren't particularly forthcoming and have no 'small talk'.

### Theorist

*Strengths*

Logical 'vertical' thinkers.
Rational and objective.
Good at asking probing questions.
Disciplined approach.

*Weaknesses*

Restricted in lateral thinking.
Low tolerance for uncertainty, disorder and ambiguity.
Intolerant of anything subjective or intuitive.
Full of 'shoulds, oughts and musts'.

### Pragmatist

*Strengths*

Keen to test things out in practice.
Practical, down to earth, realistic.
Businesslike – gets straight to the point.
Technique-oriented.

*Weaknesses*

Tendency to reject anything without an obvious application.
Not very interested in theory or basic principles.

Tendency to seize on the first expedient solution to a problem.
Impatient with waffle.
On balance, task-oriented not people-oriented.

*You may find it useful to complete the learning styles self-assessment in Chapter 2 of Honey and Mumford's book entitled* A Manual of Learning Styles *(full details in reference section of this book).*

There is, of course, a danger in this approach that if someone decides they belong to a particular category, they will regard this as fixed and permanent. It could indeed be argued that a major purpose of professional development ought to be to enable teachers to teach and learn in a progressively greater variety of ways. Nevertheless, it could be useful to be aware of your present learning preferences. The descriptions of learning styles put forward by psychologists, such as Honey and Mumford, provide yet another lens through which to view the planning of your professional development. They enable you to look for a match between your preferred learning style(s) and the professional development that you undertake. This is not to say that you should go for an exact match and only consider professional development, which *only* consists of methods that fit your preferred style. It is, however, to point out that too much of a mismatch may lead you to feel dissatisfied with the professional development that you undertake.

It is perhaps also worth referring again at this point to the ideas on effective professional development of Joyce and Showers (1980) which we considered in Chapter 3. You will recall that in their model of professional development there are a number of possible components:

- presentation of theory/description of skill or strategy;
- modelling or demonstration;
- practice in simulated or classroom settings;
- structured and open-ended feedback;
- coaching for application.

Their argument is that an effective professional development opportunity is likely to consist of a mixture of these components. They also suggest that changes in skill depend upon going beyond presenting information and demonstration to practice, feedback and coaching. It is useful to set these ideas alongside individual learning preferences in order to develop a fuller picture.

## Task 25

Review your outline professional development plan in the light of the ideas in this section on professional learning. Look carefully at the type of professional development that you are planning and think about how well each element matches your learning preferences. Make any appropriate changes to your plan.

---

In the next section we move away from the individual aspects of professional development and consider its institutional context. We look at the context created by school and team needs and also raise wider questions about the impact and value of professional development.

## THE INSTITUTIONAL CONTEXT FOR PROFESSIONAL DEVELOPMENT

This section is concerned with the broader context for professional development and reviews the organisational setting and implications of professional development. It also returns to the question of the impact of professional development. It is designed to help you consider how far your own professional development plan relates to the need of your school and of the department(s) or team(s) of which you are a member.

As has been noted previously, it is possible to think of professional development as serving the needs of a school, department, team or an individual and of individual professional development needs as varying in terms of how far they relate to school department or team priorities. It has been argued that 'teacher development and school development must go hand in hand. In general, you cannot have one without the other', (Watson and Fullan, 1992). It has also been suggested that, whereas in the past there has often been a preoccupation with helping both individuals and schools handle individual changes, there is now an increasing need to 'deal with second-order changes – changes that affect the culture and structure of schools, restructuring roles and reorganising responsibilities, including those of students and parents' (Fullan, 1992). As discussed in Part I of the book, this is now a policy requirement on schools in England and Wales, fed through a number of statutory initiatives for CPD. As discussed in Chapter 4, the challenge is to create a culture in a school, which empowers individuals to learn and develop and enables the school to respond to change effectively. At the root of these issues is the need to harmonise and balance the professional development needs of schools, teams and individuals and to ensure that the needs of each are prioritised and provided for as far as practicable.

This section reviews these issues from a number of perspectives to help you look at the way your outline professional development takes account of school and department or team aims, priorities and development alongside your own individual needs. It deals with:

- school development planning
- staff development and appraisal
- school effectiveness and school improvement
- school culture
- the impact of professional development on school, or department/team.

## School development planning

The organisational context for individual professional development can be made clearer by the presence of a school or department/team development plan. Such a plan usually sets out aims and priorities for action within the context of the values of a school or department/team. To be effective, plans for action needs to be linked to resource and training needs and individual responsibilities. As noted in Chapter 3, development planning is often seen as consisting of a number of stages:

- audit i.e. a review of strengths and weaknesses
- construction i.e. identifying priorities for development and turning these into specific targets
- implementation i.e. carrying out the plan
- evaluation i.e. checking the success of the plan.

Usually, the plan is split into a long-term (three-year) strategic plan and a short-term (one-year) development plan. Development planning of this type increased in popularity over recent years and has been seen as a way of handling change by identifying priorities and assessing the value of particular changes to the aims of an organisation. The success of the planning process is seen as depending upon rooting the plan in a clear vision of what the school or department/team is about. Hargreaves and Hopkins (1991) would argue that development plans provide a context for the professional development of teachers by clearly setting out what staff development is needed to enable school aims to be realised.

They argued, at the start of the 1990s, that 'the growth in school-focused and school-based staff development, the existence of professional training days, and the experience of appraisal schemes are beginning to lead to better policy and practice for staff development.' They suggested that development planning built upon this trend as follows:

- The plan focuses on the school's needs and the professional development required to meet these needs.
- Appraisal schemes provide links between individual needs and those of the school as a whole.
- Every teacher is seen to have rights to professional development so there is a more equitable distribution of opportunities for CPD.
- Since professional development is directed to the support of teachers working on agreed topics (the targets and tasks), the knowledge and skills acquired through CPD are put to immediate use in the interest of the school.
- Staff who undertake CPD have a framework for disseminating their new knowledge and skill.
- There is improvement in the design and use of professional training days.
- Information on external provision is collated and checked for relevance to the school's needs.
- School-based CPD and external forms of provision are used to complement one another.
- Staff development is included in the school's budget.

(adapted from Hopkins and Hargreaves, 1991).

They see development planning as a means of developing the culture of a school so that, among other things, the school becomes better at responding to change; a view which we developed in some detail in Part I of this book and which underpins the school improvement movement.

The danger, of course, in this approach is that individual development needs can be squeezed out if individuals have no ownership of the development plan. Institutional needs and individual needs have to be carefully balanced. In reality, the construction of an institution and development plan is not a purely rational process; in other words, to be most effective it needs to involve at least some communication, and even consultation or collaboration, acknowledging individuals' roles within the organisation.

---

## Task 26

If you can, look at the current copies of your school and department/team development plans. Take a look at these and think about the extent to which your own plans for professional development tie in with what is there. Are there any school department or team priorities for which you feel you may need professional development but which you have overlooked? Write your ideas in your notebook.

## Appraisal/teacher review

Appraisal can be used to foster school, department/team and individual needs. Above all, it provides a means of harmonising these needs and of sorting out priorities. Furthermore, it provides an opportunity for individual needs to be placed on the agenda alongside the school needs set out in a school development plan.

Appraisal has been presented in this book as potentially a positive and developmental process, which places professional development on the agenda of all teachers, even in the context of an increasingly accountability-based model. It can provide opportunities for professional development in its own right, by encouraging reflection and enabling teachers to work collaboratively and learn from each other. It can be used to identify

---

## Task 27

Consider whether the above comments match your own experience of appraisal/review. You may find it helpful to think about what has come out in your appraisal process, as appraiser or appraisee, and to consider how far this is reflected in your outline professional development plan. Write your ideas in your notebook.

---

and prioritise future professional development requirements. It can also be used to evaluate professional development and to consider how effective this has been. Appraisal is potentially well-placed to identify and ensure provision of professional development that is closely integrated into practice. (A fuller discussion of appraisal/teacher review was provided in Chapter 2 and you are advised to refer to that if you wish to think more fully about the implications of appraisal at this point.)

## School effectiveness and school improvement

As discussed in Chapter 4, over the past decade or so, there have arisen two complementary movements – the school effectiveness and the school improvement movements. The school effectiveness movement has been concerned with identifying characteristics of effective schools. The school improvement movement has been more concerned with the processes that enable schools to achieve their goals better and respond to change. Put rather crudely, school effectiveness research tries to show what an effective school looks like, while school improvement studies tend to focus on how it becomes that way.

As noted in Chapter 4, the different school effectiveness studies are not totally consistent, varying in the emphasis they place on particular factors and on the factors they include. Reynolds and Cuttance (1992), Sammons, Hillman and Mortimore (1995) and Sammons (1999) provide useful summaries of this body of research and highlight the shortcomings of the movement. In particular, school effectiveness research is relatively light in terms of longitudinal studies (i.e. studies over time) and secondary school studies and is sometimes fairly narrow in terms of what is held to be evidence of effectiveness.

With these cautions in mind you may find it helpful to look back at the characteristics of effective schools identified by the major British studies, given in Chapter 4. They can be read in conjunction with the following characteristics, identified by Fullan (1985), which highlight some of the cultural features of an effective school and the summary of effectiveness factors which follows it, produced by Sammons, Hillman and Mortimore (1995) for OFSTED.

## Process factors making for effective schools

1   *A feel for the process of leadership*: this is difficult to characterise because the complexity of factors involved tends to deny rational planning – a useful analogy would be that organisations are to be sailed rather than driven.
2   *A guiding value system*: this refers to a consensus on high expectations, explicit goals, clear rules, a genuine caring about individuals etc.
3   *Intense interaction and communication*: this refers to simultaneous support and pressure at both horizontal and vertical levels within the school;
4   *Collaborative planning and implementation*: this needs to occur both within the school and externally, particularly in the LEA (or EA).

(Fullan, 1985)

### Eleven key characteristics of effective schools

1   Professional, participative firm leadership by 'leading professionals'
2   Shared goals and vision
3   An orderly and attractive working environment
4   Concentration on learning and teaching, focusing on achievement in academic areas
5   Purposeful, efficient and organised teaching
6   High expectations and intellectual challenge, clearly communicated to learners

7   Positive reinforcement including fair and clear discipline
8   Monitoring of pupil and school progress
9   Pupil rights and responsibilities developed through focus on esteem and involvement
10  Home–school partnership in learning
11  School as a learning organisation (i.e. involving school-based staff development).

(adapted from Sammons, Hillman and Mortimore, 1995)

Together, these lists with those in Chapter 4 provide an agenda of issues to be addressed through professional development, which has a school focus. In particular, they are relevant to management development. They also suggest processes for school management, such as collaborative planning and implementation, which, if adopted, can, in themselves, provide powerful strategies for professional development.

*How far do the factors identifed by Reynolds, Rutter, Mortimore, Creemers, Scheerens, Fullan and Sammons et al., reflect your own experience?*

*You may like to contrast these with the characteristics of a good school, identified in* Choice and Diversity *(Secretaries of State for Education in England and Wales, 1992):*

- *parental involvement,*
- *freedom from excessive external control and regulation, leaving more power in the hands of the individual school to plan its own priorities within national guidelines, and*
- *teachers of high quality under the strong leadership of the head teacher.*

The issue for this book is how far professional development can contribute to the various characteristics of an effective school. In particular, professional development might address teaching issues or 'process' issues. In this context, a school might aim to:

1   treat the teacher as a whole person;
2   establish a school culture based on norms of technical collaboration and professional inquiry;
3   carefully diagnose the starting points for teacher development;
4   recast routine administrative activities into powerful teacher development strategies.                                   (Leithwood, 1992)

This last quotation takes us into the territory of school improvement. As discussed in Chapter 4, the school improvement movement has been concerned with process issues of this type and has focused on how schools can better achieve their aims and better respond to change. The movement has been concerned with developing ways of strengthening the organisational and problem-solving capacity of schools. It has focused on areas such as school-based review, organisational development, school development planning and the nature of educational change. For the purposes of this course, the essential point is that school improvement strategies can provide opportunities for professional development as well as helping to develop a culture conducive to professional development. For example, staff working collaboratively to review an aspect of a school's practice in order to identify areas for change and development are engaged in a form of professional development as well as in the process of school development planning. Our contention is that professional learning is part of professional development, for the individual and for the school, a view espoused by many researchers in the field as discussed in Chapter 4 (Blandford, 2000; MacGilchrist *et al.*, 1997). It is a view which is now built into government policy for identifying, funding, monitoring and accounting for (including inspecting the outcomes of) CPD, as documented by Blandford (2000). Thus a 'learning' organisation is one which is changing and developing. There is an assumption built in to the view that a developing school is more likely to be effective – since it is more likely to be responsive to change. You may not agree with this view, since of course the extent to which a school is 'effective' will depend on the criteria by which it is judged.

## School culture – building a learning organisation

The culture of a school can both influence and be influenced by the professional development of individual teachers. There are several different ways of describing the kinds of culture found in organisations; for example, Charles Handy has written about a wider range of (mainly business) organisations; Jenny Nias has written about 'collegiate culture' in primary schools. The set of categories we are going to look at here are those put forward by Harrison (1987), quoted in Aspinwall *et al.* (1992). He suggests that there are four dominant cultures to be found in organisations. Normally schools exhibit a mixture of these but one culture may well be predominant. The four cultures are:

- power culture (where decisions and direction depend on senior staff)
- role culture (where there are clearly defined roles and lines of responsibility)
- task culture (where flexible teams are set up to deal with issues) and
- support culture (where emphasis is on caring for people).

Aspinwall *et al.* (1992) describe these as follows and illustrate their impact on evaluation:

In the *power culture*, evaluation processes are primarily concerned with control... Information is likely to be collected informally, especially from individuals whom the senior manager trusts, and evaluated personally by senior staff. This approach is designed to ensure that the leader's vision for the organisation is being interpreted and undertaken appropriately...

In the *role culture*, in contrast, evaluation processes are undertaken in ways that fit the notion of administrative necessity. They are likely to be systematised with clear lines of responsibility and well-defined reporting procedures ... Evaluation responsibilities will be clearly defined in relation to the organisational hierarchy ...

In a *task culture*, the emphasis is on using evaluation activities for problem-solving ... Responsibilities for evaluation are likely to be shared and shifting, being based more on expertise than on formal authority ...

In a *support culture*, people are encouraged to like and support each other ... Competence in this sort of organisation is defined in terms of the ability to give and receive care and support. In such a school or college, evaluation would be undertaken in counselling mode in a supportive environment ... Processes of evaluation would be facilitative and would be person-centred ...

The quotation stresses the impact of culture on evaluation and this may be of interest to you in the light of the discussions of evaluation in Part II of the book. Similar points can, however, be made about the impact of culture on other activities, including professional development, again subject to the proviso that cultures can co-exist in the same school.

Aspinwall *et al.* (1992) are doubtful of the value of power culture but argue that role, task and support cultures have certain strengths:

The task culture has considerable strengths in terms of ability to cope flexibly with changing demands and to make good use of organisational expertise. There is a good deal of evidence that many teachers, given the choice, prefer it (Handy and Aitken, 1986). On the other hand, it can lead to problems in relation to the more routine, mundane aspects of work. The strengths and weaknesses of the role culture, in contrast, are the opposite of these. It has a tendency to encourage rigidity and stifle imagination; but it does ensure that roles are clearly demarcated and understood and that the procedures are in place to enable routine activities to be carried out efficiently. The support culture is consonant with much current management literature that stresses the development of shared values: it can perhaps be seen as the 'people' side of the task culture.

A feature of any organisation today – including schools and colleges –

is a move towards decentralisation and hence a decline of the power and role cultures and a rise in the task and support cultures. If an organisation is to learn, the total learning that occurs in it must somehow add up to more than the sum of the learning by the individuals involved.

This point is closely aligned to a key point made in this course that professional development can be seen as part and parcel of helping schools to become learning organisations. In particular, collaboration on both day-to-day activities and on professional development can help transform the culture of a school and facilitate learning at all levels.

## The impact of professional development on a school or department/team:

Whether or not it is reasonable to expect some impact of a particular professional development activity on a school as well as on the individual concerned will depend on the purposes of the activity. If the activity undertaken can reasonably be expected to have an impact within the school, then there are various strategies that can be used to maximise this effect. In particular, attention might be given to:

- encouraging teachers to present a written or verbal report about their professional development to the staff development committee or the CPD co-ordinator;
- enabling a teacher to run a school-based in-service activity to disseminate what has been learned;
- setting up classroom observation or some other feedback mechanism specifically to help someone analyse the impact of a piece of professional development on their own practice;
- building review and evaluating processes into the cycle of school development planning;
- setting up a network of teachers to build on and implement what has been learnt; this might include exploring the options offered by ICT.

It need hardly be said that in the past, schools have often failed to make use of the professional development of their staff. This state of affairs can both impoverish schools and frustrate teachers, who feel they have something to offer. By contrast, each of these strategies enables a school to harness the professional development of its staff and also provides a further opportunity for professional development.

*What opportunities are available within your own school to enable people to disseminate their experiences of professional development?*

## Summary of Chapter 12

This chapter has been concerned with individual teachers' learning, and then with the context in which teachers develop, i.e. the school.

We began by highlighting the issue of how teachers learn and to suggest that teachers can have a range of preferred approaches to learning. In particular, it was suggested that you think about your professional development plans in terms of:

- the types of opportunity commonly available for professional development (as part of your work, through participating in opportunities specifically provided by your school or through taking part in externally provided events),
- your preferred learning style(s),
- your purposes in professional development.

In considering the institutional context for professional learning, we suggested:

- school and department/team planning together with wider policy requirements, provide the context for individual professional development;
- teacher appraisal/review can provide opportunities for professional development and be used to harmonise and prioritise school, department/team and individual professional development needs for individual teachers;
- the ideas to be found in the school effectiveness and the school improvement research provide areas to be addressed in professional development and can help develop a rationale for professional development;
- strategies can be developed within the culture of a school to provide increased opportunities for professional development and to ensure that, where appropriate, the outcomes of professional development are disseminated – thus creating and fostering the school as a 'learning organisation'.

# Chapter 13

# Megatrends in CPD

In this book, we have been exploring professional development as we move into the first years of the twenty-first century.

By way of a conclusion, we should like to present two contrasting perspectives on professional development. The first is an extract from the 1972 James Report and takes the form of a series of recommendations for in-service training made twenty years ago, which are still of interest today. The second is a list of megatrends in education and provides a reference point with which to evaluate some of the changes in CPD which are currently in process. First, then, the James Report.

> The third cycle covers the very wide range of activities which serving teachers should undertake at intervals throughout their working lives, to continue their personal education and extend their professional competence. In no area covered by this Inquiry has criticism of present arrangements been more out-spoken or more general. In no area do the proposals of this report deserve greater emphasis. The proposals for the third cycle are clear: all teachers should be entitled to release with pay for in-service education and training on a scale not less than the equivalent of one term in every seven years and, as soon as possible, on a scale of one term in five years. This entitlement would be satisfied only by release for designated full-time courses lasting at least four weeks, or their approved part-time equivalents, and would be in addition to any shorter term third cycle activities in which teachers took part, whether or not these involved release from school. There should also be a considerable expansion of these shorter-term opportunities. To commit energies and resources to a development of the third cycle along the lines envisaged here would be the quickest, most effective and most economical way of improving the quality of education in the schools and colleges and of raising the standards, morale and status of the teaching profession. For third cycle activities on the scale proposed it would be essential to set up appropriate machinery to identify needs and to co-ordinate arrangements to meet them.

This book has been based on a similar belief in the importance of professional development for serving teachers. Yet, thirty-odd years on from the James Report, the climate has changed. The prospect of regular secondments seems increasingly distant and the notion of professional development as involving a greater proportion of on-the-job competence-related training has come closer and become far more of a reality. We have put forward in this book a broad view of what constitutes professional development and have argued for a balance to be struck between using professional development to serve 'national', school, department/team and individual needs. And we have suggested, as does Hargreaves (1994), that, given the continuous context of change, the continuing professional development of teachers must reflect, respond to and help support change and restructuring.

As documented in Part I of this book, some significant changes have taken place in some parts of the UK during the 1990s, changing the focus and place of CPD as part of a teacher's professional responsibilities. These include an increasing policy/government involvement in defining national standards such as those for subject leaders, special educational needs co-ordinators, aspiring and serving head teachers (although this is softer in Scotland where Education Authorities still have much greater influence). The introduction of the National College for School Leadership seems likely to feed into and support such initiatives and thus potentially to close some avenues for CPD whilst holding others open. For not only are certain types of activities, leading to certain types of outcome, likely to be funded when others are not, there is a level of compulsion involved in some, as discussed in Chapter 1. The introduction in England of national bodies such as the National College for School Leadership seems likely too to herald a move toward attempts at national definitions of what to prioritise in education and thus in CPD.

It is possible that the introduction of the General Teaching Council for England will soften some of the impact of these changes, in that its role will involve mediating between the profession and the government. However, it remains to be seen whether it will be able to rise to that considerable challenge given the apparently inexorable tendency toward powerful centralisation and policy-defined practice. Such centralisation, combined with performance-related pay for teachers and head teachers operated at school level, mediated by an increasingly accountability-driven model of appraisal, and subject to a national inspection system, seems likely to have a major influence on the scope, nature and type of CPD undertaken by teachers in the future.

Other major shifts have included the increasing role of ICT in teachers' professional development (and, indeed, the potential roles which ICT may increasingly play in pupils' learning, thus shifting the teacher's role). This seems likely to have a fast-moving impact on teachers' CPD also.

## Task 28

Read the following extract, which is based on a list of 'megatrends' in education which was written by Naisbitt and Aburdene (1990). Prior to some of the changes discussed above, they provided a wide agenda for both those providing and those undertaking professional development of all types, suggesting the idea of lifelong learning and re-learning; a value implicit in this book (and also in many policy statements written after their ideas were published).

- How does this agenda for professional development compare with your own experience of recent policy development? Note down any observations you may have on this point.
- How does this agenda for professional development compare with your own experience practice? Make some notes on the ways these trends are played out in your professional practice.
- What other megatrends do you see exemplified in your work, if any? Write your own megatrends down.
- What are the implications of these megatrends for you and/or your institution's professional development needs? Make a list of needs as you see them in relation to your list of megatrends.

### MEGATRENDS IN EDUCATION

1 Formulating goals, deciding on goals and priorities, and creating accountability frameworks will increasingly become the role of *central authorities*.
2 These will be informed by *national and global considerations*, especially in respect to curriculum. The education system will need, increasingly, to be responsive to national needs within a global economy.
3 State funded schools will become *largely self-managing*, within a national framework of accountability. Distinctions between these and privately-funded schools will narrow.
4 *Concern* for the provision of a *quality* education for each individual will reach unprecedented levels.
5 Telecommunications and computer technology will contribute to the *dispersion of the educative function*. Much learning which currently

occurs in schools or institutions at post-compulsory levels will occur at home and in the workplace.

6 The *basics in education will be re-formulated and expanded* to include problem-solving, creativity and a capacity for lifelong learning and re-learning.

7 *The arts and spirituality,* defined broadly in each instance, will have a significantly expanded role to play in educating; there will be a high level of 'connectedness' in curriculum.

8 *There will be many more women leaders* in education, including the most senior levels.

9 The *parent and community role* in education will be claimed or reclaimed.

10 *Those who support the work of schools (whether voluntarily or as part of their job) will be subject to deep concern for quality of service.*

(Naisbitt and Aburdene, 1990)

# Appendix: The gender debate in professional development

This appendix is based on two contrasting sets of views put forward by prominent figures in the field of teacher professional development. The first, by Jocye and Showers (1988) has in many ways been considered to be among the 'received wisdom' in professional learning for over a decade. Recently, however, Robertson (1992) has challenged a part of the model which they put forward as being masculine and insufficiently recognising the lifestyles and aspirations of many women. The part of the Joyce and Showers model which we examine here is the discussion on personal growth within an organisation.

The piece presents the two sides of the discussion, as food for thought for all teachers and schools who are learning and developing.

## THE JOYCE AND SHOWERS THESIS

Expounded in Chapter 10 of their book *Student Achievement Through Staff Development*, Joyce and Showers describe a theory of teacher growth based on a study of teachers' professional and personal lives (Joyce, Bush and McKibbin, 1981, 1982, 1984). The study involved was large-scale and longitudinal, looking at staff development and school improvement practices in California, aiming to learn about opportunities for growth for individuals within the institutional context of the school and its associated support agencies. They worked with both elementary and secondary teachers.

They started with the assumption that in any given school, there would be equal opportunity to participate in staff development activity. Thus inequality of uptake would demonstrate differences inherent in the individual staff in their 'disposition to interact productively with the environment', as they put it.

They studied levels of activity in formal, peer-generated and personal domains of learning for each participant in the research, discovering that the levels of activity correlated across the domains. In other words, those more active in the personal domain were also more active in the professional domain.

They came up with an explanation which turned on both the propensity of the individual to interact with the environment in which they were placed, as offering potential for learning and growth and also the social influence surrounding each individual. To take the environmental part of the theory first. According to their interpretation, 'high activity' meant greater tendency to see the environment as offering potentially rich learning experiences; 'low activity' meant less awareness of potential, even greater amounts of indifference to the possibilities offered by the environment. Joyce and Showers hypothesised that those people who were active also attracted more and more opportunities to themselves, as they became known as being interested and actively developing in a range of local networks and were approached regularly to trial a new variety of approaches to teaching and learning and generally to get involved in new initiatives.

Turning next to the social influence element of the theory, Joyce and Showers suggested that the social context at work and at home moderates teachers' dispositions toward opportunities for growth and learning. Thus, encouraging and active colleagues and friend support teachers in being more active than if left to their own devices. They argued that without a high level of activity within a workplace, organisational growth would be slowed.

Set against this context, Joyce and Showers suggested that over time, individuals develop a particular pattern of response and attitude toward personal learning and growth, and that there are essentially three 'types'. These they described as:

*Gourmet omnivores*   People who have learned to scan and exploit their environment successfully. They refer to 'gourmet omnivores' as 'mature'. They are the 'movers and shakers'; they initiate new schemes and find ways of influencing policy, bringing a positive and active approach to initiatives brought by others. They seek similar-minded teachers to work and learn with. They characterise the 'gourmet omnivore' style as highly active, in the personal and the work context; and also as highly persistent. Joyce and Showers comment that they are 'more likely than others to bring the ideas they gain in their personal lives into the workplace and use them in their teaching.' They described approximately 20 percent of their sample as fitting this category, although only half of this group were very active.

*Passive consumer*   People who demonstrate conformity to and dependence on the environment, so that their level of activity depended on whose company they were in; this pattern extended into the home and personal life. The teachers in this group did not object to growth and development, but simply took a much more passive attitude toward it than those in the 'gourmet omnivore' group. The 'passive consumer' attitude also affected, as one would expect, the follow-up to professional development, so that 'passive consumers' did not as a matter of course integrate professional development experiences into their working and personal lives. Joyce and Showers claimed approximately 70 per cent of their sample matched this category.

*Reticent consumers*    People who actually go out of their way to avoid growth and development, or as Joyce and Showers put it, 'expend energy actually pushing away opportunities for growth' – in both professional and personal contexts. The teachers in this group resented being asked or required to participate in professional development, engaged at the minimal acceptable level, and tried to avoid following up professional learning. The reticent consumer described by Joyce and Showers had a suspicious and conspiracy-theory attitude to those in authority, as well as sneering with cynicism at peers adopting a 'gourmet-ominivore' approach, believing them to be naïve. Joyce and Showers claimed approximately 10 per cent of their sample matched this category.

As discussed in Chapter 11 of this book, Joyce and Showers relate these 'types' to conceptual development and self-concept, drawing on systems theory (Harvey, Hunt and Schroeber, 1961) and also self-concept theory (Maslow, 1962). They see 'gourmet omnivores' as having the most sophisticated and complex conceptual development. They also see gourmet omnivores as having 'strong self-concepts .. accompanied by self-actualising behaviour, a reaching out toward the environment with confidence that the interaction will be productive.' At the other end of the continuum, they see reticent consumers as having less well-developed conceptual frameworks and relatively weak self-concepts and feeling unsure of their surroundings and of their ability to cope.

    Joyce and Showers begin to tease out some of the implications of these ideas for teacher development, stressing the need to consider carefully the degree of support, interaction, encouragement and energy that will be needed to develop people at different stages of development. They emphasise this from the point of view both of engaging and supporting the individual, but also from the stance of the collective, the organisation.

## THE CRITIQUE BY ROBERTSON

Published in a recent book entitled *Understanding Teacher Development*, edited by Hargreaves and Fullan (1992), Robertson offers a feminist analysis and critique of the Joyce and Showers model described above, in a paper entitled 'Teacher Development and Gender Equity'.

Robertson claims that education systems, including those which support teacher professional development, are operated on male-orientated systems, set up from a male point of view. Two things follow, she argues, from this. First, this requires all who are in the system as teachers or learners, to explicitly value male values and characteristics, including competitiveness, certitude, hierarchical power, heavy reliance on rationality, the valuing of conflict and dominance, and a tendency to rely over-heavily on quantifiable and objective information rather than what is valued and subjective. Second, it means a denial of other realities, and the propagation of the masculine stance as universal, under the apparent guise of 'gender neutrality'.

The masculine values and characteristics described above (which reflect work done by other feminist researchers such as Carol Gilligan,1982, 1986, 1988) pervade, argues Robertson, staff development as well as all aspects of the system which supports teaching and learning with school pupils. Indeed, she notes that recent attempts to reform education in the USA involve trying to make the profession more 'competitive, cerebral, efficient and focused on instrumentalism' – masculine values. Her point is that reforms, school practice and also approaches to staff development appear to be 'gender neutral', when in fact they are not.

So, how is Joyce and Showers' model not gender neutral?

Robertson analyses their approach by looking at a number of themes: the purposes of professional development, the nature of teachers as learners and as teachers, appropriate knowledge in professional development, the requirements of leadership, the choice of targets, and processes considered to be appropriate for professional development, as follows.

## Purposes of professional development

Robertson notes that Joyce and Showers use a competitive framework as justification for professional development; in other words the reasons for developing professionally are couched in terms of teachers' roles in supporting pupils in entering a competitive market. In Robertson's view, this presents a view of the world as having 'winners and losers' where 'even the classroom is a playing field in which competition is to be the core value and activity for teachers as well as students'. She also notes their certitude in tone, implying, she argues, that if we simply follow their models of teacher types, and formulae for planning and delivering professional development, we will achieve predictable results with teachers and pupils. Both the value given to competition and the tone of certitude are, she argues, masculine and not gender neutral.

## Nature of teachers as learners and as teachers

Robertson's response to Joyce and Showers' typology of teachers as learners as outlined above is to question the notion that varying levels of activity are outcomes of personal disposition. She asks why individual or collective circumstance are not posited as potential sources of the different attitudes embodied by the three 'types' which they describe. She points out that by characterising the 'gourmet omnivores' as the most successful at personal and professional development through their high level of activity and positive attitude to development and growth, they ignore issues which may be gender related. These include unequal distribution of family and domestic responsibilities, familiarity with being assertive, unequal distribution of power and the systemic tendency to recognise only the skills and abilities in both genders which will continue to propagate the masculine model as described under 'purposes of professional development'. Drawing on a feminist literature (Heilman and Kram; 1983, Sadker and Sadker, 1986), she provides evidence to suggest that for the 'reticent consumer' type of teacher, reluctance to engage with professional development might in fact be a response to unsupportive environmental factors, including an increasingly male-dominated culture, including the culture of discourse (from the 'not being able to get a word in' syndrome to the kinds of 'not being heard' which Deborah Tannen, 1995, has recently documented).

In particular Robertson suggests that Joyce and Showers may be guilty of the widespread societal attitude toward the multiple roles which women continue to bear – despite women entering the paid work force in increasing numbers, it continues to be the women who undertake the majority of work in the home, including the increasing burden of caring for ageing parents. She suggests that rather than 'inactivity', those teachers whom they label 'reticent consumer' might in fact demonstrate reluctance to undertake additional development because it cuts across other onerous commitments which require great activity on their part.

She challenges Joyce and Showers' recommendation that the teaching profession needs more 'gourmet omnivores', because this 'type' is based on a model of career which excludes home/personal values and responsibilities, and in effect excludes many women. She suggests that it is particularly inappropriate for a human resource model supposedly grounded in interpersonal influence and engagement, time management and leisure pursuits, to ignore such huge 'culturally-induced differences'. And in creating this model, the masculine model of interpreting social experience is reinforced as the universal reality; and its certitude contributes, she suggests, to the suppression of other perceptions or models of understanding teachers as learners and teachers.

## Appropriate knowledge in professional development

Underpinning Joyce and Showers' model of professional learning is, Robertson notes, a view that expert knowledge provides the source of leadership in motivating change in teacher behaviour. As a result there is an assumption of 'expert-dependency' in their model of teacher learning. This, Robertson suggests, demonstrates a deeply patronising and dismissive attitude toward teachers, the majority of whom are women.

The pivotal role of expert and validated knowledge is also a masculine approach to knowledge itself, which is at odds with personal and subjective knowledge which Robertson suggests (drawing on Gilligan's work (1982) on women's 'voice') is more typically female. Furthermore, she cites many instances where research studies concerned with the creation of knowledge itself ignore women's perspective and experience, by generalising from all-male samples! Carol Gilligan's own work, on moral reasoning, is built on earlier work by Kohlberg, carried out with all-male samples. The Kohlberg framework of moral reasoning, when replicated with women, appeared to demonstrate that women rarely attained the higher levels of moral reasoning. What Gilligan's research has now suggested is that women and men have different ethical frameworks. Whereas for men the ethic of rights tends to be central, for women it tends to be an ethic of care based in responsibility to others. What her research demonstrates is not that women are inferior at moral reasoning to men, but that they use a different moral system in solving moral dilemmas.

The absence or ignoring of women's experience in creating models of behaviour means that the knowledge which is produced is 'objectified' and at worst, Robertson says, women's realities are ignored. Thus, expert knowledge creates a contradiction for women, which means that some women silence their own subjective, intuitive knowledge, and others simply cannot access the masculine model of knowledge. The knowledge of women is, Robertson suggests, 'connectivist', and involves multiple ways of knowing. It involves avoidance of certitude and values tentativeness and uncertainty.

What Joyce and Showers do is to reject this, by creating a dichotomy between 'professional' knowledge, which is objective, shared and examined, and other knowledge, which 'feels right' and which is based on custom and intuition. Robertson claims that the position they adopt undermines the art of teaching which puts the relationship with the pupil at the centre of teaching and learning, rather than the 'teaching role'.

## Requirements of leadership

The model of leadership which Joyce and Showers put forward is uncritically hierarchical. More importantly, Robertson argues, many of the characteristics of 'effective leadership' put forward by Joyce and Showers, such as orientation toward people, willingness to negotiate solutions, collegiality, capacity to take risks, etc., are all feminine ones, and yet the majority of people in leadership positions in the teaching profession are male. So questions arise of how to enable men to be effective in a style which is characteristically female. Questions might also be asked of why more women are not in those roles. Neither question is addressed by Joyce and Showers.

## Choosing targets for personal growth

Robertson notes that pupils' access to curricula and learning can be affected by many factors, including gender. She expresses surprise that in discussing the setting of observable targets for professional development, Joyce and Showers do not acknowledge the impact of unequal access on how the 'effects' of professional learning might be measured. Indeed she queries why they do not recommend the prioritising of gender discrimination in curricula and assessment as an area for professional learning and growth.

## The processes of professional development

The Joyce and Showers model rests on the principles that first, transfer of new knowledge and skills back to the classroom is possible through practice, feedback and coaching. Second, participation of all staff in ongoing study groups of twos, threes and larger groupings is important for collegial feedback on learning – and they recommend ongoing peer-coaching.

Robertson suggests that the assumptions on which these principles rest are problematic for women, because the processes involved throughout, from identifying needs and supporting continuing professional development mean women engaging with male 'gatekeepers' and colleagues. Differences in conversational style and behaviour in mixed gender groupings, added to the fact that many women will be dealing with male authority figures, means that women are at a disadvantage in this kind of model. Roberston cites as evidence Sadker and Sadker's findings that men tend to dominate conversations and that their conversational style is more likely to influence the direction of group discussions. These claims have recently been documented and fleshed out extensively by Deborah Tannen (1995). Accordingly, argues Robertson, gender cannot be ignored in the process of professional development.

Robertson's claim then, is that significant and deep gender differences in values, knowing and style raise many questions about equality of access to professional learning and growth opportunities. Theorists such as Joyce and Showers who simply ignore the question of gender imply gender neutrality, which effectively contributes to gender bias, a position there is now growing evidence to substantiate.

## REFERENCES

Gilligan, C. (1982), *In a Different Voice*, Cambridge, MA: Harvard University Press

Gilligan, C. (1986), 'Remapping development: the power of divergent data', in Crillo, L., Wapner, S. (eds) *Value Presupposition in Theories of Human Development*, Hillsdale, NJ: Lawrence Erlbaum Associates

Gilligan, C., Ward, J.V. and Taylor, C.V. (eds) (1988), *Mapping the Moral Domain*, Cambridge, MA: Harvard University Press

Harvey, O.J., Hunt, D.E. and Schroeber, H.M. (1961), *Conceptual Systems and Personality Organisation*, New York and London: John Wiley & Sons

Heilman, M.E. and Kram, K.E., 'Male and female assumptions about colleagues' views of their competence', *Psychology of Women Quarterly*, 7 (4), Summer, 1983

Joyce, B., Bush, R. and McKibbin, M. (1982*), The California Staff Development Study, The January 1982 Report*, Palo Alto, CA: Booksend Laboratories

Joyce, B., Bush, R. and McKibbin, M. (1984), 'Predicting whether an innovation will be implemented: four case studies', Papers presented at the annual gneral meeting of the American Educational Research Association: New Orleans

Joyce, B. and Showers, B. (1988), *Student Achievement Through Staff Development*, New York: Longman

Maslow, A. (1962), *Towards a Psychology of Being*, New York: Van Nostrand

Robertson, M. (1992), 'Teacher Development and Gender Equity' in Hargreaves, A., Fullan, M. (eds), *Understanding Teacher Development*, London: Cassell

Sadker, M. and Sadker, D., 'Sexism in the classroom: from grade school to graduate school', *Phi Delta Kappan*, March 1986

Tannen, D. (1995), *Talking from Nine to Five*, London: Virago

# References

Acheson, K. and Gall, M. (1980) *Techniques in the Clinical Supervision of Teachers*, New York: Longman

Ainscow, M., Hargreaves, D. H. and Hopkins, D. (1995) 'Mapping the process of change in schools', *Evaluation and Research in Education*, 9(2), pp. 75–90

Alexander, R. (1984) *Primary Teaching*, London: Holt, Rinehart & Winston

Apple, M. W. (1986) *Teachers and Texts: A Political Economy of Class and Gender Relations in Education*, New York: Routledge

Aspinwall, K. *et al.* (1992) *Managing Evaluation in Education*, London: Routledge

Ausubel, D. P. (1968) *Educational Psychology: A Cognitive View*. New York: Holt, Rinehart & Winston

Ball, S. J. (1994) *Educational Reform: A Critical and Post-Structural Approach*, Milton Keynes: Open University Press.

Ball, S. J. (1996) Good School/Bad School. Paper presented at British Educational Research Association Annual Conference. September, Lancaster, UK

Barth, R. (1990) *Improving Schools from Within*, San Francisco, CA, Jossey-Bass

Bell, J. (1987) *Doing your Research Project: A Guide for First-time Researchers in Education and Social Science*, Milton Keynes: Open University Press

Bell, L. 'Approaches to the professional development of teachers', in Bell, L. and Day, C. (eds.) 1991, *Managing the Professional Development of Teachers*, Milton Keynes: Open University Press

Bennett, H., Lister, M. and McManus, M. (1992) *Teacher Appraisal: Survival and Beyond*, Harlow: Longman

Bennis, H. G. *et al.* (1969) *The Planning of Change*, 2nd edition, New York: Holt

Blandford, S. (1997) *Middle Management in Schools – How to Harmonise Managing and Teaching for an Effective School*, London: Pitman

Blandford, S. (2000) *Managing Professional Development in Schools*, London: Routledge

Bloom, B. S. (1976) *Human Characteristics and School Learning*, New York: McGraw-Hill

Bolam, R. (1986) 'Conceptualising In-service' in Hopkins, D. (ed.) *In-service Training and Educational Development: An Institutional Survey*, London: Croom Helm

Bolam, R. (1993) *Recent Developments and Emerging Issues in the Continuing Professional Development of Teachers*, London: General Teaching Council for England and Wales (GTC)

Bollen, R. (1996) 'School effectiveness and school improvement: The intellectual and policy context', in Reynolds, D., Bollen, R., Creemers, B., Hopkins, D., Stoll, L. and Lagerweij, N. (1996) *Making Good Schools: Linking School Effectiveness and School Improvement*, London: Routledge

Bollington, R. and Bradley, H. W. (1990) *Training for Appraisal*, Cambridge: Cambridge Institute of Education

Bollington, R., Hopkins, D. and West, M. (1990) *An Introduction to Teacher Appraisal: A Professional Development Approach*, London: Cassell

Bradley, H. W. (1989) *Evaluation of the School Teacher Appraisal Pilot Study*, Cambridge: Cambridge Institute of Education

Bradley, H. W. (1989) 'Training Materials for Appraisal' (unpublished)

Bradley, H. W. (1991) *Staff Development*, London: Falmer

Chambers, J., Sargeant, J., Seward, B., and Skinner, P. (1995) *Investors in People in School (Training Materials for Schools)* London: Sage and UBI (available from UBI Teacher Placement Service on 020 7931 8668)

Chomsky, N. (1980) *Rules and Representations*, Oxford: Blackwell

Cogan, M. (1973) *Clinical Supervision*, Boston: Houghton Mifflin

Cohen, L. and Manion, L. (1989) *Research Methods in Education* (3rd edition) London: Routledge

Cordingley, P. (1999) 'The Teacher Training Agency's research agenda', in Bush, T., Bell, L., Bolam, R., Glatter, R. and Ribbins, P. (1999) *Redefining Educational Management: Policy, Practice and Research*, London: Falmer

Craft, A. (1994) 'Five and six year olds' views of friendship', *Educational Studies*, vol. 20, No. 2, 1994

Craft, A. (1995) *Those Mystifying People: The Pupil Perspective on Teachers' Professional Development*, London/Oxford: UBI Teacher Placement Service

Creemers, B. (1992) 'School effectiveness and effective instruction: the need for a further relationship', in Bashi, J. and Sass, Z. (eds.) *School Effectiveness and Improvement. Proceedings of the Third International Congress, Jerusalem* (pp. 105–32). Jerusalem: The Magnes Press

Creemers, B. (1994) *The Effective Classroom*, London: Cassell

Creemers, B. (1996) The school effectiveness knowledge base, in Reynolds, D., Bollen, R., Creemers, B., Hopkins, D., Stoll, L. and Lagerweij, N. (1996) *Making Good Schools: Linking School Effectiveness and School Improvement*, London: Routledge

Creemers, B. (1997) *Effective Schools and Effective Teachers: An International Perspective*, Warwick: Centre for Research in Elementary and Primary Education

Creemers, B., Reynolds, D., Schaffer, E., Stringfield, S. and Teddlie, C. (1991) *International School Effects Research Workshop*. Kaohsiung: College of Education, National Kaohsiung Normal University Press

Creemers, B., Reynolds, D., Stringfield, S. and Tedlie, C. (1996) 'World class schools: Some further findings'. Paper presented at the AERA Congress, 1996

Dadds, M. (1997) 'Continuing professional development: nurturing the expert within', *British Journal of Inservice Education*, vol. 1, 1997

Davies, P. (1999) What is evidence-based education? *British Journal of Educational Studies*, vol. 47, 2 June 1999, pp. 108–21, London: Blackwell Publishers and SCSE

Day, C. (1991) *The Professional Learning of Teachers in Primary Schools and the Devolution of In-Service Funding*, Nottingham: University School of Education

Day, C. (2000) 'Stories of change and professional development: The costs of commitment', in Day, C., Fernandez, A., Hauge, T.E. and Moller, J. (2000) *The Life and Work of Teachers: International Perspectives in Changing Times*, London: Falmer

Dean, J. (1985) *Managing the Secondary School*, London: Croom Helm

Dean, J. (1991) *Professional Development in School*, Milton Keynes: Open University Press

Department for Education and Employment (1998) *Teachers Meeting the Challenge of Change, Green Paper*, London: HMSO

Department for Education and Employment (1999a) *Teachers Meeting the Challenge of Change, Technical Paper*, London: HMSO

Department for Education and Employment (1999b) *Pay and Performance Management, Technical Paper*, London: HMSO

Department for Education and Employment (2000) *Professional Development: Support for Teaching and Learning, 9/2/00, ref. DfEE 0008/2000*, Nottingham; DfEE Publications

Department of Education and Science (1989) *Planning for School Development*, London: HMSO

Edwards, G. (1993) *Stepping into the Magic*, London: Piatkus

Edwards, R. (1995) 'Troubled times? Personal identity, distance education and distance learning' unpublished paper, June 1995

Eisner, E.W. (1985) *Educational Imagination: on the design and evaluation of school programs* (2nd edition) Macmillan

Eraut, M. (1994) *Developing Professional Knowledge and Competence*, London: Falmer

Eraut, M *et al.* (1988) *Local Evaluation of INSET*, Bristol: NDCSMT

Everard, B. and Morris, M. (1990) *Effective School Management*, 2nd edition, London: Paul Chapman

Evertson, C. M. and Holley, F. R. (1981) 'Classroom observation', in Millman, J. (ed.) *Handbook for Teacher Evaluation*, Beverly Hills, CA: Sage

Fielding, M. (1997) 'Beyond school effectiveness and school improvement: lighting the slow fuse of possibility', in White, J. and Barber, M. (eds.) (1997) *Perspectives on School Effectiveness and School Improvement*, London: Institute of Education University of London, Bedford Way Papers

Fitz-Gibbon, C. T. (1991) 'Multilevel modelling in an indicator system', in Raudenbush, S. and Williams, J.D. (eds.) *Schools, Classrooms and Pupils*, San Diego, CA: Academic Press

Fryer, R. (1997) 'We've got to get a handle on change', *Times Educational Supplement*, 28 November

Fullan, M. (1982) *The Meaning of Educational Change*, New York: Teachers' College Press

Fullan, M. (1985) 'Change processes and strategies at the local level', *Elementary School Journal*, 85 (3) pp. 91–421

Fullan, M. (1991) *The New Meaning of Educational Change*, New York: Teachers' College Press

Fullan, M. (1993) *Change Forces: Probing the Depths of Educational Reform*, London: Falmer

Fullan, M. (1999) *Change Forces: The Sequel*, London: Falmer

Fullan, M. (with Stiegelbauer, S.) (1991) *The New Meaning of Educational Change*, London: Cassell

Fullan, M. and Hargreaves, A. (eds.) (1992) *Understanding Teacher Development*, London: Falmer

Fullan, M. and Park, P. (1981) *Curriculum Implementation*, Toronto: Ministry of Education

Giddens, A. (1991) *Modernity and Self-Identity: Self and Society in the Late Modern Age*, Cambridge and Oxford: Polity Press and Blackwell

Gilligan, C. (1982) *In a Different Voice*, Cambridge, MA: Harvard University Press

Gilligan, C. (1986) 'Remapping development: the power of divergent data', in Crillo, L. and Wapner, S. (eds.) *Value Presupposition in Theories of Human Development*, Hillsdale, NJ: Lawrence Erlbaum Associates

Gilligan, C., Ward, J. V. and Taylor, C. V. (eds.) (1988) *Mapping the Moral Domain*, Cambridge, MA: Harvard University Press

Gipps, C. (1994) *Beyond Testing: Towards A Theory of Educational Assessment*, London: Falmer

Gipps, C. and Murphy, P. (1994) *A Fair Test? Assessment, Achievement and Equity*, Milton Keynes: Open University Press

Goddard, D. and Leask, M. (1992) *The Search for Quality*, London: Paul Chapman

Goldhammer, R. *et al.* (1980) *Clinical Supervision: Special Methods for the Supervision of Teachers*, (2nd edition) New York: Holt, Rinehart & Winston

Goleman, D. (1996) *Emotional Intelligence: Why it Matters More Than IQ*, London: Bloomsbury Paperbacks

Goodson, I. (1991) 'Teachers' lives and educational research.' *Biography, Identity and Schooling: Episodes in Educational Research*, Goodson, I. F. and Walker, R., (eds.), London: Falmer

Gray, J., Hopkins, D., Reynolds, D., Wilcox, B., Farrell, S., and Jesson, D. (1999) *Improving Schools: Performance and Potential*, Milton Keynes: Open University Press

Gray, J., Reynolds, D., Fitz-Gibbon, C. and Jesson, D. (eds.) (1996) *Merging Traditions: The Future of Research on School Effectiveness and School Improvement*, London: Cassell

Green, H. (1999) *A View from the Teacher Training Agency's Educational Management and Leadership ESRC Seminar (7 May 1999)*, London: TTA

Handy, C. and Aitken, R. (1986) *Understanding Schools as Organisations*, Harmondsworth: Penguin

Hargreaves, A. (1994) 'Individualism and individuality: Understanding the teacher culture', in *Changing Teachers, Changing Times: Teachers' Work and Culture in the Postmodern Age,* London: Cassell

Hargreaves, A. (1994a) 'Collaboration and contrived collegiality: Cup of comfort or poisoned chalice?' in *Changing Teachers, Changing Times: Teachers' Work and Culture in the Postmodern Age,* London: Cassell

Hargreaves, A. (1994b) *Changing Teachers, Changing Times: Teachers' Work and Culture in the Postmodern Age,* London: Cassell

Hargreaves, A. and Goodson, I. (1996) 'Teachers' professional lives; aspirations and actualities', in Goodson, I.F. and Hargreaves, A. (eds.) *Teachers' Professional Lives,* London: Falmer

Hargreaves, D. (1998) *Creative Professionalism: The Role of Teachers in the Knowledge Society,* London: Demos

Hargreaves, D. and Hopkins, D. (1991) *The Empowered School,* London: Cassell

Hargreaves, D. H. (1996) 'Teaching as a research-based profession: Possibilities and prospects', TTA Annual Lecture, London: TTA

Harland, J. (1990) *The Work and Impact of Advisory Teachers,* Slough: NFER

Harland, J. and Kinder, K. (1991) *The Impact of INSET: The Case of Primary Science,* Slough: NFER

Harris, A. (1998) 'Improving the effective department: Strategies for growth and development,' *Educational Management and Administration,* Summer edition

Harris, A. (1999) *Teaching and Learning in the Effective School,* Aldershot: Ashgate

Harrison, R. (1987) *Organisation Culture and Quality of Service,* Association for Management Education and Development

Heifetz, R. (1994) *Leadership without Easy Answers,* Cambridge, MA: Harvard University Press

Helsby, G. (2000) 'Multiple truths and contested realities: The changing faces of teacher professionalism in England', in Day, C., Fernandez, A., Hauge, T. E. and Moller, J. (2000*) The Life and Work of Teachers: International Perspectives in Changing Times,* London: Falmer

Hertfordshire Education Services (1995) *Effective Schools: Guidance and Advice,* Wheathampstead: Hertfordshire County Council

Higgins, S. and Leat, D. (1997) 'Horses for courses or courses for horses: what is effective teacher development?' *British Journal of In-service Education,* vol. 23, no. 3, 1997

Holly, M. L. (1987) *Keeping a Personal-Professional Journal,* Australia: Deakin University Press

Holly, P. and Southworth, G. (1989) *The Developing School,* Lewes: Falmer

Honey, P. and Mumford, A. (1986) *The Manual of Learning Styles,* Maidenhead: Peter Honey and Alan Mumford

Hopkins, D. (1989) *Evaluation for School Development,* Milton Keynes: Open University Press

Hopkins, D. (1996) 'Towards a theory for school improvement', Gray, J. Reynolds, D., Fitz-Gibbon, C. and Jesson, D. (eds.) *Merging Traditions: The Future of Research on School Effectiveness and School Improvement,* London: Cassell

Hopkins, D. and Lagerweij, N. (1996) 'The school improvement knowledge base', in Reynolds, D., Bollen, R., Creemers, B., Hopkins, D., Stoll, L. and Lagerweij, N. (1996) *Making Good Schools: Linking School Effectiveness and School Improvement*, London: Routledge

Hopkins, D., Ainscow, M. and West, M. (1994) *School Improvement in an Era of Change*, London: Cassell

Hopson, B. and Scally, M. (1981) *Lifeskills Teaching Programmes, No. 1*, Leeds: Lifeskills Associates

Hoyle, E. (1980) 'Professionalisation and deprofessionalisation in education' in Hoyle, E. and Megarry, J. (eds.) *World Yearbook of Education 1980: Professional Development of Teachers*, London: Kogan Page

Huberman, M. (1992) 'Teacher development and instructional mastery', in Hargreaves, A. and Fullan, M. (eds.) (1992) *Understanding Teacher Development*, London: Cassell

James (1972) *Teacher Education and Training* (The James Report) London: HMSO

Jennings, J. (1995) 'Back to the future', *Bulleti Informatiu: Forum Europeu D'Administradors De L'Educacio a la Comunitat Valencia*, Spain: August 1995

Jersild, A.T. (1995) *When Teachers Face Themselves*, New York: Teachers' College Press

Jones, J. (1993) *Appraisal and Staff Development in Schools*, London: David Fulton

Joyce, B. and Showers, B. (1980) 'Improving in-service training: The messages of research', *Educational Leadership*, 37(5) pp. 379–85

Joyce, B. and Showers, B. (1988) *Student Achievement through Staff Development*, New York: Longman

Joyce, B. and Weil, M. (1980) *Models of Teaching* (2nd edition) New Jersey: Prentice Hall

Joyce, B., Calhoun, E., Hopkins, D. (1999) *The New Structure of School Improvement: Inquiring Schools and Achieving Students*, Milton Keynes: Open University Press

Kerry, T. and Shelton Mayes, A. (1995) *Issues in Mentoring*, London and New York: Routledge

Klette, K. (2000) 'Working-time blues: How Norwegian teachers experience restructuring in education', in Day, C., Fernandez, A., Hauge, T.E. and Moller, J. (2000) *The Life and Work of Teachers: International Perspectives in Changing Times*, London: Falmer

LEAP (1992) *Quality in Schools*, Milton Keynes: Educational Broadcasting Service Trust

Leithwood, K. A. (1992) 'The principal's role in teacher development' in Fullan, M. and Hargreaves, A. (ed.) (1992) *Teacher Development and Educational Change*, London: Falmer

Loucks-Horsley, S. *et al.* (1987) *Continuing to Learn: A Guide Book for Teacher Development*, Andover: Regional Laboratory for Educational Improvement of the Northeast and Islands and National Staff Development Council

MacBeath, J. and Mortimore, P. (1994) 'Improving school effectiveness: Proposal for a research project for the Scottish Office Education Department', Glasgow: Quality in Education Centre, University of Glasgow

McCormick, R. and James, M. (1983) *Curriculum Evaluation in Schools,* London: Croom Helm

MacDonald, B. (1976) 'Evaluation and the control of education', in Tawney, D. (ed.) *Curriculum Evaluation Today: Trends and Implications,* London: Macmillan

MacGilchrist, B. Mortimore, P., Savage, J. and Beresford, C. (1995) *Planning Matters,* London: Paul Chapman Publishing

MacGilchrist, B., Myers, K. and Reed, J. (1997) *The Intelligent School,* London: PCP

McMahon, A. (1999) 'Educational leadership, administration and management', paper presented at the ESRC Seminar, 6–7 May, West Hill House, Birmingham

McMaster, M. (1995) *The Intelligent Advantage: Organising for Complexity,* Knowledge Based Development Co. Ltd

Miles, M. B. (1986) *Research Findings on the Stages of School Improvement,* (Mimeo)

Millett, A. (1996) 'Chief Executive's speech, 1997–8', *TTA Annual General Meeting,* London: TTA

Mortimore, P., Sammons, P., Ecob, R., Stoll, L. and Lewis, D. (1988) *School Matters: The Junior School Years,* Salisbury: Open Books

Naisbitt, J. and Aburdene, P. (1990) *Megatrends 2000: The Next 10 years – Major Changes in your Life and World,* London: Sidgwick and Jackson

National Committee for the Inservice Training of Teachers (Scotland) (1984) *Arrangements for the Staff Development of Teachers,* HMSO

National Primary Centre (NPC) (1990) *Practical Issues in Primary Education (PIPE)* Issue 3, Oxford, NPC

National Union of Teachers (NUT) (1993) *Appraisal,* London: NUT

Nias, J. (1989) *Primary Teachers Talking,* London: Routledge

Nonaka, I and Takeuchi, H. (1995) *The Knowledge-Creating Company,* Oxford: Oxford University Press

NSG (National Steering Group for Teacher Appraisal) (1989) *School Teacher Appraisal: A National Framework,* London: HMSO

Nuttall, D. (1990) *Developing Evaluation in the LEA,* London: ILEA Research and Statistics Branch

Office for Standards in Education (OFSTED) (1999) *News Release* 9, May 1999: London

Oldroyd, D. and Hall, V. (1988) *Managing Professional Development and INSET,* Bristol: National Development Centre for School Management Training

Oldroyd, D. and Hall, V. (1991) *Managing Staff Development,* London: Paul Chapman

Raymond, D. *et al.* (1992) 'Contexts for teacher development: Insights from teachers' stories', in Hargreaves, A. and Fullan, M. (eds.) (1992) *Understanding Teacher Development,* London: Cassell

Reynolds, D. (1976) 'The delinquent school', in Woods, P. (ed.) *The Processes of Schooling,* London: Routledge & Kegan Paul

Reynolds, D. (1982) 'The search for effective schools', *School Organisation,* 2 (3) pp.215–37

Reynolds, D. (1992) 'School effectiveness and school improvement: An updated review of the British literature', in Reynolds, D. and Cuttance, P. (eds.) *School Effectiveness: Research, Policy And Practice*, London and New York: Cassell

Reynolds, D. and Cuttance, P. (eds.) (1992) *School Effectiveness: Research, Policy and Practice*, London and New York: Cassell

Reynolds, D. and Parker, A. (1992) 'School effectiveness and school improvement in the 1990s', in Reynolds, D. and Cuttance, P. (eds.) (1992) *School Effectiveness: Research, Policy and Practice*, London: Cassell

Ridley, M. (1996) *The Origins of Virtue*, London: Penguin

Robertson, P. and Sammons, P. (1997a) 'Improving school effectiveness: A project in progress', paper presented at the Tenth International Congress for School Effectiveness and Improvement, Memphis, Tennessee, 5–8 January 1997

Robertson, P. and Sammons, P. (1997b) The improving school effectiveness project (ISEP): Understanding change in schools, paper presented at the British Educational Research Association annual conference, University of York, September 1997

Rogers, G. and Badham, L. (1992) *Evaluation in Schools: Getting Started in Training and Implementation*, London: Routledge

Rudduck, J. (1981) *Making the Most of the Short In-service Course*, London: Methuen

Ruiz, M.A. and Pares, N.S. (1997)' The professional development of teachers by means of the construction of collaborative thinking', *British Journal of In-service Education*, 23(3) pp. 241–52

Russell, T. and Bullock, S. (1999) 'Discovering our professional knowledge as teachers: Critical strategies and learning from experience', in Loughran, J. (ed.) (1999) *Researching Teaching: Methodologies and Practices for Understanding Pedagogy*, London: Falmer

Rutter, M., Maughan, B., Mortimore, P. and Ouston, J. (1979) *Fifteen Thousand Hours: Secondary Schools and Their Effects on Children*, Wells: Open Books

Sammons, P. (1994) 'Findings from school effectiveness research: Some implications for improving the quality of schools' in P. Ribbins and E. Burridge (eds.) *Improving Education: Promoting Quality in Schools*, London: Cassell

Sammons, P. (1999) *School Effectiveness: Coming of Age in the Twenty-First Century*, Lisse, The Netherlands: Swets & Zeitlinger

Sammons, P., Hillman, J., and Mortimore, P. (1995) *Key Characteristics of Effective Schools: A Review of School Effectiveness Research*: A report by the Institute of Education for the Office for Standards in Education, London: OFSTED

Sammons, P., Thomas, S. and Mortimore, P. (1997) *Forging Links: Effective Schools and Effective Departments*, London: PCP

Scheerens, B. and Creemers, B. P. M. (1989) 'Conceptualising school effectiveness', *International Journal of Educational Research*, 13(7) pp. 789–99

Scheerens, J. (1992) *Effective Schooling: Research, Theory and Practice*, London and New York: Cassell

Schön, D. A. 'The reflective practitioner: How professionals think', *Action*, London: Templesmith

Schwandt, T. A. and Halpern, E. S. (1988) *Linking Auditing and Meta-Evaluation: An Audit Model for Applied Research*, Beverly Hills, CA: Sage

Scott, D. (1985) *Everyman Revived*, The Book Guild

Scott, D. (1997) 'The missing hermeneutical dimension in mathematical modelling', in White, J. and Barber, M. (eds.) (1997) *Perspectives on School Effectiveness and School Improvement*, London: Institute of Education University of London, Bedford Way Papers

Secretary of State for Education and Science (1991a) T*he Education (School Teacher Appraisal) Regulations*, London: HMSO

Secretary of State for Education and Science (1991b) Circular No 12/91 *School Teacher Appraisal*, London: DES

SOED, *School Development Planning Support Materials* (HM Inspectors of Schools, 1992) Performance Indicator Series

Southworth, G. (1994) 'The learning school', in Ribbens, P. and Burridge, E. (eds.) *Improving Education: Promoting Quality in Schools*, London: Cassell

Stacey, R. (1996) *Complexity and Creativity in Organizations*, San Francisco: Berrett-Koehler

Stenhouse, L. (1975) *An Introduction to Curriculum Research and Development*, London: Heinemann

Stoll, L. (1992) 'Teacher growth in the effective school', in Fullan, M. and Hargreaves, A. (eds.) (1992) *Understanding Teacher Development*, London: Cassell

Stoll, L. and Fink, D. (1996) *Changing Our Schools: Linking School Effectiveness and School Improvement*, Milton Keynes: Open University Press

Stoll, L., Reynolds, D., Creemers, B. and Hopkins, D. (1996) 'Merging school effectiveness and school improvement: practical examples', in Reynolds, D., Bollen, R., Creemers, B, Hopkins, D., Stoll, L. and Lagerweij, N. (1996*) Making Good Schools: Linking School Effectiveness and School Improvement*, London: Routledge

Styan, D. *et al.* (1990) *Developing School Managment: The Way Forward* (Report of the School Management Task Force) London: HMSO

Tannen, D. (1995) *Talking from Nine to Five*, London: Virago

Teacher Training Agency (1998) *National Standards for Teachers*, London: TTA

Teacher Training Agency (TTA) (1995) *Survey of Continuing Professional Development*, Research Conducted for the TTA by MORI, June 1995, published by the TTA

Teddlie, C. and Reynolds, D. (1998) *The International Handbook of School Effectiveness*, Lewes: Falmer

Troman, G. (1996) 'The rise of the new professionals? The restructuring of primary teachers' work and professionalism', *British Journal of Sociology of Education*, 17(4): pp. 473–87

Universities Council for the Education of Teachers (UCET*) Summary Report of Annual Conference, 1999: The Challenge of the Future*, held at Bosworth Hall, Market Bosworth, November 1999. London: UCET

Watson, N. and Fullan, M. (1992) 'Beyond school district-university partnerships' in Fullan, M and Hargreaves, A (eds.) *Teacher Development and Educational Change*, London: Falmer

West, N. (1992) *Classroom Observation in the Context of Appraisal: Training Manual for Primary Schools*, Harlow: Longman

Wideen, M. (1986) 'The role of the evaluator', in Holly, P. (ed.) *Cambridge Journal of Education*, 16, 2, pp. 126–30

Woods, P. (1994) 'Adaptation and self-determination in English primary schools'. *Oxford Review of Education*, 20 (4): pp. 387–410

Wragg, E.C. (1987) *Teacher Appraisal: A Practice Guide*, London: Macmillan

Yin, R. (1984) *Case Study Research*, London: Sage

# Index